NELSON'S LEGACY

LADY HAMILTON:

HER STORY & TRAGEDY

BY

Julia Frankau

i

Gibbons' Rare Books

41 Wooster St.
SoHo, New York

Contents

AUTHOR'S NOTE

THE following is a true and authentic account of the birth, life, and death of the notorious adventuress, sometime Emy Lyon, but ultimately the wife of Sir William Hamilton, his Majesty's Minister at Naples, together with the story of her many lapses from virtue both before and after her connection with Immortal Nelson, the Hero of the Nile. It has been compiled from contemporary documents, the writings of eye-witnesses, and other reliable evidence. We trust that sufficient excuse will be found for the relation in the moral lesson conveyed. The features of the unhappy subject of this memoir were limned by all the most illustrious painters and designers of the century. To gratify the curiosity of those who would fain investigate the charms of one who provoked so much controversy whilst she lived, and has been the occasion of so much argument since she paid the final debt of nature in the poor lodging-house at Calais, has proved a task not wholly uncongenial.

Our acknowledgments and those of our readers are due to many ladies and gentlemen who have added their quota to our knowledge, and allowed generous access to their treasures for the benefit of our illustrations.

NELSON'S LEGACY

CHAPTER I

Introduces Henry Cadogan and relates the events that led to his strange situation at Great Nesse.

IT happens frequently in the case of persons who rise to eminence, that the envy of those whom they defeat in the struggle for Fame seeks to belittle their origin, and discredit their breeding, failing to perceive by how much the more the disgrace attaching to their own failure is thereby increased. It happened no otherwise in the case of the incomparable beauty whose adventures it is attempted to trace in the following sheets. And since legitimate birth into a family of ancient lineage and fine tradition is a valuable possession for anyone, even though the marriage that has so resulted be not one of social equality in the contracting parties, I purpose to set forth at the outset the events which led to the introduction of a future ambassadress into the world in circumstances so humble as those belonging to the smithy in the remote village of Great Nesse.

The father, then, of that Emma whom the vicissitudes of fortune conducted to the nuptial bed of Sir William Hamilton, His Britannic Majesty's Ambassador to the Court of Naples, whose beauty lives through the unrivalled art of Mr. Romney, and whose wanton charm

1

captured the heart, and made happy the last years of the Hero of the Nile, the victor at Trafalgar, immortal Nelson,—the father of this remarkable woman was Mr. Henry Cadogan, nephew and heir to Mr. George Cadogan, a gentleman of small estate, but not so small importance, in the village of Hawarden, which lies about six miles west of the city of Chester. His house was the next largest to Broadlane Hall, the residence of Mr. and Mrs. Thomas, of whom we shall hear more as this history progresses. It lay on the bank of one of the three brooks that fed the iron foundry and the boring mill, but away from the smoke of the one and the noise of the other.

Here, in a house already old, set in an ordered garden, the leaden statues and stone sun-dial diversifying the clipt yews and formal flower-beds, lived Mr. George Cadogan, a scholarly man, of refined and fastidious tastes. And here, being a bachelor, he installed, as mistress of his establishment, the widow of his deceased brother, with her only son, to whom, in course of time, he purposed to bequeath all his worldly goods.

Mrs. Cadogan did not long survive her husband. She died before her little Henry's tottering baby feet had learnt to stand firm, but not before she had directed them on the right path and shown him a light by which to steer his wavering course. He knew, already before the death of his mother, that he must not hurt other people, and that he must be gentle as she was gentle. So much of the rules of conduct she inculcated in him. Afterwards he strove to interpret them in action, imperfectly perhaps, even incorrectly. But Providence having removed her before she had carried his education farther, he was left to the care and tutelage of a man who, never having known the joys of fatherhood, lacked, and was unable to acquire, that sympathetic understanding of the development of youthful character which is one of fatherhood's natural attributes.

Mr. George Cadogan was, nevertheless, one of the worthiest of his sex, and if the enunciation of abstract principles had been sufficient to form an entirely virtuous character, his nephew could not have been committed to a more desirable preceptor. Henry was an obedient pupil, somewhat unchildlike, and apt to melancholy. In truth, he felt a mother-want about the world, and groped after it silently; giving but an inattentive ear to the apothegmata of a long-deceased Roman Emperor, or the moral conclusions arrived at after repentance by an uninspired Bishop of Hippo.

Henry Cadogan perhaps deemed Marcus Aurelius but a dull dog, and the holy Augustine's career interesting only up to the point when he sat under the fig-tree in the garden at Milan. Having read the rest as an academic exercise with his estimable uncle, he would dismiss the whole story, with its valuable lessons, from his mind, and go forth into the garden, or into the country beyond, to employ his leisure hours in his own way, making sketches of such objects as pleased his growing sense of beauty, for he was ever zealous with his pencil, or attempting to express in verse some of the vague thoughts and emotions which overcharged the heart of a youth whose disposition was naturally romantic. To such of these as he ventured to submit to his uncle's eye,

3

the older man gave a kindly and a tolerant attention. Mr. George Cadogan took pleasure in his nephew's society, and encouraged him in his poetical exercises, regarding them, however, only as essays in one department of literature, and not as the first immature expression of a nature that might crave and exact more substantial satisfaction in the days to come.

Yet this, in truth, is what these romantic and heroic poems presaged. And as their author passed from childhood to adolescence, and felt the throb of the blood in his body, he ceased to be content with visionary Lesbias as objects of his amorous lyrics, and with imagined Evadnes and Cassanas as heroines of his romantic narratives. The mother-craving left him, and now he desired some inamorata, whom he might idealise, and who in return should inspire his genius to flights that should set him far up on the slopes of Parnassus, and at the end, perhaps, secure him a resting-place in the Temple of Fame. Desiring, he sought, and seeking, found. No society is so small but what it contains one maiden at least, endowed with charms of person, or witchery of sex, sufficient to qualify her to be the divinity of a youth in love with love. Hawarden certainly was not so small. And in Mary Kidd, the daughter of an honest labouring man, living in a little thatched cottage at the far end of the village, Henry Cadogan discovered a new outlet for the strange emotions that had hitherto found their expression only in verse.

Of the first passages of their courtship there is no history. First love is ever shy and shuns observation. But even if proven facts were the only material with which it is the historian's business to deal, I venture to suggest that there would still be no necessity for me to reconstitute what every reader can imagine for himself. This much, however, it is not impertinent to observe: that the natural shyness and pretty reluctance of young lovers to engage the attention of any save the single object of their mutual affection, are in themselves justification for that rigid fence of etiquette by which, in polite circles, young females are protected. The proprieties, in short, are the unwritten laws of behaviour which society, as the sum of its experience, has found to be necessary for the safeguarding of the morality of its inexperienced members, and in insisting upon their observance it shows rather a prudent knowledge of the temptations to which those members are liable to be exposed while their characters are still in process of formation, than mistrust of the ultimate efficacy of the virtuous principles which it simultaneously labours to instil.

Unhappily, in the lower ranks of society, to which Mary Kidd belonged, no corresponding code of etiquette exists, and the temptations to which a young female is exposed can be resisted only by her own invincible religious sense or by the unceasing vigilance of her proper guardians. In the case of Mary Kidd no vigilance could be exercised. Her family was for ever labouring with dire poverty. She herself had to assist in its maintenance by hard and unremitting labour in the fields. Life had meant naught but labour in the thatched cottage until Henry Cadogan saw timidity yet aspiration in a pair of blue eyes, and showed a counterpart of them in his own. There followed long interviews, sweet, because stolen, meetings in the moonlight, sighs and mutual

5

protestations, quick pleading, and presently surrender. Then, one day, Mary had that to tell which sent Henry back to his uncle's house with face flushed by pride or shame, resolute to tell him what had happened, and thus test the practical value of his great store of abstract virtuous principles.

Mr. George Cadogan heard his nephew's confession with steadily increasing astonishment. He was at first so disconcerted by such amazing intelligence that for the moment he even forgot the habitual Latinity of his diction, and the hitherto invincible courtesy of his manner. He took a pinch of snuff before he spoke, but even that failed completely and immediately to restore his calm.

'You've gotten the wench with child!' he exclaimed, at the end of the long narrative, interspersed with rhapsodies, and punctuated by sighs, which his nephew inflicted upon him. Then there was another pause, and another pinch of snuff. 'It is indeed a painful circumstance, a most lamentable occurrence. I trusted I had implanted in you the seeds of virtue.'

> 'Virtuous and vicious every man must be,
> Few in th' extreme, but all in the degree,'

quoted Henry respectfully.

Mr. Cadogan was somewhat mollified by the response, which had the literary flavour and was therefore to his taste.

'True, true,' he answered. 'Most true. 'Twas the trollop herself that led you to it, no doubt. Yet if the responsibility be truly yours, you must e'en shoulder it. What does Mr. Samuel Prior say?

'Amongst all honest Christian people
Whoe'er breaks limbs maintains the cripple.'

He would not be outdone in quotation by his nephew. 'And who is the wench?'

'Mary Kidd.'

'Ah! Comely?

Henry indulged in the exaggeration incidental to his state. And his uncle heard him with patience, almost with complaisance, relating an incident of his own youth, not, however, without shaking his head, and sighing, and having recourse to his snuff-box. But Henry could see he was secretly not ill-pleased to recall the story, and remind himself that, although a scholar and a recluse, he was also a man of the world.

The trouble between them only arose when Mr. Cadogan suggested that ten guineas should be raised from Henry's small patrimony and given to the companion of his vice on condition that she left the neighbourhood. It was then Henry showed the result of his mother's early teaching. He protested that Mary loved him, and that he would not desert her. He vowed that he would make an honest woman of her, cover her frailty with a marriage ring. . . .

'Marry! *marry*, forsooth! Marry the strumpet! 'Quite a flush came into the thin old cheeks and the hand that held the snuff-box shook. 'Have you taken leave of your senses? Where do you propose to live, and upon what do you propose to maintain a wife?' Mr. Cadogan strove after dignity and composure, but both eluded him. When Henry urged his point with persistence his exasperated uncle resorted to dark threats of

7

'spinning-houses for waistcoateers, and pounds for loose puppies.' He threatened to make use of his commission of the peace to bring the pair of them to heel, uttering a denunciation of all loose women, including Mary by name in a manner that roused all the mistaken chivalry and impotent anger of the boy. For, in truth, at this time Henry was little more than a boy. And Mr. Cadogan pursued the subject with further quotation, more snuff-taking, and a growing calm. He held the power of the purse, and other powers, was bitter in argument, and now that his self-possession had returned could play rapier-like with sharp speech. His words bit, and the wounds bled, letting out self-esteem and courage. Henry became as a whipped child before him; he could have wept in his rage and revolt, and found himself with no word or argument left. But there was heat in his cheeks, and in his heart, and a great blaze of pity and tenderness for the maid who had given him in love that which his uncle coarsened and brutalised in argument.

He was dismissed from Mr. Cadogan's presence presently, with contemptuous coldness, and a parting adjuration in the Latin tongue.

He had not regained his spirit when Mary herself was in his arms. She had waited for him in the orchard, beside two nymphs who guarded a stone fountain where clear spring water gushed from the mouth of an infant Triton. Underneath the apple blossom, and the young spring green, were tearful eyes, and tremulous lips that yielded as they trembled, lips cold with fear, and hot with love. What could Mr. Cadogan ever have known of love? *His* story was but of lust.

Henry heard the piteous appeal not to abandon whom he had betrayed; and it was not in him to hear it unmoved. Incoherent murmurings of love proved more potent than logical statements of worldly facts. He vowed fidelity as the shadows fell and the evening closed about them, when love held out its wanton charms, and persuaded them that which is beautiful and natural is also surely right. The night guarded their secrets.

Next day, and on many succeeding days, the struggle between uncle and nephew was renewed. Now it took a literary, and again an academic form. Mr. Cadogan cited authorities, and Henry refuted them. Mr. Cadogan argued, and Henry demurred. In the course of this conflict of will and reason the weakness of the lad's character, which was responsible for the injury he had done the girl, manifested itself in obstinacy to persist in what his uncle described as the folly of his intentions with regard to her. And then the last word was spoken; the ultimatum given out. Henry could pay the girl off generously, for money, if not plentiful, was not wanting; or he could carry his Quixotism to the end, and marry her. In that case he could go where he pleased, and 'take his wanton' with him. But go he must. And if he went, he went for ever.

It was the old story. Once more youth was given the choice between the world and love, and once more youth counted the world well lost for love.

As almost any girl in a like situation would have done, Mary Kidd accepted the sacrifice made on the altar of her frailty. She was more mature than her boy-lover, and was the counsellor in much that followed. It was on her advice that Henry Cadogan took another name, both in order to avoid awkward questions, and to elude his uncle's threatened reprisals. In the name of Henry Lyon he was married to Mary Kidd, by the Rev. C. Gardener, curate, in the parish church of Neston. With a pathetic pretence of equality suggested by his native chivalrousness—or perhaps it was with an as pathetic desire to make discovery still more difficult—Henry signed the register, as Mary did, with a mark. Thenceforward he would have no use for scholarship.

But he had a wife, and soon would have a child, and must redeem the hostages he had given to fortune. Dame Fortune gave him small choice as to the way in which he should do so. For fifty years John Hales had been blacksmith at Great Nesse, and now the old man was failing, and needed help. Henry Lyon bound himself apprentice to him, in hopes to learn the trade. But after four months John Hales died, leaving Henry's education incomplete. All the money he had, independently of his uncle—it represented his mother's little savings—the unfortunate young man invested in the goodwill and stock-in-trade of the forge. Thus it came about that he who so short a time before was Henry Cadogan, gentleman, and heir to a respectable estate, was now become Henry Lyon, smith, of Nesse.

It would have been difficult for him to have picked a trade for which he had less aptitude. He was disqualified for it by something more than the tenderness with which he had been nurtured in the solitude of his uncle's house. The rich luxuriance of his red-gold hair, the transparence of his temples, showing blue tracery of veins, the moist redness of his mouth, shaped like a Cupid's bow, the soft roundness of his white and slender arms, the hectic ebb and flow of colour in his face—these were so many outward signs of a consumption that was no less his inheritance than the little savings. He did not know this yet, but each day left him more exhausted by the unaccustomed toil, each day found him less equal to the demands it made upon him. Only the pride that comes of race sustained him in the losing battle.

The end came suddenly.

Old Sir Thomas Mostyn, Squire of the Parish, rode to the forge to have his mare shod, and Henry Lyon, though wearied more than ordinarily, dared not disappoint so valuable a customer. Sir Thomas sat on the wooden bench that was all the furniture the forge afforded, and watched the young smith at work, noting the effort needed to swing the heavy hammer, and the uncertainty of its fall upon the metal. He grew impatient of such incompetence.

'Plague on it,' he said testily. 'You fiddle about with a hammer like any fool of a woman. Let it swing free, man, let it swing free.'

Henry made no answer but redoubled his efforts. The squire watched him as he finished beating out the iron, heating and shaping it, then, stooping down to take the mare's hoof upon his apron, fitted and fastened the shoe. The sweat beaded on Henry's forehead and trickled down into his eyes; he breathed with difficulty. Squire Mostyn noted the hairless whiteness of the exposed chest, and the womanly slimness of the arms, bare to above the elbow.

11

'You're no smith,' exclaimed Sir Thomas, 'and not even John Hales could have made 'ee one. The work's too hard for you.'

'There are worse things than hard work,' Henry answered breathlessly.

'Want of it, for one,' put in the squire, dryly.

'Very true, very true. But you'd have no need to be afraid of that if you'd buckle to and master your trade. There's not another forge within twenty miles, and would not be, if you learn to give satisfaction to your customers.'

Henry was touched both by the encouragement and the warning. He knew he must struggle on, at least until after his child was born. Yet but a boy himself, that which was coming to him would need all his strength and courage.

He rose and straightened himself painfully, answering respectfully. Then he led the newly shod mare to the ghost stone outside, which the squire, an old man now, was perforce obliged to use as a mounting block. The squire was mollified by his attitude, perhaps moved by his appearance, and as he settled himself in the saddle, he said, 'A man ought to be fitted for his business.' He gathered the reins in his hands. 'Belike smithing is not yours. Why don't 'ee turn barber, man, or schoolmaster, or both? You could attend to both sides of the children's heads then, inside and outside; and 'twould be an easier job to knock learning into them, thick though they be, than 'tis to beat out horseshoes. Give the matter your thought, young man; and if you're needing help, come up to the house. . . .'

He tossed the smith a crown for his labour, and rode off, unaware of the desperation smouldering behind him. The air of patronage and the scarcely veiled scorn, had flicked Henry Lyon on the raw. He would be neither barber nor schoolmaster. He was a scholar and a gentleman. . . . When Sir Thomas had jogged away out of sight he flung the crown upon the bench. And yet he could not but give the matter thought, as he had been enjoined.

Leaning against the door of the forge, he rested his eyes on the wide estuary of the Dee, and on the Welsh hills, showing purple in the distance. It was a beautiful place to which his folly, or his virtue, had brought him, a peaceful and prosperous place. But the fairest prospect is powerless to soothe the heart that is not at rest; and Henry Lyon knew already that he was the victim of irremediable discontent. Marcus Aurelius and all the philosophers were proven fools, and their maxims foolishness. How often had he repeated to himself the adage, *Leve fit quod bene fertur onus,* only to convince himself of its falseness.

In the first ardour of his emancipation from his state of pupilage he had thought to prove his independence by making a living by his hands, work was to have been the panacea for all his troubles. But instead of curing the malady, it was killing the patient. For already, this afternoon, the lad knew that he had come almost to the end of his powers of endurance. He did not regret his courtship or marriage—by it he had proved his spirit, and established his manhood's estate. But all at once he was nauseated by the conditions into which they had brought him; by the dirt and the sweat of labour; by the foetid atmosphere of the

13

cottage which he shared with Mary, and which pleased her so greatly; by the coarseness of his meat, and the spiritual loneliness of his days. The squire had brought it all home to him; he was removed from his equals in education and politeness. Man cannot live by bread alone, and feeding on sacrifice is less than bread.

Henry could work no more that day, and anon, doffing his leathern apron, washing the worst of the dirt from his hands and face, and closing the smithy door, he betook him to the old quay fields, there to lie for awhile on the warm bosom of earth, to watch from afar the slow approach of the Irish packet, to see the sails catch the breeze, and to dream, futilely, that some day he too might sail to a new haven, where there would be peace, the wind and sky for sweet company, and rest in sight.

In the cottage Mary waited the return of her husband, at first with patience, then with growing anxiety. When the night fell, and still he did not come, anxiety gave place to panic, and she sought her neighbour's aid. Gaffer Dowling, from next door, and Mary Lyon, swinging their lanterns, uncertain where to look, sallied forth into the cold grey of the spring night. The gaffer was bent and old, but Mary bore herself erect, albeit there was fear at the back of her mind. She was truly of stouter heart, and of more judgment, than her husband, and if more time had been given her, she might well have made a man of him. But his weakness had won upon her, so that now she loved her husband as she had never loved her lover. She knew that he was delicate in health, and she guessed too, as wives will, that he was unhappy in his spirit. He had striven to keep it from her, but she knew. Women are fain to know such things.

Now she and the old gaffer went first to the empty forge, and then to the village inn, where they had tidings that the young blacksmith had been seen to leave the forge, and to go toward the quay, many hours ago. Other villagers joined them, with more swinging lamps, and there was talk of murder and highwaymen, and much rough sympathy and foreboding.

And, indeed, when they found Henry, coming upon him suddenly, and with many an exclamation and loud lament, it looked as if a murder had been wrought. For he lay upon his back, and there were patches upon his clothes, and on the ground about him, darker than the night. The sky might have been his pall, so still he lay, and the murmur of the sea beneath might have been his dirge. There were no stars, and no moon; truly the bracken might have hid an assailant. But Mary, who was soon beside him, on her knees, pillowing his head on her breast, crying to him, saw that it was no murder.

'I went to sleep, and woke coughing. My mouth was full of blood. . . . it is coming again! Mary . . .'

They carried him back to the cottage presently, and it seemed he would have died before they brought him there, so great and so constant was the flow of blood from his mouth. They halted him at the inn, and tried the sovereign remedy, but without avail. The village barber, who was also the apothecary, was in the bar parlour, and he let blood from his arm to stay the blood from his lungs. For awhile the treatment

15

seemed to avail. It was a living man they brought home before the morning, to linger a few weeks under his Mary's tender nursing. Whatever fault may have been hers in the beginning, she strove to atone for it now, tending him night and day, offering to send for his uncle, or go to Hawarden herself to entreat forgiveness. For it was that that weighed on the sufferer, a sense of ingratitude, and a great home-sickness. But he could not make up his mind to let her leave him. It was always of her situation, and never of his own that he murmured in his last days. He was full of concern for her and her coming child. But for himself, it seemed that death would bring him ease, both of mind and body; his fretting conscience saw no other way. He knew now that for manual labour he was unfit, and he had forfeited his right to his uncle's affection and estate. Mary was his wife, and would be the mother of his child, but it was not true love he felt for her. The burden of concealing from her that he was aware he had made a mistake was a burden he would lay down gladly.

Henry Cadogan lived to see his daughter. With eyes fast glazing in death, he gazed upon her lovely face, a replica in miniature of his own, and with that strange gift of vision of the future which Providence so often vouchsafes to dying men, he appeared to have some foreknowledge of her destiny. He uttered a broken blessing and entreaty.

'Oh, Mary,' he cried to the weeping woman, 'my Mary, let not her weakness, nor the weakness she inherits from her unhappy father, deprive her of maternal love. Cherish her, I beseech you; cherish her as you cherish my memory, and love her whatever displeasure she may cause you. . . .'

And how well and truly she obeyed him the pages of the following history will duly testify. She was a woman of the people, and the child she bore was a gentleman's child. He had sacrificed much to her honour, and she too must make sacrifices; and, as will be seen, she did not spare them. The little Emma, so early fatherless, was ever surrounded with the love and devotion of the best of mothers. Her low estate notwithstanding, Mary Kidd had in truth a noble spirit.

CHAPTER II

Little Emma is carried to Hawarden and repudiated by Mr. George Cadogan;
welcomed by her grandmother, she is sent to school, where she meets her first
suitor; and, worldly prudence dictating, she accepts her first engagement on
life's stage.

A TENDER heart can scarce bear to contemplate the desolate plight in
which a young woman finds herself when prematurely bereft of the
husband of her girlhood, and the father of her new-born babe. Even Pity
is fain to steal away from that dark chamber where the widow Lyon
kneeled and mourned her dead. Yet was it not a manifestation of Pity
from Him who knows the human heart that cajoled the mourner from
the bier whereon her husband lay to the cradle where her infant woke,
and cried, and made its new demand?

This was the substance of the second act in the tragic comedy of Life
which the great dramatist, Fate, provided for Mary Lyon. And were it
Mary Lyon instead of her babe with whose person and history this
narrative is concerned, an author would be remiss in discharging the
obligations imposed upon him by his art, who failed to point the morals
that are to be derived from so affecting a situation. It is the daughter,
however, and not the widowed mother, who is to be the heroine of this
chronicle, and therefore it is unnecessary to pause to depict the anguish
brought by a loss of which she was too young to be aware. Only what is
pertinent to herself, shall be recorded, and in respect of Henry Lyon's

death all that has to be told therefore is how it affected the worldly position of the child whom he had begotten.

All the money Henry possessed had been sunk in the purchase of the forge, an investment than which nothing could have proved more completely the lack of prudence in worldly matters, with which his uncle, Mr. George Cadogan, had been wont to charge him. For, as it had provided him with an occupation for which he was entirely unfitted, and subjected him to an exertion to which he was so unused that it undoubtedly hastened his end, so now it represented a business which his widow could not carry on, and which, had she been unable to dispose of it, would have been as completely useless in supporting her as any of the lyrical poems which he had been in the habit of addressing to her in their ante-nuptial days.

It was the lady of that Sir Thomas Mostyn, who had chafed at the smith's lack of craftsmanship, who now came to the assistance of his widow. Gaffer Dowling, Mary's neighbour, had a nephew, a smith who had learned his trade in Chester, and was willing to avail himself of an opportunity to practise it in his native village. Through the good offices of my Lady Mostyn, negotiations were entered into between Thomas Dowling and Mary Lyon, and brought to a happy conclusion, whereby young Dowling covenanted to take the forge upon lease, paying to Mary Lyon a rental of eight shillings a week. The plan proved perfectly agreeable to all the parties. Dowling, an able-bodied and industrious man, restored the business to the prosperity it had known in the days of old John Hales, and Mary found the income accruing to her amply sufficient for her modest needs. Both she and her babe throve upon it.

Common consent consented for once with maternal pride, and the little 'Emy, daughter of Henry Lyon of Nesse, by Mary his wife,' was agreed on all sides to be the most beautiful babe in the three villages. The sympathy that at first had been the young widow's chief solace grew to be less necessary as she found happiness in her child. Her love for her young husband was merged in an affection both stronger and more sacred when his blue eyes smiled on her from the infant's face, and the red-gold curls grew under her caressing hand. Mary forgot to be unhappy when the babe crowed and kicked, forgot to grieve for the rose, as she watched the bud unfolding beneath her care. She set too much store by it, the neighbours said, and bid fair to spoil the child to whom she devoted every minute of her time. But Mary paid no heed to them. It was a tyranny to which she was the willing subject, and it was a sweet picture of innocence and domestic happiness that, all unconsciously, she formed when playing with her child.

Yet, such is the ironical humour of Fate, Mary's very happiness in her new condition was the cause of her soon being driven from the place where she had found it. Young, lovely, and already relying upon him for her maintenance, she appeared to Thomas Dowling in every respect a desirable helpmeet. Affection followed where self-interest led the way, and affection developed into a truly passionate desire. But Mary had no love, or even affection, to give. That of her heart which lay not in her Henry's grave was centred on the child with which he had so grandly dowered her. She repulsed Thomas Dowling's advances, and told him plainly she thought it showed his ill-breeding to press them upon her. Yet she should have known, none better, that it is idle to attempt to counter love's assaults with argument. To Thomas Dowling it seemed wholly fitting that Mary Lyon should take as her second husband a man who was also a smith, and already her tenant. She might scorn his advances, and taunt him with his ill-breeding, but in truth in that respect she was no better than himself. Only Mary knew, although she could not explain, that a man is not a blacksmith merely because he chances to work at a forge. Henry Lyon was a gentleman, and intimate association with him had made intimate association with anyone his social and intellectual inferior for ever impossible to her. Great love can hardly condescend from its ideal, and it was great love that Mary had lavished upon her husband, whom she had idolised in life, and, dead, idealised.

So she persisted in her denial of all that Dowling sought, and when he pursued her with ever-growing pertinacity she determined to find safety in flight. Her thoughts turned involuntarily, and often, to Hawarden, and now to Mr. George Cadogan. She would ask his protection for herself and for her child. It was her right and her privilege to appeal to its father's relatives for the child's maintenance, and though he might be harsh to herself, the fond mother deemed it impossible that any man with a heart in his breast could resist the appeal of her child's beauty and innocent helplessness.

It was at the end of a long day's journey that Mary found herself once more in Hawarden. Without pressing forward to pay her duty to her mother, who lived at the extreme end of the village, she made her way direct to that other dwelling beneath whose roof her beloved had grown to man's estate. If some tears suffused her eyes as she tenderly recalled her happy conversations with him the pledge of whose affection she now pressed to her bosom, no lack of courage made her feet falter. Widowhood lent her dignity, motherhood gave her confidence. She walked up to the thatched porch of the old house, by the open door of which a heavy iron bell depended. But while she was in the very act to pull it, Mr. George Cadogan, in person, stood before her. He had a large pair of scissors in hand, and was about to engage in the congenial task of shearing a rosebush. He peered at Mary through his horned glasses, without recognition, although with some appreciation of her comeliness, and as Mary waited for him to address her, she observed that he looked older and more frail than the passage of so few years since she had last seen him would seem to warrant. Time, though inexorable, is not cruel; it is Care that graves the deepest lines upon the human countenance, and corrodes the frame.

She dropped him a curtsey: 'An' it please you, sir,' she began, 'I am Mary Lyon that was Mary Kidd.'

'Ay,' he said, 'ay?' His hearing was a little dull. 'Mary Lyon, that was Mary Kidd,' he repeated with the usual recourse to his snuff-box. 'And what may you be wanting of me? Speak freely, girl, speak freely. 'Tis a burden you carry.' She hugged the burden closer. 'What does our poet say?

> 'To mortal man great loads allotted be,
> But of all packs, no pack like poverty.

You seek relief?'

The hand that restored the snuff-box to the pocket, lingered there to draw forth a netted purse, somewhat slenderly furnished:

> 'In faith and hope the world will disagree,
> Of all Mankind's concern is Charity,'

he quoted, not without sententiousness. 'Here is a florin for you; now go your way in peace, wench.' For still she lingered, the coin in her hand. 'I must to my roses; the day grows late. . . .'

She curtseyed again: 'You are good, sir, and most truly kind. But if it please you . . .' and again she repeated, 'I am Mary Kidd."

The name had brought nothing to his mind. Of Kidds there were not a few in the district, sailors and labourers for the most part, all of the humblest station.

But some dawn of knowledge must then have been his, for into the thin old cheeks came a reddening and his head shook a little, as if from palsy. Could this be the trull for whose sake his ward had defied and shaken off his authority, with incredible ingratitude treated as naught the affection and solicitude of an uncle who had been father and mother in one, and thrown away all the fair prospects of inheritance to an honourable position in the country? Was this the trollop through whom he had lost the young and animated companion of his solitude, and through whom his old age was lonely? And had she the hardihood and boldness to attack him here? All the bitterness and anger that had been pent up within his breast for so long, rushed to his lips in an eruption as dreadful as that which *Ætna* belches forth when *Typhon* struggles beneath it in a paroxysm of impotent rage.

'You . . . you trull, the strumpet, that ruined my nephew!' he stammered. 'Begone, begone, or I'll set the dogs on you, you baggage. . . .' All his philosophy had left him, all his reticence and dignity; he presented only the spectacle of a palsied old man in an impotent rage. 'Begone, before I do you an injury. I'll have you in the pound by the heel, I'll have no loose women in Hawarden. . . .'

'I'm an honest woman, and your nephew's widow,' she faltered out, alarmed nevertheless by his demeanour.

'You're a witch, you're a . . .' He used another word with which I dare not disfigure my page. 'An honest woman, forsooth! A pretty honesty, I warrant. You played upon the simpleness of a love-sick boy, who, to give him his due, was more fool than knave, forcing him into the marriage which led to his death.' And at the thought of what had come to the lad, and his untimely end, emotion overcame him, and he stayed a moment in his ungoverned speech. 'Poor lad! poor lad!' he murmured. 'A blacksmith's forge, a blacksmith! But perhaps I was overharsh with him. . . .' Then he recalled her presence again. 'As for you, I wish to Heaven I had made out a mittimus to Bridewell, where you might have cooled your blood what time the lad came to his senses. You married him, and then you killed him. Ay, it was through you the boy died. And now, with no husband, and none of the fortune for which you plotted, you have the impudence to come to me. I'll have nought to do with you, nor yet with the child. How do I even know it's his, or with what Dick, Tom and Harry you have had commerce?'

'God knows, sir, I was a true wife to him, and had commerce with none but my Henry before or after we were wed. Nor ever will, an' it please you, seeing what came of it. . . .' But Mr. Cadogan, philosopher and scholar though he was, was beyond listening to reason, more particularly when it spoke to him from the lips of his nephew's despised wife.

' 'Twas a clever thing you thought you were doing when you laid your bastard at my poor boy's door, and snared him into a clandestine marriage. And it's a pretty pass to which you have brought yourself. But it's Heaven's judgment on you, and I'll not interfere. Begone, I say.'

She confronted him with unfailing courage, though her limbs were tottering, and for the child's sake she strove once more to melt his wrath. But he drowned each faltering word of hers in a new torrent of passionate invective, until in very hopelessness she was compelled to turn and leave him. In truth, he drove her from his door, but when at last she passed from his view, neither his roses nor his philosophy availed him; he was conscious only of his bereavement, and of the vanity of man's hopes.

Mary went down the long street hugging her living burden yet closer to her bosom. She held her head high, conscious of her own integrity, but the colour burned in her cheeks and her eyes were dry and brilliant. The harsh words hammered on her confused brain, and now she was conscious of a great fatigue. She came at last to her mother's cottage. Motherhood meant so much more to her now than it had when, nearly three years ago, she had fled from its protection. But memory, instinct, hope, told her that here succour awaited her. And hope this time told no false, or flattering tale. Mrs. Kidd, old in her forty-seventh year, weighted with cares and poverty, was stooping among her cabbages, and for a moment failed to note the suppliant fumbling at the latch of her little gate. Then she looked up and saw. Irresolute, but only to believe so great a happiness, she stood silent for a moment. 'I've come home,' Mary faltered. 'I've come home,' . . . she held out her baby, 'with my burden.' The tears streamed down her face. 'Mother, mother, you'll not turn me from your door?'

For answer there were open arms, and crooning words of love for exhausted mother and hungry babe. There were no questions, and no reproaches, it was enough that Mary had come home again; more than enough, a great joy, an overwhelming mercy. She could not make too much of the pair of them. For Mrs. Kidd, the labouring woman, no less than the philosopher in his garden, had missed the young life about her. Mary's welcome here lacked nothing in warmth; and gradually her grief was assuaged and her courage to face life again, restored.

Nevertheless the situation of which our Emma's dawning consciousness became aware, and which furnished her with her earliest memories, was one of bitter, grinding poverty. The cottage at Hawarden was even smaller than the one at Great Nesse, containing only two bedrooms under a thatched roof, and downstairs a single living-room. A patch of garden grew the potatoes which often formed the only food for the family, and although Mrs. Kidd gladly shared her all with daughter and granddaughter, that all amounted to little more than six shillings a week. Hunger was familiar in the little cottage. Nevertheless the wolf starvation kept from the door, and this small family, females of three generations without one pair of manly arms to work for them, furnished a living proof that it is possible to be healthy and hungry at one and the same time.

Health, at any rate, was Emy Lyon's dowry in her babyhood, and with it a double portion of the beauty that is health's proper attribute. Already in her tenth summer, her hair was a miracle of length and thickness. Her skin was almost transparently fair, eyes lustrous with dancing blue, lips red and laughing, wondrously shaped. The large cotton bonnets in which she went to and fro to school, enhanced these beauties by the modesty with which they half concealed them. Her gentle parentage gave her a refinement which the other village children did not possess, and affected both her mother and her grandmother with a sense that hers was a higher nature than their own, to be more carefully nurtured, and more tenderly controlled. Remarkable was her capacity for affection; but with the warmth of heart and generosity of disposition that made the little creature adorable to all who knew her, she had a passionateness of temper, and a waywardness that were difficult to meet.

Variety of life, and the distractions of gaiety, were hard to come by in so remote a village, but already the child's heart inclined to them, and of such excitements as were provided by the great cattle-fairs held every spring and autumn she took full advantage, sorely trying the loving discipline of her natural guardians. There were rough men and boys about on these occasions, and maternal love was racked by anxiety; it could not be wholly blind to the dangers lying in wait for one so beautiful, but withal so fitful in mood, so emotional, and so captivating. Yet, if fear was latent in the mother's heart, pride and hope flourished there too, and these were not all unhappy days for Mary Lyon.

And now there was woven into the pattern of the child's life a thread, in close context with which the weft of her own career was afterwards to be entangled and knit in complicated design.

In the west corner of the churchyard at Hawarden stands the Grammar School, founded and endowed by good George Ledsham. Here the child was taught the first beginnings of that education which, later, she was at great pains to carry further; and here she met the first of the opposite sex to pay her those attentions which, later, some of the greatest in the land vied in laying at her feet.

Will Masters, like herself, was an only child, and his mother, too, was a widow. Will Masters singled Emy out from the others for his chosen companion, and soon between the two children a pretty and idyllic intercourse was established. He was her knight, championing her cause when other boys grew too rude and violent in their play, teasing, and being teased in turn by her, and in quieter moments weaving simple stories of what they should do when they were grown up, and Emy had become his wife. Heaven, that allows the heads of little children to be filled with harmless fancies, knows that in this early sweethearting there was nothing that was not pure and innocent. And yet the place the boy won in the maid's affectionate heart was so secure that, later, she was to pay a bitter price to save him from distress. Even now this first courtship was destined to make a change in her situation.

Mrs. Thomas, wife of the squire living at Broadlane Hall, found something ominous of danger in this attraction of boy to girl and girl to boy. In her position of leading lady in the parish of Hawarden she was well qualified to judge of the difficulties Mary Lyon might find in safeguarding the virtue and modesty of her daughter when she should come to marriageable age. Had not Mary Lyon's own mother found some difficulties not so long ago? Mrs. Thomas and the schoolmaster held conference together. Already it was impossible to ignore the beauty of the little cottage girl. The schoolmaster and the Lady of the Manor combined in disapproving of the romping games and too early courtships that were so prevalent in the village. More than once evil had come of such games. At the Hall, under the discipline that prevailed in that well-ordered establishment, impropriety was impossible, and danger kept at bay. So, Mary Lyon consenting, Mrs. Thomas took Emy, who now was thirteen years of age, into her service, to act as nurse-girl and maid to her own three children, and be taught to earn her living Christianly and virtuously under Mrs. Thomas's own supervision.

On the face of it the arrangement appeared entirely good. For at home Emy's natural gaiety and the lightness of her nature, robbed reproof of all its force. Neither Mrs. Kidd nor Mary Lyon could find it in their heart to punish her as beseemed them when thoughtlessness carried her beyond the bounds of prudence.

Emy's loving and lovable disposition, her impetuous repentance and easy tears won her quick forgiveness. To her mother she was the living representation of romance and the joy of life. Mother and grandmother combined in her spoiling, and indeed they acknowledged it to each other. Already little Emy was almost beyond parental control, and Will Masters was a yet further complication. The household of Mrs. Thomas presented a solution of all difficulties. There she would be well provided for, and placed out of reach of temptation. And if she were not happy, was not the cottage door always open to her? To Broadlane Hall, then, Emy was duly conveyed, on the understanding that she might visit her home every week, and that every week her mother and grandmother might come to see her at the Hall.

Thus it came about that on her thirteenth birthday Emy made her first venture into the world, beginning, as many another great actress hath done, with the humble part of a serving-maid, to rise in after years to be the accepted queen of the theatre.

But the little Emy was destined also to play her part, not in the stilted tragedies and comedies of the stage, but in the great drama of contemporary history.

CHAPTER III

Master Will Masters creates a diversion at Broadlane Hall, and Mrs. Thomas decides that Emy must shine in some other sphere.

HAPPINESS dwells in ordered ways as surely as doth security. Nay, it were apter to the fact to declare that Happiness is the offspring of Security, but for whose maternal labour and ensuing vigilance it could neither have its being nor endure. Yet such is the perverseness of human nature, it often finds in security naught but tedium, and would adventure happiness for variety, not knowing the value of its most valuable possession. Even of those of gentle disposition there are some who forfeit the satisfaction of quietude, disturbing the placid atmosphere by the admission of elements which the wisdom of their guardians deems it necessary to exclude. And this was the first misfortune of our heroine, who, in childish ignorance of all that it might entail, was a consenting party to the intrusion of her old associations into her new.

For assuredly in that first year she found happiness at Broadlane Hall. It was her disposition to be happy, and there was nothing in her new circumstance to war with her disposition. From the poverty of old Mrs. Kidd's cottage, where there was seldom meat enough to stay healthy hunger, where fuel was too scant to dispel the cold that rose from the flagged floor, she had come to the enjoyment of the creature comforts, the warmth and plenty of the spacious Hall. In a less conscious degree she was grateful for the sense of safety it afforded, for that very protection which it was the excellent Mrs. Thomas's object to secure her. She strove to requite kindness with good service, minding the children when she took them on expeditions in search of nuts or berries, playing with them decorously in the house or garden when they were not permitted to go further abroad, listening soberly to the instruction of her mistress, and accepting praise or rebuke in a becoming spirit. It seemed now as if a fair breeze filled the sails of her life's little barque, to waft it evenly to the haven of good fortune. But of a sudden and without premonition, the breeze fell away, the sky altered, and a horrid tempest broke, driving the barque on an uncertain course into the open sea of perilous adventure.

Within the limits of his not inconsiderable fortune Mr. Thomas gratified his wife's taste for the Fine Arts and, in particular, for painting. His eldest daughter had already acquired some proficiency in this pleasing accomplishment, and had made a portrait of Emy Lyon, than whom she herself was but little less attractive in exterior appearance. Her eyes were blue, though of a lighter hue than those of her lovely model, and her hair was ringleted, albeit fairer than were Emy's auburn curls. But to her fond mother's thinking, Miss Thomas at the age of sixteen, possessed a more elegant shape. Emy had not yet grown to her full height, and was inclined to be buxom in the figure.

Mr. Rumney was at this time but a journeyman artist, with his reputation still in the making. But recommendation of him was spreading far and wide, and flattering accounts of his skill in portraiture had reached the ears of Mrs. Thomas. That lady entered into communication with the artist, and ascertaining that his circumstances were poor, prevailed upon him to travel from Colchester, where he then was, to Hawarden, for the purpose of painting a composite portrait of her husband, attended by herself and eldest daughter.

It was while he was engaged in the execution of this commission that the storm broke on Emy Lyon's head, and that Mr. Rumney first beheld her who later inspired so many of his exquisite achievements.

He had been painting in the great oak parlour, Mr. Thomas standing before him, straight and stiff, Mrs. Thomas, in all the glory of a new purple paduasoy, sitting in an arm-chair, Miss Thomas reclining at her feet. It was a truly admirable composition, and Mr. Rumney, walking back from the easel, palette swinging from his thumb and brush in hand, was able to assure his patron that this was one of the best things he had done. He begged Mr. Thomas to step down and look at it, and even now was perpending his criticism. Mr. Thomas could find no fault with the likeness, which indeed was excellent, nor with the painting, which was spirited and lively; but he felt it obligatory upon his reputation as a connoisseur, and his dignity as a patron, to take exception to something in technique or in detail. He therefore expressed himself as being hardly satisfied with the representation of the red coat he had donned for the occasion.

'It sags under the arms, mister, for all the world as if 'twas a sack, and no coat at all.' He went up to it, thrusting a broad first finger on to the wet paint. 'And what's worst of all, these buttons be too far apart.'

Mr. Rumney's pride as an artist was touched, but his discretion deterred him from arguing the point. When a man's pocket is empty, the first thing he puts in it—and he be wise—is his pride, and *de gustibus*, especially *non est disputandum*, 'twixt client and patron. So poor was Mr. Rumney in these days that he had been obliged to leave his wife and son behind him while he travelled up to London to make his fortune, painting portraits by the way, at five guineas a head, with reduction on taking the quantity. There were ten guineas at stake on this very canvas, enough to mitigate a much greater mortification than could be caused by the censure of one whose qualifications as critic Mr. Rumney had the lowest opinion. So the artist pursed his lips, and affected to be considering of the matter, whilst in reality he was framing a speech whereby he might tell Mr. Thomas to go to the devil, and take his buttons with him, yet so as not to give any offence.

How Mr. Rumney would have yoked civility with candour—ever a difficult pair to drive in double harness—will never be known, for at that critical moment a shriek resounded from the kitchen quarters, followed by shrill ejaculations, the sound of blows, and yet more screaming. Consternation seized the party in the great oak parlour. The complaisant smile which Mrs. Thomas had worn until her lips were stiff was drawn into a round O of amazement and alarm; her daughter's angelic sweetness was lost in excited curiosity. Both of them were on their feet in a trice and hurrying to the kitchen, where it was evident a battle was proceeding. Mr. Thomas retained his composure long enough to possess himself of a stout cudgel wherewith to enforce his authority if need be. Then he followed the ladies, hurriedly, yet not without dignity. Mr. Rumney brought up the rear of the procession, allured by the same curiosity that will draw an entire town to see a dog fight, and quite forgetting the discomfiture into which he had been thrown by Mr. Thomas's criticism of his fine oil painting.

The kitchen was in a dreadful turmoil, the principal figure in which was Mrs. Ogle, a woman of most ample proportions, whose face, always red, was now scarlet and moist with sweat. With one huge hand, she grasped Will Masters, with the other a poker snatched from the hearth. She was belabouring him, and he grappling with her, kicking and trying to bite, the while the pair of them revolved about the room, crashing against the chairs and table, alternately screaming and shouting most terrible invectives.

'I'll learn you to come thieving into my kitchen, you lazy, idle, blubbering loon,' the angry woman bawled. 'I'll learn you, I'll learn you.' And indeed it seemed that a lesson so rubbed in could not lightly be forgotten.

All the children were in the kitchen, each one setting up his separate scream of fright or delight at such noise and confusion. The gardener's boy was there, too, grinning and calling out encouragement to both the combatants. Joe Codgers, from the stables, was spurring Mrs. Ogle on to greater efforts.

'That's right, mother. Lay it into him. Shouldn't be surprised if 'twas him that was busy in my harness-room; get on to him.' Joe gave her a yell of encouragement, a species of tally-ho, that would have struck terror into the heart of the stoutest old dog otter that ever fought terrier; it delighted the children, and almost outvoiced Will Masters's howls. For he was howling in earnest now, his scarcely adolescent strength beaten down by the weight of the angry woman's blows.

Such was the scene upon which burst Mr. Thomas, his wife, eldest daughter and Mr. Rumney.

'Ha' done, woman, ha' done before you kill the lad. Is this a Bedlam or a bear-pit? Let un go, I tell you.' Mr. Thomas forced his way between them, sending Will Masters reeling against the wall and thrusting Mrs. Ogle back into a chair.

Then arose a babel of explanations, of how Mrs. Ogle had found Will Masters hiding in the wood cupboard, and charges of thieving were shouted against the boy, who gave back through his sobbing breath loud and fierce denial. But it was not to these that the itinerant artist gave heed, nor to the screaming children and excited servants. *His* gaze was fixed upon a face pale with terror, a pair of dark blue eyes drowned in tears, lips of incomparable beauty, quivering and trembling in distress, upon a mass of auburn ringlets escaping from under a mob cap.

'What an exquisite child!' he murmured to himself. The scene in the disordered kitchen was forgotten, and he feasted his eyes upon every line of beauty and wonder of colouring. And now, gathering courage, Emy darted forward and poured out a passionate defence of the friend and champion of her school-days. It was 'only Will Masters,' she said, 'Will Masters from the village,' and she protested that he was not thieving, and he was not a thief, that it was her he had come to see, and

36

he meant no harm at all. Then she fell to sobbing, and Mr. Rumney thought she was even more beautiful than before. When Will Masters presently drew close to her for mutual society, help and comfort, Mr. Rumney whipped out his pocket-book and began to make a pencil drawing of the pair of them.

Order was restored with some difficulty, the children pacified, the servants sent about their proper business, and Mrs. Ogle interrogated. Such scenes could not be permitted in Broadlane Hall, both Mr. and Mrs. Thomas insisted, and they pressed for further explanation.

A very slight investigation led to the dismissal of the charge of theft against Will Masters. But it had to be admitted that he was concealed in the wood cupboard for an unlawful purpose, the said unlawful purpose being to intercept Emy on the way to the nursery with the dinner, and persuade her to let him walk home with her that day from Broadlane Hall to Mrs. Kidd's cottage.

Mrs. Thomas's face showed grim disapproval. Such scenes could not be permitted in her house, she repeated, and if this one had truly arisen on Emy's account, Emy must go back to the cottage. And at that the girl wept afresh, more curls coming down, and Mr. Rumney noted that they fell far below her waist. He could not but observe, too, the whiteness of her neck and the perfection of its moulding. His fingers itched for the drawing of her.

But Mr. Thomas fell to laughing, and seizing Emy by the arm, looking into her face rather rudely, he swore that the lad had good taste.

37

' 'Tis as pretty a wench as ever I saw,' he declared, pinching her cheek. Then, more soberly, with Mrs. Thomas's eye upon him, he bade her 'be a good girl and mend her ways.'

'I do try, sir,' she answered, dropping him a curtsey, 'I do, indeed, for my mother's sake, and because Mrs. Thomas has been so good to me.' There was no sign of softening on Mrs. Thomas's countenance. That good lady was, indeed, becoming more and more displeased by the admiration of her little nurse-maid so openly shown by both Mr. Thomas and Mr. Rumney. Emy was not unobservant, and now she addressed her appeal to her master rather than to her mistress.

'And Will here, sir, believe me, he meant no harm, he only wanted to ask me to walk with him. Do, sir, do beg Mrs. Ogle to forgive him, for indeed she has used him sore.'

She looked up at him with such pleading eyes, luminous through their blue depths, and humid with tears, that he pinched her cheek again, and did as he was asked.

'Leave off railing at the boy,' he said to Mrs. Ogle, 'and see if you can't put something inside of him to make up for the bruises you've set on the outside. A full belly's a fine cure for a sore head. As for his walk home with you this afternoon,' he went on to Emy, 'that's for your mistress to decide. For my part, I think it's tempting the lad too far. If he ben't a thief now, 'tis putting him in the way of becoming one.' And at that he gave another great laugh, and turned on his heel. But Mr. Rumney lingered and noted again the pretty wondering flush on the child's cheek, and the grace of the curtsey she dropped as Mr. Thomas left the kitchen, followed by his indignant wife.

Will was duly fed, and further comforted by a stoup of small ale. Mrs. Ogle was not a bad-natured woman, only one of quick temper, and in truth the unexpected appearance of Will Masters in the wood cupboard had greatly alarmed her. She was willing to make up for her violence at her master's bidding, and was so generous with the ale that it came about Will walked not home at all with Emy Lyon that afternoon, but slept instead, heavily, and without dreams. His place was taken by Mr. Rumney, who said afterwards that, child though she was, only in her fifteenth year, Emy had charmed him by the sprightly nature of her discourse, and ravished him by the grace with which she moved by his side.

It may be that Mr. Rumney spoke too warmly of her, or perhaps it was the generosity with which Mr. Thomas concurred in the praises, that confirmed Mrs. Thomas in the resolve, nebulous during the melee in the kitchen, but soon to take shape and form. No woman, least of all one of experience like the lady of Broadlane Hall, could have failed to notice how particularly the two men looked at the pretty nurse-maid in the following days, Mr. Rumney following her in her walks and begging her to sit for him, Mr. Thomas pinching her cheek and asking her where she found her roses.

Miss Thomas was pale and languished modishly. Mr. Thomas vowed that he liked to see a girl buxom and as if her food nourished her. Emy's roses deepened under his attentions, so he told her again that she must

39

be a good girl and come to him if the boys plagued her; which she promised to do, thanking him for his kindness, but adding in her childish way, that Will Masters never plagued her, but was her old schoolfellow with whom she had been sweethearting until Mrs. Thomas told her mother it was unbecoming, and that she had better be nurse-maid to the young ladies.

'And I'll warrant the schoolmaster gave a good account of you to Mrs. Thomas.'

Emy had to confess roguishly that she feared 'twas but indifferent good.' At which Mr. Thomas expressed surprise, and would have continued his inquiries, but that Mrs. Thomas came out at that moment, reproving Emy for standing gossiping when she ought to be at work, and sending her to her duties.

Mr. Thomas vowed she was hard upon the girl.

'A little beauty like that won't long be nursemaid to a parcel of brats. Any man with half an eye in his head can see she's fit for something better. Why, Mr. Rumney, who has painted half the fine ladies in the county, says her beauty is most uncommon.'

' 'Tis to be hoped her beauty won't bring her into a worse situation,' his lady retorted tartly.

This incident, with other passages of a like nature, determined Mrs. Thomas that Emy Lyon could not be serving-girl in her establishment much longer. Mr. Thomas blustered, but the grey mare was the better horse, and 'twas only in his cups he held his own.

'A curse on women's jealousy,' the squire said to Mr. Rumney. 'They can't deny beauty when they see it, but they'd go to the gallows sooner than acknowledge it. What a shape, man! What a shape! She'd set London by the ears if she appeared at Ranelagh.'

Mr. Rumney thought so too. He may even have told Emy as much, and so set Heaven knows what visions moving before the girl's lively mind. Emy was quick to see a future in which ease and gaiety might take the place of work and frowning reprimands from Mrs. Ogle and her like. She had no opposition to make to any plan that should set her in new scenes and give her new experiences. The lightness of her nature rejoiced in any prospect that promised change. Mary Kidd trembled and feared, and the good grandmother was full of misgivings, but no foreboding or presage of evil entered the mind of the girl who was now to be exposed to all the evils of the great metropolis. She was still little more than a child. But Mrs. Thomas thought that a child Will Masters could not leave alone, to whom Mr. Thomas was complaisant, and Mr. Rumney attentive, was better away from Broadlane Hall.

And Mrs. Thomas was wise in her generation, as the event proved.

CHAPTER IV

Emy misbehaves in Chatham Place and follows it by indiscretion at Mr. Linley's. She meets Mr. Harry Angelo.

IT was in the house of the learned Dr. Budd, a surgeon of eminence living in Chatham Place, near St. James's Market in the Blackfriars, that Emy Lyon first found shelter in the great capital. Dr. Budd was Mrs. Thomas's brother, and Mrs. Thomas deemed that a young person even more addicted to frivolity than Emy had yet shown herself to be, might profit by the advantages offered her in such a situation. To the ordinary solicitude for the welfare of her servants felt by every conscientious mistress there would be added the personal interest arising from the fact that Emy came from the establishment at Broadlane Hall where Dr. Budd had a worthy relative, and where so often Mrs. Budd had been an honoured guest.

Without evincing partiality, which would have been to do less than justice to her other servants, Mrs. Budd was undoubtedly disposed to bestow favour upon a girl sent to her with such credentials. But as it chanced, unfortunately—although, perhaps, there are persons who would rather use the word 'providentially,' for it so happened that all Emy's misfortune led her upwards, and not downwards—there was at this time, also in the domestic employment of Dr. Budd and his lady, a young woman named Jane Powell. In addition to an outward appearance very pleasing, and a refinement of manner unusual in persons of her station of life, Jane Powell was the possessor of histrionic talents wholly exceptional, which in after years carried her to eminence in the theatrical profession. No generous heart can fail to sympathise with the efforts of genius to rise from sordid circumstance, or refuse applause to that perseverance which enables it to triumph over obstacles. But sympathy cannot be permitted to deflect justice, and we are compelled to censure the impropriety of conduct which is not infrequently indulged in by persons of an artistic temperament who devote to the gratification of their tastes, and the indulgence of their propensities, the time for which they accept pecuniary reward to give to other employments. Seen in proper perspective such behaviour is dishonest, and deserving of reprobation.

It was precisely this fault which Jane Powell frequently, wellnigh habitually, committed, and with which all too soon she infected her new fellow-servant. Tasks were performed perfunctorily, and with unbecoming haste, in order that these two young females might the sooner fall to practising steps in the kitchen, hastily disordered for that purpose, to dressing their heads in imitation of actresses whom Jane had seen at Drury Lane, to posturing and striking attitudes for the admiration of vast audiences that as yet only existed in their fecund imagination. Their talk was ever of the glitter and excitement of the theatre, their waking dreams were of the triumph Jane at least was confident she would achieve.

Mrs. Budd, although perennially dissatisfied with her maid-servants, disappointed with Emy's levity, and disheartened by Jane's idleness, had yet for a considerable time no conception to what lengths these faults would carry them. She, no less than her sister-in-law, was a conscientious woman and good housewife. But if she had often to reprove these young women for their negligence of duty and looseness of behaviour, which seemed ominous to her as indicative of bad habits in formation, she had really little idea of the degree which these faults had already attained. And her indignation at her discovery was the greater for the way it came about.

The doctor had engaged himself to dine with friends occupying a considerable position in society, and early in a certain evening he departed to their house, which was in another quarter of the town, carrying his lady with him. Mrs. Budd left her home with little misgiving. Jane Powell and Emy Lyon were bidden to finish their not too onerous duties and ordered to retire early, after snuffing the candles, and seeing that all doors were barred save the one on the latch, which would serve for the entry of Dr. and Mrs. Budd. But the rare opportunity of the absence of the mistress of the house was one not to be lightly lost. Jane and Emy projected a frolic the like of which they had often contemplated. Mrs. Budd's wardrobe was not kept locked; they would dress up and give an entertainment! Their audience might consist of the kitchen cat and the cockroaches that made their sluggish disposition about the warm corners of the hearth, but in imagination the scene was a crowded theatre, and not Mr. Garrick himself would evoke more tumultuous applause.

Jane, in Mrs. Budd's most cherished possession; the white satin wedding dress that had lain these seven years past enwrapped in lavender; danced, sang, and pirouetted. A touch of soot served for patches. Her hair was piled high, flour served her for powder, and material for a week's puddings had gone to its elegant whiteness. The red for her cheeks she had found in Mrs. Budd's bedchamber, although afterwards, to her husband, that lady expressed both surprise and wonderment at its appearance. Emy had draped the auburn abundance of her curls with a mantilla of valuable lace; she had disembarrassed herself of her frock and modest kerchief, and candour compels the admission of the fact that nothing but the mantilla and her chemise hid the elegance of her form.

The room was brightly lighted with candles abstracted from the stores cupboard, the key of which Mrs. Budd had so trustfully left at home. Their hilarity waxed with the occasion, soon they forgot all but the exuberance of their spirits and the exercise of the talents which assuredly were the birthright of both of them. The kitchen table, which had been set against the wall so as to leave a greater area available for movement, was discovered to be the ideal stage. Jane was the first to jump upon it, and now with loud voice, and the poker for baton, she sang and directed the dance that Emy began to perform in her character as a wood nymph; she was a dryad inviting unwilling faun, the very spirit of the wood was in the intoxicating laughter of her eyes and the wildness of her unbound locks. Hers was really the poetry of motion, her wantonness an irresistible appeal.

And thus it was the doctor and Mrs. Budd found them when, startled by the sound of voices and laughter as they made their sober entrance, they descended to the kitchen and burst upon the scene that had so different an effect upon each. Mrs. Budd, although she did not take in all at once the tragedy of the wedding dress, the lace mantilla, and all the desecration of her wardrobe, was for the first moment overwhelmed and speechless with indignation. Whilst Dr. Budd, good man, warmed with port and the conviviality in which he had taken part, lost sight of the heinousness of the offence against decency and order on which he was gazing, and could do naught but wonder at the beauty revealed by Emy's indecorous toilette. Her arms were bare, her bosom exposed, all the promise of her budding womanhood revealed. Since she had been in London she had become slender, and the slenderness, so white and exquisite, had already a warm and sensuous appeal. Emy's beauty was only in the bud; but in thin chemise, with her wild curls and dancing eyes, 'twas already a thing to wonder at. If Mrs. Budd for the moment was speechless with anger, that which kept the good doctor silent for the same space had another name. For in truth the make of the girl was beyond compare, and would have inflamed any man's blood.

The girls had been too absorbed in their playacting to hear the entry of their master and mistress. The doctor had time to note those slender white arms of Emy's, the dimplement in the elbow, to watch the graceful movements making play under the revealing chemise, and then . . . Well, what befell needs the Homeric pen, and Heaven forfend that ours should attempt it. Mrs. Budd recognised all at once the genesis of Jane Powell's masquerade, the treasures of her wardrobe, and the wastefulness of the flaming candles. It was upon Jane her first rage

46

descended. Jane was dragged in a trice from the table, the dress was torn off her back, and her reputation torn no less quickly. 'Thankless,' and 'brazen,' and 'abandoned' were epithets that descended like blows on the bare shoulders; the powdered hair was pulled down violently, the flour descended on Mrs. Budd's second best silk dress, but failed to cool her violent speech, or the red that inflamed her cheeks.

Meanwhile Emy, startled and terrified, was being upbraided by her master. But was it upbraiding? Mrs. Budd certainly did not think so when, diverting her attention for a moment from the dishevelled and panting Jane, she perceived that her husband had his arms about the hussy, and was admonishing her for exposing herself with something that seemed to be warmer than professional solicitude. 'Wanton' was the word Mrs. Budd used on that occasion, and would have said worse, no doubt, but that the doctor checked her, and spoke of the girl's youth and, in mitigation of punishment, said it was only a frolic in which they had been engaged, and harmless, but that the night was chill and the draughts dangerous. He kept his hand on Emy's bosom with the object of feeling if her heart were sound. And indeed it was palpitating; but that may have been from the dance. Dr. Budd suggested she should come up to the consulting-room and let him investigate with a stethoscope the condition of her health. But Mrs. Budd was firm in resisting the proposal. The turn affairs had taken startled her into prompt measures. Both girls were ordered immediately to their attic. In the morning, she said, ominously, she would deal with their offence, which now, however, seemed light in comparison with the one of which she saw the possibility dawning in her husband's eyes. Mrs. Budd was not without experience of his complaisance with his female patients. He adjured her to compose herself, suggesting that if she stayed to recover her finery, put out the candles, and restore the kitchen to its wonted order, he would himself see the culprits upstairs. But she flouted his suggestion, and there were warm words between them, during the passage of which she intercepted a glance passing between Jane and Emy, in which there was not penitence, but some amusement. Then, indeed, her wrath grew beyond reason or measure, and 'twere well to draw a veil over what followed. But the mischief, no doubt, lay in the doctor's interference, and if the result showed that a *modus vivendi* had been arrived at between husband and wife, and perhaps a reconciliation in the solitude of the bedchamber, it boded evil, and not good, for the two girls, who, having been caught *in flagrante delicto*, could oppose no argument to the cold morning justice that was meted out to them.

The doctor had departed to his duties at the Hospital of St. Thomas what time their fate was communicated to them and no appeal to him was possible. Otherwise Jane Powell, who already knew the world better than her young friend, had determined to make it. They had been locked in their attic all night. Emy had spent the time in tears, Jane in preparation for the dismissal she felt was inevitable. She tried to encourage Emy, and raise her drooping spirits. She told her there was no doubt Dr. Budd looked favourably upon her misdemeanour, or upon her, and she drew a most favourable augury from his attitude.

But, as has been seen, she reckoned without Mrs. Budd's promptitude and the absence of her spouse. Mrs. Budd had recognised, even as Jane had observed, the inclination of the doctor to befriend the young and beautiful girl who was in his charge. And her measures were taken accordingly. She dismissed both girls from her service, laying credit to herself, in her severe admonition of them before their departure, that she adventured no stronger steps. She talked of Bridewell and the stocks, of the whipping-post, and the way the law had of dealing with untrustworthy servants. But for herself she was satisfied to see the backs of them.

Thus it came about that before ten o'clock Emy Lyon found herself standing outside the closed door of Dr. Budd's house, her few possessions in a box in her hands, the only human being whom she knew in the whole of the crowded city standing beside her, outcast and friendless like herself.

Her situation appeared desperate, bringing tears of self-pity to her eyes. And truly it was a situation full of grave peril to one so lovely and ignorant of the world. Yet who can gainsay the justice of her punishment?

'We'll go to Drury Lane and see Mr. Sheridan,' Jane declared; ' 'tis acting has brought about our trouble, and maybe 'tis acting we are best fitted for, and not service at all. My aunt has a place about the theatre, and will help to opportunity of speech with him. Our looks must do the rest,' she added flippantly, smiling to herself, as one who knew her stock-in-trade was saleable.

49

She encouraged her companion with much shrewd philosophy, and led her directly to the great theatre in Drury Lane. Success is often to the adventurous. The manager could not refuse an interview prayed for so urgently and with aspirants of whose looks he had heard so glowing an account. He had the young women admitted, and examined them straitly about their story and their qualifications for the stage. When Jane Powell put the facts before him he laughed, thus inspiring hope again in Emy's doubting heart. Jane had the glibber tongue, and was ready to show her quality by immediately singing and dancing. To Mr. Sheridan's great entertainment she gave also a spirited imitation of the scene in the Chatham Place kitchen that had led to their present dilemma. But Emy's eyes were swollen and disfigured with crying, and she had neither the courage nor the spirit for exhibition.

Mr. Sheridan consented to give Jane Powell a trial, but he would make no such promise to Emy.

'What am I to do?' Emy pleaded. It was the first, but not the last occasion, that the same cry rang from her lips when her own imprudence brought her to a critical situation.

Mr. Sheridan looked at her, with the practised eye of a man whose business it is to appraise female appearances. He was struck by the wonderful innocence of the great blue eyes, arrested by the mute appeal of virginity still unsullied and in peril. There was little of life that Mr. Sheridan did not know, either at first hand from experience, or at second hand as mirrored in the playhouse he controlled. It seemed certain that evil would befall the child if she were left to her own resources. And he was ever a man of heart.

'I will give you a letter to my father-in-law,' he said, after a minute's reflection. 'He is in need of assistance with an invalid son, and may possibly give you a trial with my recommendation. The boy is in a consumption.'

'My father died of a consumption,' Emy interposed eagerly. With hope of employment her light spirits reacted quickly; and now Mr. Sheridan was struck by her animation. She was not yet ripe for the stage, had shown no talent like that of Jane Powell, but already he was loath to lose sight of her.

Emy accepted the suggestion to take service with Mr. Linley, uttering a thousand protestations that she would never betray such generosity. Mr. Sheridan put an end to them with the air of one who sets small store by words, and bade the girl make it her business to please her new master. He added carelessly 'twould do her no harm in her spare time to study a play or two, and later he would hear if she made progress in elocution.

Thus, by a stroke of good fortune which they could not have expected, and by the benign interposition of a Providence which they had done so much to offend, both girls were saved from the worst consequences of their folly. Jane Powell obtained, and kept, her engagement in the theatre, of which she subsequently became a brilliant ornament, and Emy Lyon found a refuge in the house of respectable and worthy citizens. The lesson was a sharp one, and its effect might well have been permanent.

Nevertheless, it would seem that Emy had not learned prudence. Certain it is that the issue of this affair was not satisfactory to her rescuer, nor entirely creditable to herself, although the fault imputed to her on this next occasion was due to excess of sensibility, and not lack of decorum.

Mr. and Mrs. Thomas Linley already mourned the death of a son, cut off in the bloom of youth, and now they were watching with dreadful apprehension the fell progress of a consumption which sapped the vitality of another, full of promise, who carried the barque of their high hopes.

Mr. Sheridan's letter, and the proffer of Emy's services, came in the nick of time. They made no investigation into her antecedents. Mr. Sheridan's letter was enough when, coupled with it, was the fact that Mr. Linley was impatient of the sick-room and Mrs. Linley worn out with her services there.

It is a matter of common observation that hope, and confidence of restoration to health, wax higher in the bosom of consumptives the nearer they approach their inevitable end. One might imagine that Mother Nature spreads this fond delusion before their eyes that the gloom of despair might not be added to the melancholy perception of failing forces. This was Lieutenant Linley's condition; the brilliancy of his eyes and the colour in his cheeks, as he saw them reflected from the mirror, seemed to promise complete recovery. He spoke hopefully to his new nurse, and told her stories of what he had done in the days of his vigour, making clear what he would do again when these should return. Emy listened to him with increasing interest, and soon he felt that he was deriving advantage from her abundant vitality, from which there seemed to emanate a health as contagious as is disease.

The young man drew benefit from the propinquity of the beautiful young girl who waited upon him, but it was an artificial rather than a natural benefit, and presently the inevitable happened. Emy had a compassionate heart, to which the weakness of her patient appealed. She soon became to him something more than attendant and he was not willing she should be a moment out of his sight. He craved a love that she was not ripe, nor ready, to give him, but a simulation of which at first made him content. Pity was what she had for him, but they both misnamed it. In truth, he came in the end to repel, rather than to attract her. For his illness made him fierce in his desires, and her virginity shrank unconsciously from a morbid condition that she could neither understand nor escape. He prayed his parents to consent to a marriage between them, and they could refuse nothing to the dying lad. But it may be imagined that they had no tender feelings towards Emy! They consented, but insisted that the ceremony should be deferred for his convalescence. They reprobated her for not yielding to him more cheaply, blaming her for that which indeed was culpable in neither of them. They would have blamed her equally, or more, had she given him that which as yet she had hardly learnt to value. Her situation was full of difficulties. She wanted neither to marry Samuel Linley nor to become his mistress. She was still little more than a child, and the feelings she evoked, and was doomed always to evoke, found as yet no response in her own breast. Yet was she no longer completely ignorant, for her circumstances in the sick-room, the physician in attendance, and Mr. Linley himself, to say nothing of Samuel's fevered pleading, combined to open her eyes. But she was still innocent, and her youth should have pleaded for her when the event happened for which they had all been waiting.

Samuel's excitement at the prospect of the hurried wedding he craved brought on a violent fit of coughing; it was followed by high fever and prostration. He never rallied, lingering too short a time to make provision for the girl upon whom his ill-starred attachment worked so dire an ill. His death relieved his parents, or so they deemed it, of any duty toward her. They had been jealous of his attentions to her, and now they were in anguish at his loss. That was their excuse for their treatment of this young and beautiful girl, but indeed 'twas a poor one. Immediately his son was dead, Thomas Linley drove Emy from his house, and once more the weeping girl was without a home, alone in London.

Beauty in distress is more quickly evocative of pity than plainness in a like strait. This is not merely the apothegm of the cynic; it covers matter for the reflection of a philosopher and a religious, and for the pen of poet and historian. Emy Lyon now provided another illustration of its truth.

At sixteen years of age she was so beautiful that all who passed by turned to gaze after her. Clad in poor mourning, with her eyes brimming with tears, and every mark of agitation upon her countenance, she walked along Rathbone Place, wondering whether she should turn her steps towards Drury Lane and Jane Powell, or where else she might find a refuge in her desolation. She had given little love to Samuel Linley, yet was she distressed at his death, and distracted by her own situation.

In this disconsolate condition she was stayed by a gentleman of fashionable appearance, who, with every expression of sympathy and good breeding, declared his regret for her manifest unhappiness and his ardent desire to be of service to her. Prudence dictates caution, but necessity refuses obedience to law. Emy raised her eyes to the stranger's face, and, realising her immediate necessity, responded to the amiability written upon it. She acquainted him with the recent events of her life, and wept anew when she spoke of Lieutenant Linley's death.

'Indeed I but did my duty to him, and fondled him no more than he compelled me, sir,' she protested, 'and there was no truth in what his father said, nor the harsh names he called me. Indeed I am an innocent girl. Oh, sir, if you know anywhere where I can find a shelter, or can devise any means whereby a virtuous girl can earn a decent living, tell me, for I am indeed sore distressed, and know not which way to turn.'

'What is your name?' he asked, and when she told him, added: 'Confidence for confidence; mine is Henry Angelo, and I am not without acquaintance in the polite world. Even now I am on my way to visit a lady of quality, and if you will accompany me, I will present you to her. Then you can repeat your story, and if you receive no comfort there, I will try to devise some other plan.'

Cheered by his easy kindness, and with confidence somewhat restored by the gentleness of his demeanour, Emy accompanied her new acquaintance, not failing to perceive how frequently he had occasion to acknowledge the salutations of men no less fashionable in appearance than himself, and, bare-headed, how often he would bow, with inimitable elegance, to the fair occupants of passing carriages. Such familiar acquaintance with the great world on the part of her cicerone could not fail to impress the humble girl, and her timidity was lessened by the affable candour of his conversation.

She ventured an apology for walking with one who was on terms of such easy familiarity with people of the first fashion of both sexes. He replied:

'I will make no pretension to nobility, with a view to deceiving a confiding girl. My father is the first master of equitation, and is equally famous as a professor of the art of defence. Peerless as a swordsman in England, he has been patronised by the highest in the land, and at his table I have become acquainted with many great and eminent people, some of whom, as you have seen, have done me the honour of recognition to-day.'

Engaged in such conversation as this, the strangely met pair arrived at Arlington Street, in the near neighbourhood of the Palace of St. James's, and being instantly admitted, Mr. Angelo left Emy temporarily alone whilst he was received by his friend, whose name he informed Emy was Kelly. It was not long before he reappeared, and delighted her with the assurance that everything had gone well.

'Mrs. Kelly will presently grant you an interview,' he informed her, 'and I have every confidence that my introduction will secure you an engagement in some capacity suited to your qualifications. No, say no more; I am delighted that good fortune threw me in your way. Be as happy as you are beautiful, and I shall be enchanted to have done you a small service.' And with a most elegant bow, he took his leave of her, as it proved, for ever.

The imputation of motives is a delicate task, involving a moral responsibility not lightly to be undertaken. In the case just recorded in this narrative it is charitable, as it is sufficient, to suppose that in introducing Emy Lyon to the house of this so-called lady of quality Mr. Angelo was actuated only by a desire to find an unfortunate fellow-creature, not far removed from his own sphere of life, an immediate shelter from the inhospitable streets. But in actual fact he could hardly have introduced her to conditions more favourable to the development of that side of her character which most needed restraint, or presenting greater or more obvious temptations to a girl of such rare loveliness.

Mrs. Kelly's house was the favourite resort of gentlemen of the fashionable world, the majority of whom were dissipated and extravagant, without principle, and devoid of morality. As for the lady, her sole object in life was to provide the means of gratifying the love of pleasure of those who at the same time ministered to her own. In such an establishment anything like moral discipline was out of the question. Night was prolonged far into the day, devoted to riotous festivity, in which sobriety and decorous behaviour had no place. Regularity in the performance of their duties was not incumbent upon the servants, who gave sufficient satisfaction if their work was not discovered to have been left undone. They were permitted to employ the rest of their time as they pleased, without reference to the propriety of their amusements, or the company they kept. Modesty, delicacy of sentiment, virtuous reflection, could not endure in such an atmosphere as this. Familiarity with every form of licentiousness bred indifference to the result, custom furnished specious justification for gratifying inclination. Mrs. Kelly, at Harry Angelo's request, took Emy into her service, but 'twas a doubtful charity.

Soon, all too soon, Emy became acclimatised to her surroundings. Something of the country bloom had been brushed from her at the Linleys'. At Mrs. Kelly's that which, but a short time ago, would have filled her with horror, now provided her with ever-increasing interest. Her own beauty was conspicuous, and this was a more powerful recommendation to her mistress than virtuous character. The lovely girl, ostensibly occupied in domestic work, became the object of ardent pursuit by the young bloods who frequented the gay house, and in their pursuit they had the encouragement of their hostess. Emy's perfect shape, her regular features, her graceful movement, her indescribable sweetness of expression were capped, crowned, and made peerless by an air of artless innocence. On many occasions was Emy compelled to call

all her spirit, and even her strength, to the defence of her virtue. Nevertheless, it is to her credit that for a time she defended it successfully.

In houses such as that of Mrs. Kelly social distinctions are but indifferently observed. Emy Lyon rose insensibly from the kitchen to the withdrawing-room. Endowed by nature with a musical voice, a fair ear, and a retentive memory, she acquired the art of singing the songs in vogue at the moment with considerable effect. Her natural gift of mimicry was encouraged, and presently, instead of the safety of domestic employment, she was assisting to entertain Mrs. Kelly's guests by the exercise of her newly found art. Mr. Sheridan heard her again, but, perhaps prejudiced by his father-in-law, he vowed he detected in her nothing of the genius of which he was told. He pointed out also that her ear was fair only, and not good. She frequently sang out of tune, was still the victim of embarrassment and uncertain of her place. Where none is virtuous, virtue is apt to become a reproach. Emy was made to feel by Mrs. Kelly, and other ladies of the same quality, that her chastity betrayed her humble origin. They found in her anxiety for its preservation a subject for humour, and she had hardly sufficient strength of principle to disregard entirely their quips and jests at her expense. Her mind was ever in a turmoil, sometimes her blood was inflamed by what she saw or heard, sometimes her delicacy was outraged. But no real temptation assailed her, in the true sense of the word, in the young bloods and old roues who were the patrons of Mrs. Kelly's house of accommodation. There was none to move her to the

59

sentiment that is the first temptation of young females. Emy's virtue was to fall by dint of the generosity of her nature, not by any weakness that might deprive her thus early of the sympathy of our readers.

Among the visitors to the Arlington Street house was Dr. Graham, the young and handsome empiric, whose intelligence was already being proved by the manner in which he was using his knowledge not so much of medicine as of men. He it was alone of all that community of loose women and debauched men who perceived the quality of Emy's resistance to the surrounding atmosphere. And it was only he to whom she listened with pleasure, and who, had he chosen, could no doubt have accomplished the downfall which he set himself rather to avert. He encouraged her in her attempts to raise herself from her lowly position. A very pleasant friendship was soon established between Dr. Graham and the young girl whose position was so uncertain in the house, the girl who was now scrubbing in the kitchen, and anon singing in the drawing-room, but who, whether in one or the other case, was conspicuous by something of personality. Truly Dr. Graham felt for her, and promised her his countenance and protection. But his own fortune was yet in the building. He could exhibit his interest, promise his friendship, but he could do little more for her at the moment. Yet when peril was at hand, he was able to mitigate the force of the blow, as will be seen by those who have the courage to pursue the relation of Emy's history.

Another of the young men of fashion whose acquaintance Emy made in Mrs. Kelly's establishment was Charles Willett Payne, a naval captain employed in the regulating service. A gallant officer, and a man of good feeling, notwithstanding some small taste for debauchery, he was one of the few who had refrained from persecuting Emy Lyon with his attentions. Her youth and ingenuousness were her protection from his gallantry; he was not a seducer, only a man of pleasure. He accepted Emy Lyon's presence in the gay house, but in point of fact he had taken little notice of her, for his light affections were otherwise engaged. One evening, however, when the fun was waxing furious in Arlington Street, a clamour and tumult arose in the street outside. The noise excited no attention in Mrs. Kelly's reception-rooms, where, indeed, there was sufficient noise already. Emy had been summoned from her place in the kitchen to give an imitation of a singer now drawing the town to the theatre in Lincoln's Inn Fields, and, flushed and excited, she was receiving the applause and encouragement of her audience. The group was joined by a young Irishman, whose admiration had already kept pace with his indiscretion.

'Faith, Mistress Emy,' he began, 'and can't ye be satisfied with filling the house, that ye must be filling the street as well? As I walked up to Arlington Street from my club in St. James's, 'pon my honour, I thought there was a riot.'

'What d'ye mean?' she asked him nervously, and indeed he was regarding her with intentness.

'The folks are swarming round the door like bees round a queen in July. 'Tis no exaggeration that I had to fight my way through. Your admirers are being driven away by force, and necessary force, I assure

61

you. There's a lad amongst them that calls himself Will Masters, who speaks of you by name. Fists are going, cudgels swinging, cutlasses flashing . . .'

'Will Masters?' she echoed. 'Will Masters from Hawarden! And cutlasses! '

'Aye, cutlasses. The constables have much ado to keep the mob in order. Before Gad! I'm telling you the truth.' Then seeing that her colour changed, and her beautiful blue eyes were suffused with tears, he added: 'And if it's the fellow outside on whose account you've refused every gentleman that frequents the house, you're likely to remain a virgin. For the pressgang have taken him; there's work before the Navy for many a year, and a great lack of men.'

Emy now burst out crying, and was quickly surrounded by the curious, whose wit saw fresh food for laughter in the transition of the merry songstress into 'Niobe, all tears.'

Mr. Dennis O'Flanagan explained the jest.

'There is a young gallant outside, fresh from the country, but, by my troth, he looks more bucolic than gallant, clay-caked, with something of the ploughboy about him, who has tramped a hundred miles or more for the chaste embraces of this lady.' He bowed to Emy mockingly, and she averted her eyes, for indeed she could not stomach his pleasantry. 'And now the pressgang have him instead,' he continued mockingly.

But others in the company were more compassionate, and one, moved by the girl's real distress, suggested to her that if her friend were not yet embarked, and if 'twere true, as she sobbed out, that his mother

62

was a widow, and he an only son, Captain Willett Payne had it in his power to effect an enlargement.

Emy's unhappy impulsiveness took fire at the thought of saving her whilom playfellow from his dreadful situation. She knew the gallant young officer as one of the few who had not singled her out for unwelcome attention. She would make an appeal to him, an immediate, urgent appeal. The task was not wholly an uncongenial one; it fell in with her restless humour and spirit of adventure; it satisfied her sense of loyalty; and any scruple she might have had on the score of prudence was silenced by the memory of how little notice Captain Willett Payne had taken of her or her looks. Perhaps she had been piqued at his abstinence, perhaps her taste for histrionic effect liked the prospect of making the appeal of beauty in distress to the handsome sailor who had regarded her so indifferently. Whatever the true genesis of her action, Emy Lyon ventured forth that night to seek the rooms of Captain Willett Payne, a gallant, and a man of fashion, with no other armour than her beauty. Which is as much as to say that she adventured an encounter with a highwayman with no other weapon than her filled purse.

She knew where he lived—only a few yards away, in Piccadilly. Hurrying to her room, when night had fallen and the house lay enwrapped in its wicked silence, she pulled on a cloak and hooded her head and face. Then, without staying to ask for leave, or to reflect on any possible consequences to herself, she ran through the streets, and soon was hammering at the door of the captain's lodgings. She was admitted by the captain's own servant, who first stared with undisguised surprise at her belated entry, but presently with no less disguised admiration. For, under the hood, the blue eyes were bright, and her eagerness for the chance of pleading for Will broke through the necessity for caution in showing her face.

' 'Tis late for visitors,' said Captain Willett Payne's servant, hesitatingly. The fair visitor was unknown to him, and he knew not what to do or say. 'Are you sure it's the captain you want?' And he added, out of the grossness of his nature, 'He's not the one to disappoint a lady, and if he did, dammee, my pretty, I'll oblige ye myself.'

She did not rebuke him, scarcely heard him indeed, and in another moment found herself in Willett Payne's sitting-room, where the captain was already preparing to retire for the night. He was standing near the fireless grate, in his shirtsleeves, breeches, and slippered stockings. A dresscoat and laced vest were thrown over the back of a chair, and through the opened folding door which led into his bedchamber Emy saw lighted candles before a great mirror, and all the toilet paraphernalia of a man of fashion. He stifled an oath of astonishment as she halted abruptly and nervously. The man may have been drinking; the master was certainly far from sober. He took a step forward:

'Why, 'tis Emy, Emy from Mrs. Kelly's. Well done!' he cried, 'I'm in the humour for adventure. 'Tis a miracle of happiness, or a message you're bringing me? 'He bethought himself suddenly of the friend he had in Mrs. Kelly's house, and that Emy might well be her delegate.

'I'm no messenger, sir, but a poor suppliant,' Emy cried, and threw herself quickly on her knees. Her hood fell back, her hair escaped; her histrionic power had not failed her, truly she presented a picture to excite any man's kindness. The captain's gallantry was moved, the more, perhaps, that his generous potations had loosened his tongue, unsteadied his legs, and inflamed his eyes.

'By Gad!' he cried, and drew a long breath. 'You are a suppliant, you say! Then whatever you ask is granted. But get you up from the floor,' and he raised her as well as he was able, seeing he was unsteady himself. Still holding her, he subsided into a chair, dragging her down upon his knee. Her struggle was faint, for she was come to ask him a favour, and durst not offend him. Besides, he was a personable man, and once on his knee her heart beat too fast for prudence to be heard. Falteringly she began her tale:

'By Mrs. Kelly's order to-night I was singing to amuse the company . . .'

'And 'twas a lucky company, by Gad!'

When there came an uproar in the street . . .

"I can well believe it,' he said. 'The sound of your beautiful voice might well turn the head of the whole mob,' he hiccoughed. Already, as he held her on his knee, his blood was inflaming, and colour came into his cheeks. She made to get away from him, but he held her closer. 'Be still, be still,' he said, 'go on with your story. Tell me what you want of me. 'Fore God! you little beauty, you shall have it.' She was beginning to take alarm, and sat obediently quiet.

65

'Someone I knew had come to London to see me. I don't know how he found out where I was staying, but he did, and he tried to come in. They turned him away, and he fought. And then the pressgang came along, and oh! your honour, they stunned him and carried him away, and oh! I'm the unhappiest girl in all the world.' She commenced to cry.

'Then, by the Lord, who is a man of war, I've a mind to make you the happiest. Dammee, I'm no man if I can't dry those pretty eyes.'

There was no misunderstanding him now; Emy tried to struggle from the chair and the arms that had her so fast, although not roughly.

'Don't struggle, my bird, you've flown into the cage; we'll find sugar for you there. Give me your lips.'

'No, no, no!' she cried, and almost got away from him. 'I came to you because they told me you could make the pressgang set Will free. Oh! sir, do not persecute a poor girl who is unhappy, but set my William free.'

'Your William,' he repeated stupidly; 'what's the odds about William?—my name is Charles.'

'Will Masters from Hawarden. We were at school together, and he sweethearted with me.'

'And showed good taste. But I'm sweethearting with you now, child. Have a care and don't anger me.' He caught her closer to him, and now indeed she knew fear. ''Tis a good school you've been at with Mrs. Kelly, and no doubt she's taught you to make terms. But terms or no terms . . .'

It were impossible to dwell on the scene that ensued. How Emy, terrified, fought for that which was more precious to her than Will Masters' freedom, and how yet she only secured the one at the expense of the other. Captain Willett Payne was not wholly to blame. It was past midnight, and 'twas the fashion to drink deeply; not that he was past reason, but the girl was very beautiful, and came to him out of a house of accommodation. Only the finest honour is proof against the temptations offered by certain situations, and that honour is not fostered in the world of fashion in which moved Captain Willett Payne. Our poor Emy, landed by her own indiscretion in such a situation, could not properly, nor long, defend herself. And perhaps her virtue had been weakened by the bad example that had been set her. The man who entreated her and, when entreaty did not serve, showed her how much stronger he was than she, was a man of fashion, a man of parts, in the vigour of health, handsome. Perhaps she compared him with poor Will. It is likely, too, she thought of him next to Samuel Linley. And he spoke her fair, promised her his protection, Will's release, a life of ease . . .

Emy fell, but it is difficult to apportion the blame of her undoing. In truth, circumstance had not been kind to her.

CHAPTER V

EMILY LYON'S first lapse from virtue had an immediate effect in altering her demeanour. Her expressed intention, in visiting Captain Willett Payne's lodgings alone at midnight, had been to procure the release of Will Masters from the clutches of the pressgang. She attained her object, but having done so at a cost not calculated, and only afterwards fully appreciated, she ceased to display any desire to meet the early lover whom she had liberated. He represented the days of her innocency, which being ended, shut out the desire for his companionship. Her fall was followed by a half-childish, half-philosophic acceptance of the position. She remained with Captain Willett Payne at his rooms; she considered herself under his protection. When she was not ashamed of her loss of her virtue, she was proud of the price it had brought. Mind and body were as yet unformed; nothing but the lightness of her disposition was established. After she had become used to her position—and that was an affair of days, one had almost written of hours—she danced and sang for Captain Willett Payne as she had danced and sung at Mrs. Kelly's for the amusement of her guests. She also looked after his wardrobe, and began to manifest some of those housewifely qualities, the acquisition of which she owed to Mrs. Thomas. Although light, she was not a wanton; although consent was so quickly given to what duress had first compelled, she could still maintain a shifting self-respect.

Had the captain been willing to regulate her position by marriage, or had he had the means to make permanent provision for his mistress, Emy could have been regarded as one whose fall had a mitigating aspect. But the one idea had never entered his head, and the other was not possible for his purse. Ashore, however, and, for the time being, off duty, with credit at his command, he entertained his new and delightful mistress lavishly. Neither he nor she took thought for the morrow. He was charmed with her budding beauty, delighted with her obedience and what remained of her modesty, proud of having been the first to possess her. He bade her hold no communication with Mrs. Kelly, or the 'Abbess of Arlington Street,' as it was the fashion to name her. He wished her to depend on him alone.

But though he loved pleasure and his Emy, Captain Payne loved honour more. He had the Englishman's native fondness for blue water, and was ever eager to rise in his profession. No true sailor would allow a wife to interfere with his career in the service, and it is not to be imagined that such a one would be more considerate of a mistress. Thus it chanced that when Captain Payne was ordered on active service, which came about quickly and unexpectedly, he not only omitted to make suitable provision for Emy, but was without the moral courage to inform her of more than a temporary departure from town. He rejoined his ship, leaving her plunged in young and easy tears, in light and thoughtless grief which for the moment rendered her oblivious of such mundane affairs as monetary arrangements, and temporal provision.

He left her, indeed, all the guineas at his disposal. To the girl who had had no experience of the management and prudent expenditure of money, the amount appeared to represent a guarantee against penury for some time to come; at the end of which period she supposed that her King Charles would return with further supplies. She faced her future, after his departure, with the gaiety which belongs to the irresponsible nature of light character. But not many weeks passed before she discovered that the stout sailor had left with her yet another pledge of his affection.

The operation of the maternal instinct is one of the most amazing and varied phenomena of nature. Emy contemplated the future, as it appeared with this new complication, with alarm, and without any other sentiment towards the child she carried than aversion and resentment. She was little but a child herself; and now, the period for which Captain Payne had paid in advance for his rooms having expired, she had to find herself a fresh lodging. Already she knew that he was on the high seas, and the time of his return uncertain. One is fain to admire her spirit, for her situation was desperate, and her courage rose to it. She retired to the most modest lodgings, and disposed of many of the presents she had received from her lover, in order to check the shrinkage of her little capital. As her position grew daily more critical, she racked her brains to discover some way of lessening the distress in which her folly had involved her. She went, in thought, over the names of all those whom she had met since her arrival in London, and made the mortifying discovery that among them all there was not one upon whose virtuous charity she might rely excepting Jane Powell. And to Jane Powell she was ashamed to apply. The profligate men who patronised Mrs. Kelly's withdrawing-rooms would scatter guineas in the lap of any young woman whom their sensuality made them anxious to debauch, or whose attractions held when the charm of their novelty had fled, but they had no money to waste in unselfish relief of one already spoiled. And the abandoned women who were their companions in Arlington Street had nothing but laughter for a sister in vice, who had given what she should have sold, and thus reduced herself to a disreputable distress. To them it appeared that there was nothing but the gutter for the unfortunate whose grossest error lay in miscalculating the market value of her charms.

And to the gutter Emy Lyon might have sunk, had she not in the nick of time recalled the name and personality of Dr. Graham. She remembered the aloofness of his carriage, the kindness of his demeanour, and, too late, the good advice he had given her. She heard accidentally how high a reputation he was building up as a disciple of Æsculapius, and how all the world was now flocking to the Temple where he practised the art and mystery of healing. To him, therefore, Emy determined to repair in her present distress, to solicit his attendance in her travail, and perhaps his assistance in securing some means of supporting the result.

To his house, accordingly, Emy betook herself, shrinking a little from the approaching exposure of her condition, but hoping for an amelioration of her affairs with the sanguine light-heartedness of the young and thoughtless. The house was one of those that form the Adelphi Terrace, confronting the fine panorama of the Thames. A single step separated the narrow pavement from the hall, and here, on each side of the door, stood a gigantic porter, each near seven feet in height, to regulate the traffic of the doctor's clientele. Attired in gorgeous liveries, wearing cocked hats elaborately laced, and holding long staves crowned with silver heads exquisitely chased, these imposing servants at once advertised the material prosperity of their employer and kept in check the crowd of gaping people who sought to discover the identity of the domino-covered ladies who were his visitors. Among these Emy now insinuated herself, and ere long was admitted to an apartment, magnificently furnished, where she was but one of many silent females, carefully maintaining their *incognita* until they should be compelled to discover themselves *sub rosa* to the fashionable father confessor.

But Emy's incognita was a question of moments only. Dr. Graham recognised his visitor, and soon was in possession of her trouble. Unlike the majority of those charlatans who depend for their living upon the exploitation of the weakness of their fellow-men, Dr. Graham had a good heart and a sound understanding. He was sorry for the girl whose beauty had already engaged his admiration, and he promised to assist her, only insisting that she should be guided entirely by his advice and should place herself unreservedly in his hands. If he had an *arrière pensée,* and thought, already, that she could be of assistance to him in his business, nevertheless it must be conceded to him that he behaved with great kindness to one who was sorely in need of it, and who, but for his intervention, might have found herself in so much worse a strait.

When Emy left him that morning it was only to make the necessary arrangements for giving up her present lodgings, prior to removing into Dr. Graham's own house in the Adelphi. For this, after reflection, was the plan which he proposed, deeming it the most convenient place to attend her during her lying-in, and one which, being the residence of a medical man, would cause little or no scandal if the fact of her presence became publicly known. Here, accordingly, Emy removed, assuming, at the doctor's instruction, the name of Emma Hart, and here, when her time was accomplished, she gave birth to a girl child.

In narrating the adventures of one who had so chequered and so variegated a career as the Fates allotted to the heroine of this true chronicle, the historian has many temptations to diverge into the side issues presented by the lives of the men and women with whom she was brought into personal relation. Such a one is Dr. James Graham, who is interesting as an example of the empiric with a knowledge of the credulity of human nature, and a contempt of the passions by which it is swayed. He exploited the vices he had no inclination to share. Beauty of form made to him an appeal that was scientific, utilitarianism was the keynote of the coldness of his regard. Whereas our heroine, alack! had an inflammable disposition, and knew little more than the meaning, and possibly not that, of the word utilitarianism.

Dr. Graham occupied at this time a unique position in the town, being denounced by many as an impostor and a charlatan, whilst countenanced by the great world, who were ready to declare that his system had already benefited them. Among his distinguished patronesses was Georgiana, Duchess of Devonshire, whom he had recently treated by means of his electrical apparatus; and there were others, scarcely less highly placed, ready, after experience, to testify to his ability, and who by their patronage secured him in his position as a fashionable practitioner.

But if Dr. Graham was not susceptible to the passions of humanity which affect the relations of the sexes, he was perfectly willing to play upon them for his own pecuniary advantage, and, measuring the credulity of his age to a nicety, he founded the famous Temple of Æsculapius. It was his public profession that he could teach the laws of life and health, prolong lives that appeared to be drawing to a close, arrest and repair the degeneration of a decadent society, and cure sterility. In his methods there was an admixture of imposture and of truth. He had experimented largely in the as yet little known properties of electricity, and there is little doubt that the actual effects of this new force were beneficial in many cases where the vital powers had been exhausted by immoderate indulgence. His treatment by baths was also of great efficacy, and it is easily credible that his system of dietetics was judicious and curative.

Having, however, brought the world of fashion to his doors, Dr. Graham could not refrain from pandering to its follies. He proceeded to make fresh pretensions, which the moralist must condemn as vigorously as did the faculty. Three galleried rooms, superably ornamented, and hung with pictures, chiefly from the nude, were opened to his patrons; crystal pillars, manufactured under his own superintendence, were supposed to contain the electrical apparatus whereby he undertook to restore vitality and energy. They also served incidentally to focus and reflect the myriad lights with which the apartments were refulgent. In one of the chambers was his most notorious institution, the 'Celestial Bed.' It was flanked by a figure of Fecundity, and crowned by the inscription *Dolorifica res est si quis homo dives nullum habet domi suae successorem.*

The doctor attached high importance to appeals to the emotional side of his patients. His addresses were mystical and religious in their tone, and he relied much upon music and painting as influencing the body through the mind. Solemn music vibrated through the air of the inner chamber, where the canopied bed stood in the dim light afforded by the stained-glass window. Oratorios and cantatas were employed to attune the senses of the votaries of the Temple to the mysteries about to be practised upon them; classical representations brought them into sympathetic relation with this arch-priest of the art of healing.

And it was here that Dr. Graham saw that Emma might be of service to him. He had witnessed performances by her in the house of the 'Abbess of Arlington Street,' which he frequented in his early days in order to familiarise himself with the follies and appetites of his future clients. He quickly perceived, when the girl came to him in her distress, that her unique face and form would be a further attraction to his already alluring Temple.

Emma, grateful for his timely benefaction, could not but accede to his request for her assistance as soon as it was formulated. It has not escaped general observation, and certainly it was no secret to Dr. Graham, that very young women acquire a heightened and increased beauty from maternity so soon as they have recovered from the immediate exhaustion of child-bearing. A new tenderness is added to their expression, a more delicate bloom to their complexion, a subtler curve to their lines. Within three months from the birth of her daughter, and after the child had been despatched, under Dr. Graham's advice, to the care of her grandmother at Hawarden, Emma Hart became a living demonstration of this truth. It was then Dr. Graham reaped the reward of his long-sighted philanthropy, and that Emma proved alike her gratitude and her resource. Clad in long and classic draperies, blue or white as the occasion demanded, and set in poses to compel the attention of even the most frivolous, she sang the solemn recitatives and arias which Dr. Graham wrote and composed, and lent the beauty of her voice to the spell woven by the music of the hidden orchestra.

The ritual of the Temple presided over by this so-called 'Vestal Virgin' quickly became the rage, and for one season at least the offertories brought a fortune to the high priest.

But Emma was no more secure from the attacks of immoral men of fashion in the Adelphi than she had been in Arlington Street. Captain

Willett Payne knew how to hold what he had acquired so long as he chose to do so, and he had made no secret of his conquest. Now that Emma's shape and beauty were restored, and she had ceased to be the exclusive possession of one lover, numerous pretenders were forthcoming to make a bid for the place vacated by the gallant sailor. One in particular persecuted her with his attentions. This was Sir Henry Featherstonehaugh, a baronet of considerable fortune, with an estate in Sussex, and, notwithstanding his visits to the Adelphi Temple, an unimpaired constitution. He had adventured there out of curiosity, as did so many of his compeers; for the place and its attractions its cures and its distractions, were the talk of the town. The second, and all succeeding, times Sir Henry went it was in pursuit of the lovely vision, draped after the antique, who sang in the arias and cantatas.

He wooed, and he pursued; but for some time both were without avail. The affectation of ritual, and the solemnity of the proceedings in which Emma was engaged under the supervision of Dr. Graham, set an effectual barrier between her and danger.

Towards the end of the season, however, Dr. Graham found it necessary to effect a change in his affairs. Nothing is more capricious than fashion, and the very methods upon which Dr. Graham had relied to establish his great venture contributed ultimately to its ruin. He had spread broadcast advertisements of his lectures and his methods of treatment, and had been successful in making his so-called 'cures' very widely known. Now the wits sharpened the blades of their intelligence and commenced an organised attack. A play was produced, satirising

77

the Temple and its priest under the title of *A Genius of Nonsense*. The doctor was sufficiently ill-advised to commence a criminal prosecution against Mr. Colman, who presented the piece. Witnesses were summoned on both sides, and a more than common scandal promised, when a high personage, who had been constant in his visits to the Temple of Æsculapius, and whose frequent use of the Celestial Bed was notorious, used his influence to stop the proceedings, the publicity of which threatened his own reputation. The result was the temporary ruin of Dr. Graham, and the deprivation to Emma of one who had proved a true benefactor to her.

This was the moment Sir Henry Featherstonehaugh used to press his suit. Emma had no inclination towards him, and had not the alternative offered to the establishment he promised appeared to her in a yet worse light, there is a possibility that she would have waited, with what patience she could muster, for the return of the father of her child. Not that she had much expectation from him, for no letter or word had come. In later years, when the great Admiral Nelson was captain of her heart, he found no difficulty in the despatch of missives! But Captain Willett Payne had not taken his responsibilities seriously, and by the time Dr. Graham was compelled to break up his establishment and move to Schomberg House, Emma had become convinced that his desertion was for always. Her alternative to placing herself under the protection of Sir Henry Featherstonehaugh was as follows:

Schomberg House, Pall Mall, a portion of which was occupied by Mr. Gainsborough, a painter of some repute, was taken by Dr. Graham when his fortunes were at their lowest ebb. His character and temper had suffered from the injustice with which he had been treated, and the ingratitude with which he had been met. His retort was to reopen, in the eastern portion of the house, an exaggerated form of that which had been so greatly and ruinously ridiculed in the Adelphi. He established there a new ritual, which, if his critics are to be believed, was actually of a *phallick* nature. And here he conceived the idea of presenting a living figure, in its natural state, as an object-lesson in the co-relation of beauty and health. For this purpose he required a young female who had a perfect form, and not modesty enough to shrink from exhibiting it *in puris naturalibus*. Emma Hart possessed the shape; he believed it possible she lacked the modesty. Nor was he completely wrong. Whatever history may relate—and there has been much controversy on this point—we have the best reason for knowing that Emma Hart did once appear as the illustration to Dr. Graham's lecture on 'Human Perfection.' But it was a solitary occasion.

And here it is not without interest to note the reluctance with which a sense of modesty leaves the female breast. Emma, who had remained in a gay house, cognisant of the orgies that were carried on; who, from vanity and love of praise, had appeared before its frequenters, who, since her own undoing, had posed for her benefactor before a mixed audience in costumes remarkable chiefly for their tenuity, shrank under this last demand. It would have seemed that the sacrifice made by her for the man who had given her practical help in the hour of her trouble, and had since provided her with both board and lodging, need not have overwhelmed her with confusion, since the exhibition of her person was not required to be followed by concession of its enjoyment. But to her credit it must be placed that she did shrink from the task set her. In vain Dr. Graham represented to her that undraped women posed before artists, and that their pictures had in many cases become the admiration of the whole cultivated world. Once again argument and illustration failed to obtain from reason that which natural instinct, ever stronger than philosophy, had successfully resisted.

Our unfortunate heroine may have indeed felt that she stood between the devil and the deep sea. But when her final choice was made it was found she had fled to Up Park, in the company of the aforesaid Sir Henry Featherstonehaugh.

CHAPTER VI

AT Up Park Emma entered into the first stage of that which is so inaccurately and misleadingly styled a 'life of pleasure.'

In Arlington Street she had been only a spectator of the racket and dissipation wherewith those whose profession is the oldest in the world endeavour to banish remorse and its attendant fear.

She had, perchance, supposed, in her ignorance, that women were happy whose laughter rang lightly from their lips, who moved gaily in costly gowns, under brilliant lights reflected from the thousand points of the gems that gleamed on their naked bosoms. She did not picture them in their lonely hours, scanning their faces in the cold light of day, in o'erwhelming anxiety lest they found the first wrinkle that would mean their decline from the favour of the profligates on whose extravagance they depended for existence. She had no knowledge of the way in which they paid in the solitude of their own chambers for the variety and excitement of the public rooms.

Even after her seduction she did not plumb the abyss. The passion of her lover burned and hurt her, but it kindled something in herself

81

which, knowing as yet no better, she mistook for love and deemed good compensation for all she had lost.

At Up Park she was allowed no illusionment as to her situation. Passion may enter into love and be the hallowed sacrament of chaste affection given and received in the permitted embraces of holy marriage. Nevertheless, passion is different from love, and not essential to it, since love can endure long after the natural forces are abated, and even persist beyond the grave. And passion itself is not more different from love than is lust from passion.

There was no time in her career when Emma would not fain have respected where she loved. Indeed Emma's respect and Emma's love went ever hand in hand, and Sir Henry Featherstonehaugh had not the parts to evoke either. A mere fox-hunting squire, he treated a woman with less respect than a horse, and thought as little of using the whip to correct the one as to subdue the other. The girl was naturally high-spirited and this was the first time she had been brought into personal relations with a man who made allowance neither for that nor for her sex. Her new protector frightened her by his violence and bewildered her by his capriciousness. She strove nevertheless to please him and at first succeeded only too well. He was libidinous in his disposition as he was uncertain in his humour, given over to the pleasures of the table and apt to be quarrelsome in his cups.

Nor was this the sum of her woes. Sir Henry was no lover desiring a solitude of two. He filled the house with boon companions, with whom he employed the days in coursing and the nights at cards and dice. In his first flush of pride in the beautiful young mistress he had added to his establishment he desired her attendance at every orgy. Decked out to please his eye and attract the envy of his friends, she sat at the head of his table, listening to bawdy conversation, pretending an enjoyment she did not know, encouraging admiration, for that gratified his vanity, and warding off its consequence with such skill as her youth permitted. Sir Henry Featherstonehaugh was as much enthralled by her as he was capable, and his jealousy was given to break out upon little provocation. It was she who was the victim always, for he deemed his men friends justified in endeavouring to wrest his capture from him. Emma learnt first to fear, and then to hate him, falling rapidly into that condition of recklessness which is youth's only alternative to despair.

The unhappy girl, made wretched by her days of humiliation and her nights of degradation, gradually threw away the reins of decent conduct. She would drink with Sir Henry's guests, dance for their pleasure, and gamble when gambling was the order of the evening. The one healthy pursuit in which she found herself engaged at Up Park was horsemanship, and in this she soon excelled, for she valued her life no whit, and rashness was the counterfeit that stood for courage. She won the admiration of Sir Henry by her prowess in the hunting-field, and came nearer obtaining respect from him on this account than she could ever have looked for by her conduct to him or to his friends. Yet the very masculinity of the so-called sport in which he encouraged her contributed to the deterioration of her character, and whilst affording an outlet for the unevenness of her spirits, it temporarily despoiled her of something of that womanliness which had been one of her most engaging characteristics. Her temper altered, and now, when excited by wine or fevered by riotous excess, she would confront him with a bravado not wholly assumed, would reply to warning or admonition with laughter and defiance, and bring down upon herself the rough usage which perhaps no longer could be considered as entirely undeserved.

Sir Henry Featherstonehaugh, a Nimrod in the country, but a Macaroni in town, numbered with his acquaintances some of the politest men of fashion. Among these was Mr. Charles Greville, a cadet of the noble house of Warwick, already famous for his fastidious taste in virtu and the philosophical system of his collection of specimens of mineralogy. Being the younger son of his father, and therefore unlikely, in the natural order of events, to succeed to the title and estates of the earldom of Warwick, Mr. Greville had turned his eyes to a political career. It was the only one promising to a man of such high connections as he possessed the emoluments of office commensurate to his needs. Endowed with a somewhat precocious wisdom, he pursued his object with methodical care, and was punctilious in conforming to all the customs prescribed by his social order. He was a familiar figure in the shooting parties gathered together in great country houses, and although no form of sport provided him with much personal entertainment, he was at pains to acquit himself creditably as became a man of the world. And thus, to come to the particular, it happened that he was one of Sir Henry Featherstonehaugh's invited guests the autumn that Emma Hart was the nominal hostess at Up Park.

Mr. Charles Greville presented a strange contrast to the rakes in whose company he found himself in the house of Sir Henry Featherstonehaugh. Not only was he of handsome person, but the easy grace of his demeanour, derived from noble birth and perfected by association with persons of the finest breeding, lent an additional charm to his appearance and an admirable dignity to his movements. He had an independence of mind which permitted him to indulge in the most widely diverse occupations and to mix in the most varied company without exposing him to a suspicion of hypocrisy.

Ambition, or rather might it be called aspiration, is one of the notes of a temperament such as was possessed by Emma Hart. She was daily subjected to the grossest admiration and the most debasing and capricious treatment, yet was ever conscious of virtue in her mind. Set amongst sensual and boorish country squires, whose only interests were the chase and the bottle, she discovered in herself, soon after she met Mr. Greville, a desire for the intellectual and refined company of the wits, artists, and musicians of whom he told her. Mr. Greville's aloofness first caught her attention, as Dr. Graham's had done earlier. The respectful consideration he paid to her conversation, to whom every other attention had been paid, and the courtly condescension of his manner, led her quickly to idealise him. Neither flippancy nor coarseness flourished in Mr. Greville's presence, soon his critical eyes had the power to abash and silence her. Anon she saw pity in them, when Sir Henry abused or used her roughly. Within a week of Mr. Greville coming to Up Park her manner had become subdued, and she was watching for his approval as a dog for a bone. If his eyes showed pity, hers were soon alight with something warmer.

Mr. Greville could not have achieved his great and merited reputation as a connoisseur of *virtu* had he not been gifted with exceptional discernment. His fastidious sense of decorum was outraged by the excesses at Up Park, by Emma's position there, by the immoderate expression of Sir Henry's capricious temper, by her loveliness, ignorance, and all too obvious unhappiness. His appreciation of the fitness of things was hurt by her masculine prowess in the field and her presence at the *battues* in Sir Henry's coverts. His admiration of her uncommon beauty was enlivened by her situation as the youthful and defenceless mistress of a coarse and unappreciative libertine. He knew that he himself could awaken in her something that Sir Henry Featherstonehaugh was as incapable of provoking as he would be of satisfying. He surprised her sensitiveness and discovered her tenderness all in a few short opportunities of discourse. He perceived behind her recklessness the despair of a captive without hope of enlargement.

The interest of the *virtuoso* once awakened, he resolved to prosecute his study of the fascinating problem offered by a character so complex. His visit having been timed to last a fortnight and such study being far more congenial to his tastes than field sports or games of chance, it was easy for him to devise explanations of his desire to withdraw from the

86

company of the gentlemen; the plea of necessary correspondence was always valid in the case of one who held a post in the Board of Admiralty, and was known to be so deeply concerned in political affairs. But, having discharged these duties, which he was punctiliously careful to do, Mr. Greville was wont to present himself before his hostess; who had for the nonce abandoned her habit of walking after the pheasants; and to entreat her, of her good nature, to tolerate his company for a little.

Alone with Greville, Emma was another being from what she appeared with Sir Henry and his boon companions. Gone was the gay outlaw, with loose and ready laugh, and the carelessness that challenged affront. In her place was an unhappy girl needing comfort and help, and so rarely lovely that Mr. Greville had neither the heart nor the inclination to withhold either.

She told him her story, or perhaps it was he who elicited it from her without her volition. There was enough of heart in him, for all that he was a man of the world and the organ was somewhat attenuated from lack of use, to be touched by the relation of her first betrayal, and there was enough of cultivated sensibility to revolt from the plight to which it had brought her. Above, and before all, was Mr. Greville's appreciation of contours wholly Greek, combined with a complexion such as England alone can show. He likened it to milk and roses, comparing it also to the bloom of peaches; he culled comparisons from the store of his knowledge of both ancient and modern writers. In the end he was fain to admit, with the courtly grace that so became him, that he failed in all his attempts to find an analogy for her physical charms, and that only one word expressed them and that word was . . . *incomparable.*

The 'incomparable Emma' was naturally charmed with such discernment, and under its delightful stimulus was brought to understand, without offence, that however much Mr. Charles Greville was disposed to admire her person, he found her mind uncultivated, and her conduct occasionally reprehensible. Emma's intelligence was good, and now she desired nothing so strongly as to merit Mr. Greville's approbation. Her days were spent in this endeavour and her nights in dreaming she had accomplished it. She did not perceive to what goal her thoughts were tending.

With all her experiences of false alleys and miraged glades, love was an unknown country to her. Mr. Greville's superiority to any man she had ever met was obvious; and that 'one needs must love the highest when one sees it,' was an adage truly inherent in her frailty. Mr. Greville began to occupy Emma continually and Sir Henry Featherstonehaugh and the double claim he had upon her escaped the volatility of her mind.

In the meantime, as the event proved, all unsuspected by himself, the preceptor was falling a victim to the attractions of the pupil. *Homines, dum docent, discunt,* wrote Seneca long ago, and in porches where love is the theme this is very certainly true. Mr. Greville's philosophical disquisitions took ever a more personal turn, his essays at consolation ever a tenderer note. Sir Henry Featherstonehaugh, not by a long way the most observant of men, began to notice his friend's abstraction when in only male company, and his glibness in pleading pressure of business as an excuse for withdrawing from it. But he was some time in attributing it to the real cause. In truth, his own infatuation for the beautiful Emma was on the ebb. He had subdued her spirit and brought her to a condition of obedience to his wishes. Before Mr. Greville's coming her recklessness and extravagance had begun to anger him. Now her indifference to him, which she was unable to conceal, her abandonment of the chase and the *battues*, and the alteration in her demeanour, completed what satiety had begun. He was already seeking an excuse for ridding himself of that which was rapidly becoming an encumbrance when Mr. Charles Greville, by a momentary imprudence, put the weapon in his hand for which he had been looking. The occasion was a hunt dinner, over which Sir Henry had insisted on Emma presiding. Then, having drunken more than he could carry, he was first publicly fond, and then publicly offensive. Emma, under Mr. Greville's eye, had parried the one with embarrassment, whilst the other had reduced her to tears, which she hurriedly withdrew to shed freely in the seclusion of her private parlour.

Thither the solicitous Greville followed her, anxious to commend her conduct during the trying scene through which she had passed. But the tears that fell from her lovely eyes, and the storm that heaved her snowy bosom, excited more than his commendation. Tenderness was little part of Charles Greville's nature, yet presently he found himself soothing her distress most tenderly. Indiscretion was no feature of his disposition, yet her loveliness or her distress provoked it on this occasion. And soon she was crying in his arms that she cared not for Sir Henry, his coarseness, his cruelty, nor his affection; it was only Greville, her dear Greville, she cared to please. It was after dinner, and Mr. Greville himself was no abstainer from the bottle . . .

*　*　*　*　*　*

Emma's absence from the table provoked comment, and Mr. Greville's almost simultaneous disappearance could not long escape attention. Sir Henry Featherstonehaugh was the last to notice the coincidence. But as bottle succeeded bottle, and ribald jest and laughter began to exceed the bounds of legitimate hilarity, his temper, or his suspicions, became excited, and after an observation more witty than elegant from Sir Gregory Parfitt he lurched to his feet, and with a coarse expression swore he'd 'fetch the jade back' and prove them all mistaken. He had no doubt to find her crying in her own room, or in his. As for Mr. Greville, 'plague on the fellow,' he said; 'no doubt' twas their bawdy talk had drove him away.' In truth, he was somewhat proud of having Mr. Greville as a guest, and would defend him. This was when he lurched from the dining-room to fetch his mistress to be again a butt for his boon companions, and to exhibit his mastership over her.

In national crises a prophet waits for word to be put into his mouth. In personal crises a pinch of sincerity spices a whole vatful of speech. Scratch the honour of a degenerate, and his veins will be found still to hold blood. Between each full point a truth is contained, and *quod semper, quod ubique, quod ab omnibus* finds corroboration. All Sir

Henry Featherstonehaugh's considered addresses fled from his mind when, on opening the parlour door, Mr. Greville turned to confront him; the much-engaged politician had to rise from his knees to do so, although his occupation had not been prayer. Mr. Greville rose, not only from his knees, but to the occasion.

'I was venturing to entreat your good lady not to deprive us any longer of the pleasure of her society, to promise her a toast . . .'

But Sir Henry was in no humour to be struck by the elegance of Mr. Greville's address or the dexterity of his wit. He seized Emma somewhat roughly by the shoulder, and what he said to her boots no repetition. Mr. Greville interfered, but was told Sir Henry needed no intercessor between him and his . . . Mr. Greville again objected, and this time more strongly. Sir Henry took his hand from Emma's shoulder to lay it on his sword, metaphorically, at least. And Emma slipped away in the confusion, much concerned for her dear Greville's safety, but not at all for that of Sir Henry Featherstonehaugh, although it was he who was like to fare the worse in any encounter, seeing he could scarcely stand upon his unsteady legs, nor bear himself worthily of his just anger.

Mr. Greville was master of the épée, but not anxious to exhibit his prowess on this occasion. It is possible his conscience was not as clear as his wit when he tried argument to dam the torrent of Sir Henry's rude speech. For first he combated lightly the accusation brought against him, and then he defended the conduct he denied. His rapier was his tongue, and he plied it lightly and ingeniously against the baronet's growing sullenness. Mr. Greville had his reputation to consider, he had no stomach for any other fight in such a cause, nor for the gossip that might follow the event.

'Permit me to suggest that if your mistress were really the wanton you represent her to be, you, as a man of the world need not draw your sword in defence of an honour she does not possess,' was the apothegm, as, 'perhaps you will permit me to order my chariot,' was the argument of his adroitness.

Sir Henry, whose wits were never of the nimblest, felt that he was being diverted to a side issue, since it was his own honour that was involved, if anyone's. But he was unable to overtake the rapidity of Mr. Greville's dialectical method, and had not lost all his respect for that gentleman's Chesterfieldian manner. In short, he permitted his guest to remove in a chariot instead of in the funeral hearse he had stormily pronounced the proper vehicle for his body.

Mr. Greville shortly made his adieux and set forth on the journey to his house in Portman Square. Not, however, without finding a method to convey to our heroine a reassuring message, and some franked and addressed papers that would enable her to communicate with him, if occasion should arise.

No good purpose would be served by a reconstruction of the scene in which Emma and Sir Henry Featherstonehaugh were next engaged. Restrained by no respect for her youth or her sex, wearied of the association, and angered at the loss of his valuable friend, Sir Henry put no restraint upon his language, and little upon himself.

It was yet one more of the many degrading experiences to which this unhappy girl had exposed herself by the first surrender of her chastity. It ended in her abrupt dismissal from the fictitious splendour of her situation as mistress of the great country house, and her restoration to her former condition of dreadful uncertainty.

In the first moment of emancipation from these gilded chains, which had often chafed her so cruelly, Emma was conscious chiefly of relief. Sir Henry had been intermittently generous, and had it not been for her native improvidence, she need not have been in any immediate alarm. As it was, however, she was but ill provided with money at this critical juncture. And she knew that, for the second time, she was in a fair way to become a mother. These considerations, as may be believed, proved a heavy alloy in the gold of her new freedom, and it was with a heart full of foreboding that she turned away from Up Park.

We next hear of her at Hawarden. And this was probably Mr. Greville's counsel, which had reprobated more strongly than any part of her conduct her remissness in not acquainting her good mother with her situation. He had promised to seek out Mrs. Cadogan in London, and relieve the dreadful anxiety under which she had no doubt laboured since, with Dr. Graham's assistance, the child Emma had borne to her seducer, Captain Willett Payne, had been confided, without any history or excuse, to the care of her maternal grandmother, Mrs. Kidd.

It must have been with mixed feelings, largely dominated by shame, that Emma revisited the home of her innocence. Some part of her unhappy story was already known there, communicated in its beginning by Mrs. Budd to Mrs. Thomas of Broadlane Hall, and only too suggestively supplemented by the subsequent arrival at Mrs. Kidd's cottage of the unlawfully born infant. Old scandals were now revived by her appearance, dressed in materials which the busybodies knew that honesty could not afford, and wrapped, moreover, in a mantle of reserve, which the same charitable persons declared was the pride which is destined to fall. Emma did not betray her consciousness of this shower of inuendoes. She had only her grandmother to whom to make explanations.

Mrs. Kidd received Emma much as she had received her mother in somewhat similar circumstance; she had been lonely without daughter or granddaughter. Mrs. Kidd's love for her beautiful grandchild had in no way diminished because Emma, like her mother, had erred. Rather had it increased in absence, and now was intensified by the instinct of pity and the necessity for defence. She foresaw that the situation would ere long become desperate, and it was she who first persuaded Emma to make overtures to Sir Henry Featherstonehaugh for a reconciliation. Such reconciliation might not be permanent, and if not that, could hardly be honourable, but it was worldly wise and good advice in view of the interesting event that was expected.

Emma wrote to her late protector, and then, receiving no reply, wrote a second time. She could not bring herself to believe that he would repudiate her claim upon him for assistance during her coming trouble, and she wrote yet a third time, making a pathetic, more fervent appeal. His silence remained unbroken, and now, indeed, Emma's heart failed for fear. Seven separate times did she speed her cry from Hawarden to Up Park. But there came no word from the distant Sussex Downs. At last when she knew herself deserted and penniless, within a few weeks of her travail, she brought her courage to the point of a letter to Mr. Greville. Without a single hour's avoidable delay, she had his answer, a little formal, perhaps, but speaking a true interest, somewhat solacing her bedraggled pride. It determined her to lay before Mr. Greville the true state of her affairs, and to implore his advice and help.

'Yesterday' [she wrote], 'did I receive your kind letter. It put me in some spirits for, believe me, I am allmost distracktid. I have never hard from Sir H., I have wrote 7 letters, and no anser. What shall I dow? O how your letter affected me when you wished me happiness. O G. that I was in your posesion what a happy girl would I have been. Girl indeed! What else am I but a girl in distress—in reall distress? For God's sake. G. write the minet you get this, and only tell me what I am to dow. I am allmos mad. O for God's sake tell me what is to become of me. O dear Grevell, write to me. Write to me. G. adue, and believe me yours for ever   EMLY HART.

'Don't tel my mother what distress I am in, and dow afford me some comfort . . .'

Could moralist desire, could any poet of the emotions conceive, a more impressive picture of the 'real distress' into which a female may be plunged who once lets go of virtue than is furnished by this exact transcript from Emma's letter? Distraction and despair, destitution and contumely, self-abandonment to any alternative, entreaty, madness, and again despair—to these had a 'life of pleasure' already brought Emma Hart. And seventeen summers have not yet passed over her head! If in the ears of any restless girl, discontented with her humble surroundings, sighing for delights which she imagines, but has not

95

known—if in her ears the call of the world is ringing, it would be well that she should bear in mind for one instant Emma's cry from the heart, *'Good God, what shall I dow?'*

Mr. Greville did not keep her in suspense. He wrote at once, deliberately, and at length:

'I do not make apologies for Sir H.'s behaviour to you, and I own I never expected better from him, already I began to despair of your happiness. . . . After you have told me that Sir H. gave you barely money to get to your friends, and has never answered one letter since, and neither provides for you nor takes any notice of you, it might appear laughing at you to advise you to try to make Sir H. more kind and attentive, for I have never seen a woman clever enough to keep a man who was tired of her. It would be a great deal more easy for me to advise you never to see him again, and to write only to inform him of your determination. You must, however, do either the one or the other. . . . You may easily see, my dearest Emy, why it is absolutely necessary for this point to be settled before I can move one step. My advice then is to take a steady resolution . . . I shall then be free to dry the tears of my lovely Emy, and give her comfort . . .'

The letter proceeded with other suggestions and promises. But the burden of it was that she must force an interview with Sir Henry Featherstonehaugh and explain her condition. And only then, if Sir Henry repudiated his responsibility, would he, Greville, be prepared to replace him. He sent her money, however, with prudent advice on the subject of its expenditure, and he concluded with an injunction to make her determination, and to write him again of the result.

It was the letter of a man of the world, who had an eye to his personal gratification, and yet feared to become involved. Mr. Greville made no pretensions to Christian morality. He regulated his conduct by the unwritten, yet perfectly understood, code of laws established and obeyed by polite society. Thus he was sincere when he protested his incapability of committing an abuse of the hospitality of Sir Henry Featherstonehaugh by seducing the allegiance of his mistress whilst under his roof-tree. But he saw nothing irregular in offering the same lady his protection if, and when, the earlier association should be completely broken off. Emma had indeed won all the warmth of which Mr. Greville's nature was capable. He did not hesitate to acknowledge this, but with equal candour he explained precisely how far his affection could carry him. 'Remember, I never will give up my peace,' was one of his sentences in his letter. There spoke the cold sensualist, happy to be within distance of accomplishing his desires, but not a whit less precise in dictating terms.

To Emma, however, his letter came like a gospel of good tidings, his sympathy like gentle rain upon parched soil, his pecuniary aid as manna in the wilderness. She kissed the paper a thousand times, and vowed eternal gratitude and devotion to her preserver, her hero. Then, resolved to carry out his instructions, she made preparations to return to Up Park, and thus mend, or end, her relations with Sir Henry. She did not disguise from herself that it was termination of the connection she desired, and not its renewal; her heart had turned from him completely. But there was his child to be considered, and Mr. Greville's injunctions. For the sake of these she was ready to humiliate herself and offer to return to his keeping. If he should repudiate her, she hoped he would at least make some provision for the babe. And she herself would be free to go to her Greville.

But Emma had not gauged the measure of Sir Henry's anger, nor reached the limit of his grossness. When she presented herself at the doors of Up Park, where she had reigned for a spell as mistress, insolent servants scarcely disguised their contempt and could hardly be prevailed upon to acquaint their master of her arrival.

She eventually achieved an interview, although perhaps it would have been better for her had it been refused; for Sir Henry was far gone in liquor, and first would have shown her a kindness from which she shrank, and then was made aware of her condition, and the imminence of her accouchement, at which he swore. It seemed he had never opened her letters, and now accused her of infidelity, not only with Mr. Greville, but with other of his boon companions, to whose unwelcome attentions he had so frequently exposed her. Emma's protestations of innocence fell upon drink-dulled ears. He terrified her by his violence, and, laying hands upon her, with what intent she hardly knew, he threw her into such an agony of mind and body as wellnigh cost her her life. She got away from him with difficulty, and was helped by a compassionate groom to the neighbouring village. And there her travail came upon her in every circumstance that could heighten her agony. No effort was made to keep alight the spark of life that glimmered feebly in the body of the child of which she was delivered, and little to preserve her own.

CHAPTER VII

Mr. Greville secures a mistress and a cook for one low rate of payment. But desires
a pupil more ardently than either. Emma incurs his displeasure by her high
spirits, but wins his forgiveness by the humility of her demeanour. It is arranged
that her portrait should be painted by Mr. Romney.

IN her first letter to Mr. Greville, Emma had begged him not to tell
her mother in what distress she was. But there are some situations
with which only mother-love is equal to cope, and Mr. Greville rightly
considered that Emma was in such a situation now. He therefore sought
out Mrs. Lyon, and having discovered her in the service of a friend
whose cuisine he had often admired, he contrived an interview, in which
he broke, as well as he was able, the news of her daughter's illness, and
its pitiable cause.

And here one must again admire Mr. Greville's diplomacy. Mrs.
Lyon, who had been distracted with fear and anxiety, was so impressed
with the dignity of his manner and the kindness he exhibited in
speaking of her child, that she not only agreed to proceed at once to Up
Park, but became from that day, and for all succeeding time, his very
devoted servant. *Matre pulchra filia pulchrior* was perhaps in his mind
when he showed such condescension and courtesy to his friend's cook.
But Mr. Greville was not wont to act without deliberation, and it may
well be that, seeing an opportunity to gratify, in the early future, two of
his appetites at the expense of one, he laid himself out to please the still
comely Mary Lyon. And that he succeeded the sequel proved.

99

Before Mrs. Lyon proceeded on her journey she was made aware that Mr. Greville's interest in her daughter would take the practical form of supplying her with everything she might require until she was well enough to join him in London. It was then he added the suggestion that she should accompany Emma. Nobody but Mr. Charles Greville could have thus persuaded a mother to her daughter's dishonour. But he so ingeniously worded the invitation that it seemed he was merely taking mother and daughter into his service from motives of benevolence, to which he had been moved by the pathetic letter of which he spoke.

Infinitely distressing was the first meeting between mother and daughter after their long separation. The shock was almost too great for poor Emma in her present weakness, and she wept uncontrollably. At once an answering wave of pity flooded the mother's heart, and filled every recess of it with love. Again she heard a dying voice murmur, '*Let not her weakness, nor the weakness she inherits from her unhappy father, deprive her of maternal love. Cherish her, I beseech you, cherish her as you cherish my memory, and love her whatever displeasure she may cause you.*" The parting injunction of an idolised husband had ever haunted Mary's ears and soon she was blaming herself for all Emma's misfortunes. It was she who had permitted her to come to London, and thus exposed so fair a flower to so bitter a blast. Emma's silence, that in the distance had looked so like ingratitude, was now easily explained as shame.

There is no shame so great but that mother-love can solace and console it. Mary first whispered this to her daughter, and then proclaimed it loudly. Emma took comfort from the thought, comfort of which she was in sore need. She pillowed her erring head on her mother's breast, and learnt that her troubles were all past. Never again should she be alone in the world, Mr. Greville had decreed it. She and her mother were not to be separated, his generous help and protection were to be extended to the two of them. The good news was almost too good, and mother and daughter vied in Mr. Greville's praises. If Emma withheld something of her heart, that flowed out, once and for always, like water to him who succoured her, it was only because her new susceptibility of feeling made her fearful lest her mother should refuse to accept as service that which Emma fondly hoped was meant in love. It was beyond the simplicity of her mind to conceive the great Mr. Greville, the adored and admired Charles Greville, actuated by any but the noblest of motives. Her mother and she were to be together, and both of them under his protection. Her convalescence proceeded apace under such an incentive; the gaiety of her nature quickly revived. Her past sorrows and present pensiveness riveted her afresh to her mother's heart. By the time they were able to travel to London, they were so loving and tender together that Mr. Greville was charmed by the confirmation of Emma's sensibility.

In all sensual men there is a duality of nature, and in the case of Mr. Greville this was unusually distinct. Not ungenerous where he would himself participate in the fruits of his generosity, and even extravagant beyond the proper limits of his purse in the purchase of objects of art and virtu, he was at the same time parsimonious through principle and miserly from necessity. Sensible of all carnal pleasures, and fastidious in his taste, he appreciated the gratification to be derived from a beautiful mistress, a delicate table, and a well-ordered home. He was secretly transported by the idea of obtaining all these and at the same time effecting a saving in his domestic economy. The idea had been rendered practicable by the expedient of taking both Emma and her mother into his protection and custody; and it gave the irregular alliance an air of respectability that especially recommended itself to this precise formalist.

He vacated his fine residence in Portman Square, where, although it was not yet even completed, many personages of the first fashion resided, and engaged an unpretentious residence in the charming suburb of Edgeware Row. Hither Emma travelled with her mother so soon as her health was re-established, and there did Mr. Greville receive them both with a kindness which was doubled and redoubled as the charms of Emma's beauty became accentuated in his eyes by the skill and economy of her mother's management of his small household.

Mr. Greville prided himself, and not without reason, upon the perspicacity which had enabled him, in the uncongenial atmosphere of Up Park, to recognise the exotic properties of the flower that languished there in the indifferent care of Sir Henry Featherstonehaugh. It was, nevertheless, a cardinal point of his creed that no gentleman makes a display of his emotions, amongst which is to be included gratification. Thus, in his new and modest establishment in Edgeware Row, he did not parade the elation he really felt that his intelligence had served him such an amazingly good turn upon the present occasion, nor his growing delight in the hidden grace and rare domestic virtues so rapidly developed and exhibited by the lovely Emma. At Up Park he had argued, from her restless dissatisfaction with the garish excitements of her anomalous position, a possible contentment with quieter pleasures. But now he discovered in addition a surprising modesty, a capacity for affection equal to unfailing sacrifice of self, and a talent for domesticity that neglected no detail of housewifely care which could minister to his comfort. At Up Park he had seen talent, even genius, for the alluring accomplishments of music and the dance. In Edgeware Row he discovered mental abilities of a high order, and an entirely commendable application and perseverance. He found that when Emma had bewailed her lack of education, it had not been merely to move him to leniency toward errors in etiquette, or account for her difficulty in taking an equal part in polite conversation; she had voiced a real grievance.

Whatever Mr. Greville had intended when he took Emma under his protection, she quickly became so much to his taste that he set to work to make her more so. His coldness needed a mistress less than his vanity desired a pupil. Having become enamoured, although perhaps unconsciously, by the girl's simplicity and ignorant spontaneity, he prepared to destroy both. Finding unexpectedly in his possession a rare gem, nothing would serve but that it should be cut and polished to conventional pattern. The cutting and polishing became a hobby with him. Emma must have music and dancing masters, and he himself gave her lessons in English and spelling. These last were not very successful, for even Mr. Greville found it difficult to maintain an attitude both critical and exacting when Emma's curls brushed his cheek in her anxiety to follow what he was writing for her benefit, and her blue eyes pleading, or laughing, assured him that she would rather sit on her Greville's knee than be lectured by him as to when to use the big, and when the small, *i*. Emma applied herself to all her other studies with assiduity and application; she truly had the ambition to improve and make herself more worthy. But study with Mr. Greville she could not, because the true love he had excited in her, the first and only love of poor Emma's misspent life, hungered for a larger expression of it than he was capable of giving. She was for ever wooing him, wistfully or gaily, as his somewhat perverse humour suggested. She obeyed his slightest wishes, strove to reach to his demands on her understanding, mistook his coldness for dignity, his lack of passion for an aristocratic self-restraint, his vanity for noble pride, his narrow jealousy for a fine exclusiveness. She lavished on this gentleman, who used both her and her mother as servants to his appetites, a generous wealth of childish adoration and womanly warmth; she would fawn on him for the favour of a caress, her liveliness leaping to his approval, her gaiety attuning itself to his mood. She would dance for him, sing for him, dress for him, live for him. And all of this because she was instinctively a lover, the true feminine of the word, humble and generous, uncalculating in her gifts, grateful for the smallest favours and sedulous to deserve them.

The man has never existed who is not susceptible to flattery, albeit there is nothing against which every man more prides himself on being proof. The flattery with which Emma cajoled her Greville was of the most insidious kind, the adoring humility with which she sat at his feet being her ingenuous testimony to his superlative excellence. There was not a little of the pedagogue in Mr. Charles Greville, and it was very agreeable to his vanity to instruct so lovely a pupil in the fine art of polite living. He commented, with approval, on the change she effected in her general deportment.

'She does not wish for much society,' he wrote to a correspondent, 'but to retain two or three creditable acquaintances in the neighbourhood; she has avoided every appearance of giddiness, and prides herself on the neatness of her person and the good order of her house; these are habits both comfortable and convenient to me. She has vanity, and likes admiration; but she connects it so much with her desire of appearing prudent, that she is more pleased with accidental admiration than that of crowds that now distress her. In short, this habit is not a caprice, but is easily to be continued.' And again he wrote: 'She has dropt every one she thought I could except against, and those of her own choice have been in a line of prudence and plainness which, though I might have wished for, I could not have proposed to confine her.'

Mr. Greville had reason, indeed, to congratulate both his pupil and himself upon the transformation she was so diligently achieving. It might have proved permanent, and this history never have been written, had he continued his kindness to her, been less captious, less critical, and in the end, less suspicious. But Mr. Greville saw ever himself in the foreground of his picture of life. He accepted her fondness and deemed it amply repaid by his acceptance.

It was only to be expected, however, that 'Frail Emma Hart,' as she was called in Edgeware Row, should have the defects of her qualities. Docile and obedient for six days in the week, on the seventh she would sometimes break out into an outburst of petulance and capriciousness, a childlike ebullition of emotionalism, which was the very opposite of that steadiness of mind which Greville inculcated both in theory and by his own practice. She would repent quickly, and plead or coax for pardon. But Charles Greville pardoned with difficulty. His state and dignity demanded there should be no occasion.

The coldness of his temper, opposed to her own excitability, jeopardised her position on one occasion that is worth relating.

To reward her diligence, and also, perhaps, to give himself the gratification of displaying his good taste, Mr. Greville one evening carried Emma to Ranelagh, then at its zenith as a favourite resort of the world of fashion. At first all went well. Emma was the cynosure of admiring and envious eyes and Mr. Greville enjoyed what was something like a triumphal procession. They were followed by the beaux and wits of the day. Mr. Greville was importuned for information, introduction. Who was his fair companion, where had he found her, where did he conceal her? These and other questions were pressed upon him banteringly, or earnestly. And he knew exactly how to deal with his interlocutors. He could turn a quip, parry a jest, word a paradox, invent an epigram, as well as any man in town. With Emma on his arm he was cool, witty, and most diplomatically reticent as he made the tour of the gardens, pursued and surrounded by his gayest acquaintances. But he left Emma ten minutes unguarded, albeit in the shelter of a box he had engaged for supper, whilst he busied himself with the wine list. And in that ten minutes the mischief was done that so nearly led to their separation.

Emma's ardent nature was inflamed by the brilliance and excitement of a scene so congenial and her vanity was aroused by the attention of which she knew she was the focusing point. Now, not content with the admiration she had already received, she sat well forward in her box. It was at that moment that Mr. Dennis O'Flanagan, who had known her at Mrs. Kelly's, recognised that she was not the stranger to London that she seemed. He communicated his knowledge to the gentleman nearest to him. Mr. Greville's fair incognita was 'Emy' from Mrs. Kelly's, 'The Goddess of Hygeia 'from Dr. Graham's! They called out to her in greeting, in recognition, in welcome. It would not have been Emma if she had not responded; soon she was leaning out of the box and chattering like a little bird. They had not forgotten her dancing, nor her singing, nor her imitations. Now they called upon her for both, for all. She was excited and but a wild girl for all Mr. Greville's tutoring. Her clear fine voice broke into the most popular song of the day. The gentlemen sang the chorus of it with her; they were enthusiastic, and more than one of them was enterprising. Then it was that Mr. Greville came back, not realising at once the meaning of the augmenting crowd, nor what it was they were so vociferously applauding. As the mob parted for his coming, he caught a glimpse of Emma. She was standing up, in the front of the box, singing to those below, laughing to those nearest, wimple thrown back, curls escaping, her eyes shining, and her face flushed.

Mr. Greville was mortified and angered almost beyond measure. He hurried her from the scene immediately, not concealing his displeasure, but severely silent until they were in the solitude of the hackney coach. Then, indeed, he rebuked her with the utmost vehemence, denouncing her inclination to please fools in preference to respecting his injunctions. His indignation was so hot that Emma, cold with reaction and harried with fear, suddenly realised the critical nature of the position. She broke into a frenzy of self-reproach, entreating again and again for his forgiveness. But when he handed her out of the carriage he was still unsoftened. It was then, on an impulse at once natural and theatrical, that she implored him, the tears streaming from her eyes, crying, 'You must forgive me, you must, you shall, you dear, dear Greville.' She flew to her room, and hastily rousing her mother to her assistance, she exchanged the elegant attire assumed for the Ranelagh visit for her plainest and oldest gown. Pursuing Mr. Greville to his study, she threw herself on her knees before him.

'See! I am a poor girl again, Greville, the girl you rescued, who is miserable at having displeased you. I was carried away by my high spirits, the music, and the fine clothes. But I have locked away the clothes, and the spirits is all gone.' Indeed her eyes were streaming. 'Take your poor girl in your arms, tell her that you will not cast her out. Greville, do not turn your face away, do not look so coldly upon me. I am more unhappy than when I was so distressed if my Greville spurn me. . . .'

Her self-abasement salved his wounded pride. But not all at once, not until the night was far spent did he yield to her solicitations. For the core of his heart was as hard as a stone, and she might have flung herself against it in vain, but that she added to his consequence. Mr. Greville valued his reputation for taste, and it had been stamped and hall-marked at Ranelagh to-night; he knew he would be the talk of the town to-morrow, and 'Frail Emma 'the toast.

Therefore he condescended to accord to the pleading culprit some slight reassurance, and to accept the familiarities with which she signalised her return to favour. She was permitted to fondle his hands and called him her dear, dear Greville, and to be extravagantly and exuberantly grateful in her own way. Accepting rebuke and warning in so humble and contrite a spirit, she was presently raised from the ground to the throne of his knee, from which altitude she listened to a fresh exposition of the heinousness of the offence of having drawn public attention to herself, and thus possibly compromised him at Whitehall.

What Mr. Greville feared, or hoped, came to pass, and Emma was the toast of the town. But only for a short time, for a fresh escapade of the 'first gentleman in Europe,' George Prince of Wales, was brought to light that week and filled the public ear to the exclusion of the light amours of meaner people.

The affair influenced Mr. Greville, nevertheless, to a project he had long had in mind. This was no other than to have Emma's portrait painted. It was Emma herself who begged that the commission should be given to Mr. Romney. Emma had ever an affectionate and grateful heart, and Mr. Romney had won his place in it already at Broadlane Hall, where, notwithstanding that she was only a nurse-girl, and in disgrace most of the time, he had spoken to her with kindness, and noticed her with particularity. Mr. Greville had been all for engaging Mr. Gavin Hamilton, who was among the few visitors to the little house in Edgeware Row and had already expressed his willingness, even his anxiety, to limn those lovely features and that without fee or reward. The guests Greville welcomed, and to whom he introduced Emma, were those whom genius distinguished and art engrossed, or whose sober habit and discreet age were their chief recommendation. He knew enough of physics not to expose tinder to flame.

Yet perhaps his judgment failed him when he included Mr. George Romney amongst those who were not inflammable. For he did assent finally to Emma's wish that Mr. Romney should have the commission, and it was he himself who first conveyed her to Cavendish Square.

CHAPTER VIII

Emma is taken by Charles Greville to Mr. Romney's studio in Cavendish Square, and there sits for him in many attitudes, and also in the nude. To this Mr. Greville takes objection, and much accrues from the circumstance. She makes the acquaintance of Sir William Hamilton, who at once expresses his admiration of her, and endorses his nephew's taste.

MR. GREVILLE, as has been already observed, was an authority on all matters pertaining to the fine arts, and the possessor already of a cabinet of pictures of no mean value.

A great volume of water had flowed under London Bridge since, as a journeyman artist, George Rumney, as he then spelled his name, had painted his way to London. He now enjoyed considerable repute, and by many his work was preferred to that of Mr. Gainsborough. In any case there was sufficient in his favour to make it easy for Mr. Greville to yield to Emma's wish that he, and not Mr. Gavin Hamilton, should be chosen to paint her picture.

Mr. Romney's studio was in Cavendish Square and thither Emma repaired, accompanied by Mr. Greville, one fine morning in April, a few days subsequent to the Ranelagh escapade. She was in her best attire, not without some trepidation at the prospect before her. She wondered if Mr. Romney would recognise in the great Mr. Greville's companion, in 'Frail Emma of Edge ware Row,' the little nurse-girl whose head he had almost turned by his attention in those far-away days at Hawarden.

By this time Emma was well aware of her beauty, and accustomed to the outspoken interest it excited. She was doubly prepared in this instance, since the purpose of her reception by Mr. Romney was that he might study her looks with a view to perpetuating them on canvas. Yet the event was a great one in her history, and worthy of the emotion with which she approached it. In the future it was to become commonplace to her; dozens of artists here and in Italy were to paint her for their own, her protector's, and the public gratification. But, with the exception of the amateur drawing by Miss Thomas in crayon, this visit to Mr. Romney's studio on April 17th, 1782, was the first occasion of a serious attempt being made to put upon canvas the charms of this eighteenth-century Aspasia.

Emma was entertained by the expression of half-puzzled recognition on the artist's face when, after his reception of Mr. Greville, who explained the object of their visit, he started to pose and consider his new sitter. It was followed presently by an equally apparent effort to recall any previous meeting. Much had happened to them both in the long interval and Mr. Romney's mind did not easily revert to Broadlane Hall.

'I rarely forget a face,' he said whilst he was engaged with his easel, stepping backward, and then forward, in a manner he had, his head a little on one side, and his eyes screwed up. 'I rarely forget a face, and that of your fair lady would certainly not be an exception to my rule.' He contemplated his subject with an interest in which admiration predominated. Mr. Romney was no courtier, he was not even given to courteous speech, bearing ever traces of his plebeian birth and the poverty of his early circumstances; but from the first Emma moved him strangely. He was plainly questioning his defective memory. 'For the life of me, I cannot help thinking I have seen you before.' Now he addressed himself directly to Emma, whose roguish smile was tantalisingly reminiscent. 'I even have it in my mind that I have studied or painted that hair. . . .'

Emma shook out her curls and smiled yet more.

'Shall I remind you?' she asked, and in a trice stood up and played as with her apron, dropping a little curtsey demurely. 'If you please, honoured sir,' she began, in the manner taught her by the excellent Mrs. Thomas.

'By Heaven!' Tis the little nursemaid from Hawarden, the beautiful little nursemaid,' he exclaimed. And soon everything was made clear. Emma was proud of her rise in circumstance. For to live under the protection of Mr. Greville still seemed to her a position to which that expression could be justly applied.

Mr. Romney had a good reputation, and Mr. Greville had no reason for doubting the propriety of his conduct when, as frequently happened after this, he left Emma alone at the studio in Cavendish Square.

On this occasion, after exclamation had been followed by recognition, and recognition by congratulation, Mr. Greville withdrew for a short time, promising to call for Emma when he had left a card upon his uncle, who had but this day returned from Naples. Mr. Greville was greatly attached to his uncle, whose heir he was, and who was an ambassador at the Court of Naples. He may have wished to impress the painter by making his announcement, but in truth Mr. Romney was all impatience for Mr. Greville's departure, eager to be alone with his sitter and to employ his brush on the most alluring subject that had ever offered itself to his genius.

Watching intently the delightful play of expression on Emma's animated face he led her to talk of her experiences, of which it must be admitted she gave him but a modified version, whilst he prepared his canvas. Presently he came to a pause in his attempt to rough in a satisfactory indication of her features, and going to a cabinet in which was a number of notebooks, he selected one, and coming over to the dais whereon he had placed her, he gave it into her hand. Mr. Greville found her with it on his return to the studio. Mr. Romney was now painting rapidly, and Emma was absorbed in the book, having fallen into a perfectly natural pose which greatly assisted the artist. The book was full of Hawarden sketches and reminiscences. Mr. and Mrs. Thomas and their daughter figured there, and so did the smaller children. Emma herself was delineated several times; in mob cap and apron; without a cap at all; her curls disordered. There was Emma laughing, and Emma crying, and, what delighted her more than anything else, the sketch of a struggling group, full of movement, in which figured a woman belabouring a kicking boy, whilst another bigger boy looked on grinning and in a corner a frightened child in a mob cap cried with fear.

'It's Mrs. Ogle,' Emma cried, 'and Will Masters, and that's Joe Codgers. And I am the little girl. Oh, Greville, do look! Am I like that now, but I am surely prettier?'

If he rebuked her for her vanity—for never did Mr. Greville forget his role—he did not omit to congratulate Mr. Romney on the spirited nature of the work, and he offered to purchase the book from him, to please the girl who was so enraptured with it. Which offer, however, Mr. Romney refused, afterwards, nevertheless, presenting it to her, but not until their friendship and intimacy had become fully established.

Now Mr. Romney carried on a long consultation with Mr. Greville as to the character and pose the painted figure of Emma should assume. Mr. Greville was pleased also to affect a considerable interest in the canvases that were lying about, or standing against the wall, and he promised Mr. Romney his continued patronage in the event of being satisfied with Emma's portrait, for which the agreed terms were fifteen guineas for a full length, or ten for a bust.

The sittings Mr. Romney required for his portrait of Emma were many and various. Sometimes Mr. Greville accompanied her to the studio, and sometimes her mother. There soon grew up between artist and sitter a strange friendship. In the secret heart of both of them there was what one may fittingly call a tendency to vagabondage, a lack of reverence for conventionality, an inclination towards freedom of thought and action. Emma was linked with a man to whom conventionality was as the breath of life, Mr. Romney was making a strong effort to live in conformity with the dictates of his friends and patrons. But to both Emma and George Romney their conditions were unnatural, and in each other they found a true sympathy and understanding.

Frequent visits to Mr. Romney's studio soon became Emma's chief pleasure. Her household duties accomplished, and her music master gone, she would trip singing to the gate of the little garden in Edgeware Row, and presently, taking coach, would drive to Cavendish Square, there to pass long hours posing, draped in classical robes, for a Circe, a Calypso, or a Pythian priestess; or, with floating tresses and flying draperies, as a Bacchante or a Woodland Nymph. Each character she wore, she became. And Mr. Romney found her ever a new inspiration, not only to his brush, but to his imagination. He began to live in, and for, these hours of companionship and eager work. Hundreds of meetings followed the first sitting arranged by Mr. Greville. Mr. Greville was pleased that Emma had so sober a friend. Mr. Romney's repute as an artist grew with amazing rapidity at this period, and it added to Mr. Greville's prestige as an art critic and connoisseur that he should have been a few weeks in advance of the town in discovering that 'the man in Cavendish Square,' as Mr. Joshua Reynolds called him, somewhat disparagingly, or perhaps enviously, was in a fair way to rival Mr. Reynolds himself in public favour. It redounded to Mr. Greville's credit that his mistress had been painted not once, but many times by Mr. Romney, and that the painter said that her beauty was a constant inspiration to his art. Mr. Greville was never fonder of his Emma than at this period. Mr. Romney painted her at the spinning wheel, and this picture of domesticity exemplified all Mr. Greville most esteemed. That she was so desirable, and yet so completely his, moved him to something as near conjugal love as his coldness could attain. By a thousand evidences she had convinced him of her devotion to himself, and in spite of occasional outbreaks, he was satisfied of her increasing self-command and her general prudence. In Mr. Romney's studio, she met no libertines, but many men of eminence in literature and the arts, who spurred her own intelligence into emulation, and further equipped her to be an intelligent companion of Mr. Greville's solitude. He had no fear that these gentlemen could seduce Emma from her allegiance. He encouraged her absences from Edgeware Row, which left him free to classify and catalogue his collection of minerals and otherwise indulge in the favourite employments of the virtuoso. Mr. Greville was not a man to whom the constant companionship of woman is necessary, even if that woman be an Emma Hart. Therefore, notwithstanding that Mr. Romney was a married man, who was as good as not married, since, even now that success was overwhelming him, he had not fetched his wife and children from the remote country home where he had left them long before, and in spite of the fact that Emma's ever-increasing beauty made her peerless among women, a delight to the eye, and a desire of the heart—in spite of these facts, and of his knowledge of human nature, Mr. Greville, for a long while, was oblivious of the possibility that the artist's interest in the lovely model might prove aught but professional. His vanity precluded jealousy.

An artist's professional interest in female beauty can, however, induce him to conduct his examination of it with a minuteness of detail to which the modesty of any lady and the jealousy of any protector might well object. Prudence in Emma's case was a substitute for modesty, rather than its synonym, and her adventurous career had deprived her of squeamishness. She had a frankly pagan delight in her own loveliness, which, if it had cost her much suffering, had also won her happiness in her Greville's love. For still she read as love that which might have been more truly named self-gratification.

When the time came that Mr. Romney was emboldened to ask, and she not averse to concede, although with some pretence of demurring, a fuller view of her loveliness, she had it in her mind that she thereby confirmed her Greville's taste, and that the exhibition was in his honour. That, at least, was what she said when she had to excuse herself to him.

Qualified by every gift of nature to serve as a model for Venus, 'twas a matter of small moment to her whether 'twas Venus Anadyomene or Venus Rising from the Sea whom she was invited to represent. An ell or two of transparent lawn, she had reason to know, was a poor protection for a maiden's honour. Her own feeling for Mr. Greville, and Mr. Romney's absorption in his work, was the armour on which she relied. And so it came to pass that on more than one occasion she posed for Mr. Romney clad in no more clothing than she wore on her first entrance into the world. And it is at any rate conceivable that her lavish concession was not abused.

Emma had forgot to tell Mr. Greville of these sittings and it was therefore unfortunate that he chanced to pay a visit to Cavendish Square on one of the occasions when she was delighting the artist without the draperies that might obscure his vision. It was a flawless model of Beauty Unadorned that she represented, and it was a pity that on this occasion Mr. Greville did not appreciate a picture that had so often before won his complete suffrance. For first the hot blood of a quite commonplace jealousy dyed his thin ascetic face and he moved forward quickly as if to take some definite and unguarded action. Then, his vanity coming to his rescue, he became pale and cold, a model of politeness, that struck a chill in Emma's heart.

'I am not aware that I commissioned Mr. Romney to paint a picture of Mrs. Hart in the nude,' he began. 'Are you not perhaps exceeding the limits of your instructions, sir, and of my forbearance?'

' 'Tis a study of Venus for a Judgment of Paris that Mr. Romney is making,' Emma broke in, coming forward in her eagerness from the model's throne. ' 'Twas this way I posed for Dr. Graham's lectures.'

Mr. Greville bowed and answered ironically, 'I am delighted you have so vivid a remembrance of your former condition. I should deeply regret to deprive the world too long of the enjoyment of charms I have perhaps been selfish in attempting to preserve for myself,' he added. And now his words were biting, and his voice matched them. 'Mr. Romney will, perhaps, relieve me of the necessity of saying more.'

'Oh, Greville, dear Greville, what is it you are thinking? I am but a model to Mr. Romney; he calls me his inspiration, but it is you, you

119

only. . . .' She was frightened at his voice and manner, terrified almost beyond pleading, as she poured out incoherent words.

Mr. Romney had to recall himself from his dreams of rivalling Rubens, and making Raphael look to his laurels, to consider the scene before him. Neither Rubens nor Raphael had enjoyed such a model. Mr. Romney had all and more than the artist's irritability of temperament and was ever intolerant of interruption when at work. At the present moment it was doubly unwelcome for he knew that a masterpiece was growing under his hands. His resentment was hot and spontaneous, and whilst, at first, it astounded Mr. Greville, who felt himself the injured party, it had the effect of mollifying his manner, and restoring some measure of reassurance to his mind. For Mr. Romney's anger was not that of guilt, nor of one who has stolen privileges that belong to another. It was the indignation of an artist and not of a man that Mr. Romney betrayed.

'Sir, by what right do you make rude entrance into my studio? '

'I sought the lady whom I have had for some time the honour to protect,' Mr. Greville answered, with moderation.

'The privilege . . . .'

'As you will, sir. Privilege may be the better word.'

'Neither honour nor privilege entitles you to break into my private apartment.'

'Your public studio.'

'And interrupt me in my immortal work.'

'Would it not be better if Mrs. Hart withdrew?' Mr. Greville said, growing ever cooler as the other waxed warm. 'Now that she is no longer enjoying the favour of your rapt regard, she might care to find some other covering.'

'Oh, Greville, dear Greville,' Emma sobbed, 'you are angered with me. How can I bear your displeasure? What is it that I have done that is so bad, Greville?'

'Madam, the reiteration of my name is no longer agreeable to me on your lips.'

Mr. Romney had much ado to restrain his opinion of this reply as he saw that Emma's condition of pitiable fear and her frenzied desire that Mr. Greville should hear her explanations, were momentarily increasing. Mr. Greville was cool, very cool, between the two of them, but for more reasons than one he wished Emma would robe herself.

Left with Mr. Romney, Mr. Greville was incredulous, imperturbable, but always elegant in his demeanour. He listened courteously to Mr. Romney's repudiation of the interpretation placed upon Emma's generosity to him.

'Beauty like that of Mistress Hart benefits and enriches all mankind, accentuating appreciation of its Creator. I tell you, sir, that figure,' he pointed to the glowing canvas, 'is above and beyond your poor jealousy. A representation of the sublime and perfect woman God gave to Adam in the Garden of Eden, it is Divine, not human, in its contours. Such beauty, such perfection of form, is for mankind, not for man. I am an artist, and it belongs to me, by right of my intention, if I can immortalise what you can only enjoy.'

Mr. Greville made answer:

'I do not propose to debate the ethics of art with you, Mr. Romney. Mrs. Hart is, however, under my protection, and if I obiect to her exhibition . . .'

Then he caught sight of the picture on the easel. A little colour came into his pale cheeks, and his breath was caught in his throat.

The duality of nature that I have before observed as a characteristic of Mr. Greville made him recognise instantly, even in the midst of his jealousy and just anger, that it was indeed a masterpiece upon which he was gazing. And from that moment, although the interview was prolonged nearly half an hour, the which time it took Emma to recapture her courage as well as her clothes, he said not one word more of bitterness or reproach to Mr. Romney, but accepted, if not with humility, at least with silence, the rebuke the other poured upon him for his suspicions.

'She is the most loyal, as she is the most lovely of her sex. You are unworthy of her if you doubt it. In all my intercourse with her I have treated her with the utmost respect, to which her demeanour has fully entitled her.'

'Before Heaven, that is true, my Greville,' Emma interposed. She had been listening to the colloquy whilst making her toilet behind the screen. 'Oh, believe him, dear Greville; indeed you must and shall believe him. He has been good and kind to me, no more; I swear it; and he is a great, great genius, everybody knows it now, and is leaving Mr. Reynolds to come to him. And he says it is all because of me he is being so successful, and I am his Divine Lady. Oh, Greville, do listen! What does it matter if Mr. Romney has seen me in my figure. It is only as as artist he has looked. . . .' Yet she blushed.

Mr. Greville answered her in a low voice, in his own inimitable way, 'You have been well taught, madam. I observe you have acquired Mr. Romney's phraseology.'

'I have acquired nothing from him but what is good'—now she fell to weeping again—'and for your dear interest, Greville. Believe me, in all the world it is only you I love, although I wanted to do what Mr. Romney asked, and help him in his great work. Take me home, Greville. I am tired, and frightened that I have angered you. And indeed, indeed you may trust me.'

Mr. Romney was much more easily moved by beauty in distress than was Mr. Greville. He perceived the manifest anxiety written on Emma's face and realised what it might mean to disturb Emma's present relations with one to whom she owed much. Mr. Romney had no wish to precipitate a crisis between them. Assuming an attitude more conciliatory than heretofore, he attempted to soothe Mr. Greville's dignity without forfeiting his own.

'I do owe you, and I tender you an apology, sir, for persuading Mistress Hart to oblige me. My passion for my art is my only excuse. As I have already remarked, in the whole history of the world, never had artist more perfect model. I beg you to believe that I have no thought towards this lady, but a most lively and intense admiration. I know where her heart is fixed, and that Mr. Greville can have no rival there.'

Emma shot him a grateful look, and Mr. Greville had not choice but to accept an assurance given with such an air of candour, and confirmed by Emma's pleading eyes. He took his lovely charge away with him, displaying that dignity and ease on quitting a difficult situation of which only men of the very highest breeding are capable. Nor did he revert to the matter when alone with Emma. But his manner to her was colder than before, and he was more punctilious in his address, more academic in his dissertations on *les convenances*. Emma wooed him back warmly, and eventually he condescended to be coldly won. She could not suppose that aught of rancour against her lingered in his mind.

Mr. Greville knew himself to be fortunately situated in so far as his domestic affairs were concerned. The common experience of men of fashion who set up irregular establishments is that they have planted round the columnar tree of their lives a parasite that will cling close and ever closer, until it kills the support by exhausting its subsistence. The price a loose woman exacts from the man to whom she sells her beauty is leave to waste his fortune. It is not unusual either, when this is accomplished, for her to admit that she has no further use for him, and to drop off with another, financially stronger.

Very different was Mr. Greville's experience with Emma Hart. So far from adding to his expenses, she was the direct means of reducing them. Her allowance for pin money was no more than fifty pounds a year, and the entire expenses of the establishment in Edgeware Row were never above three times that sum. And whilst thus maintaining his household with the prudence and frugality of the careful wife, she made it her first object to study the personal comfort and tastes of her Greville, whilst keeping her fascination over his senses, as a mistress is more particular in doing than a wife, since that commonly constitutes her sole hold upon the man's sense of responsibility. All this was highly agreeable to Mr. Greville, and the more so because his own position was by no means secure. The claims upon his purse as member of Parliament for his family borough were considerable, and although a minor promotion secured him a small increase of emolument, his tenure of office was precarious. As time went on he became seriously concerned as to the means whereby he could discharge all his obligations punctually and yet continue to gratify his tastes.

Therefore, although he was perfectly sensible of Emma's housewifely qualities and was still enamoured of her personal charms, even before the incident in Mr. Romney's studio, he had not omitted to debate in his own mind possible alternatives to his present situation. Such alternatives included a regular alliance with some lady of fortune and influence. Mr. Greville pretended to forgive. Emma her exposure to Mr. Romney, but his temperament, and presently his prospects, forbade it.

It was now that he received a visit in Edgeware Row from his most particular friend, whose temporary return from Naples has already been announced, and with whom he had maintained a frequent and intimate correspondence. This friend was no other than his maternal uncle, Sir William Hamilton, a man by many years Greville's senior, but bound to him in almost fraternal ties by identity of tastes and equal zest as virtuoso and connoisseur. For close upon a quarter of a century Sir William Hamilton had enjoyed his appointment at Naples, serving at the Court of the Two Sicilies as Ambassador to His Britannic Majesty, whose foster-brother he was, and of whose signal favour he had received many testimonies, including the ribbon of the Bath, Sir William's reputation as an archaeologist and man of science was worldwide and deserved, but it did not preclude him from enjoying an equal esteem as a man of wit and of fashion in a Court where frivolous amusement was the first order of the day.

Sir William Hamilton had recently been left a widower. His fortune, already considerable, was enhanced by his now coming into the sole enjoyment of property at Milford, in the county of Pembrokeshire, formerly in the possession of his wife. Mr. Greville had always acted as the manager of his uncle's affairs, and Sir William now designed to develop Milford. It was for that purpose he had obtained leave of absence from Naples, and his first visit to Edgeware Row was with the object of interesting his nephew in his scheme.

To Emma the name of Sir William Hamilton was perfectly familiar. It was constantly on Mr. Greville's lips and she had been taught to regard Sir William Hamilton reverently, as a relation who reflected credit on Mr. Charles Greville. His arrival at this particular juncture of affairs, when Mr. Greville was cool with her, and she ever bent on regaining his favour, caused her heart to flutter with anxiety to please one of whom her protector entertained so high an opinion, and she resolved to leave nothing undone for the entertainment of him whom her king delighted to honour.

For his part, Sir William Hamilton had never heard of Mrs. Hart, and he was vastly amused to discover that his nephew was so correctly incorrect. He rallied him upon it, yet took the occasion to belaud his taste and good fortune. 'I congratulate you, my dear nephew, on such a priceless acquisition. You say the connection is two years old. How is it I have had never a word about the gem of your whole collection? Did you think I should complain because you were no Stoic? I am a man of the world, Charles, a man of the world! I respect your judgment, I extol your taste. The combined genius of Phidias and Apelles, Michael Angelo and Cellini, could not have conceived a more perfect specimen of womanhood than you have here in the flesh.'

To Emma from the beginning he was vastly civil, treating her with great consideration, as if she had been his nephew's wife, or in any case his equal in birth and station.

Emma was pleased and flattered by Sir William Hamilton's manners and attention. If at first she was too awed and surprised by what she had heard of his exalted circumstance to do full justice to the liveliness of her disposition when in his presence, this was but a transient feeling. He took an ever-growing pleasure in her society, and she expanded under his appreciation, beginning to exhibit her parts, singing and dancing for his benefit, and giving little performances. Her imitation of the stiff military manner of Colonel Fulke-Greville, for instance, her

Greville's brother Robert, evoked his hearty laughter. Encouraged by her new uncle's applause, and noting that Mr. Greville raised no objection to her high spirits, she went on to mimic Mr. Willoughby and other frequenters of the house.

Whatever his engagements, Sir William Hamilton contrived they should not interfere with his daily appearance at the table of the 'fair teamaker of Edgeware Row,' as he soon came to call Emma.

She certainly laid herself out to please him. But there was neither hypocrisy nor looseness in her overtures. She knew that Sir William Hamilton's goodwill was of importance to her Greville; this, and this only, it was that actuated her in her endeavour to make his visits to the house ever more agreeable.

CHAPTER IX

Sir William Hamilton becomes more and more enamoured with his nephew's mistress. Mr. Greville sees great advantage in an arrangement which will secure his succession to his uncle's estate, whilst leaving him free to contract an alliance in accordance with his fortune.

WHETHER, as Mr. Greville suspected, Emma's exposure in Mr. Romney's studio conduced to the disorder, or whether it was due to some other cause, about this time she contracted a cold of such severity that both Mrs. Cadogan and the physician recommended by Sir William Hamilton, feared lest she should fall into a consumpton. Sea-bathing was ordered, and much as Mr. Greville regretted the expense, he had no choice but to arrange for the order to be carried into execution. He did not demur more at the expense than Emma at the separation. But the moment was opportune, for Sir William's affairs necessitated his own absence from town, and he wished to carry his nephew with him.

Emma's weakness, and Emma's tears, made further impression upon the ambassador, and he persuaded Charles, who had put him in possession of his mistress's earlier history, to offer her the company of her little daughter, still domiciled with Mrs. Kidd at Hawarden, as a solatium for his own. The proposal changed the tears of reluctance to those of gratitude. It seemed to Emma yet another proof of the incomparable goodness of her Greville's heart, and of his affectionate solicitude for her happiness. She never dreamed that it was to his uncle the suggestion was due. She accepted it with joy, and even thought that

129

this reunion with her child might perhaps become a lasting one. If little Emma were good, and had become beautiful, it was not beyond the limits of possibility that her generous Greville would allow her to bring the babe home to Edgeware Row. Then indeed would her cup of happiness be full. To live in one house together with her mother and child, all of them under the protection of the incomparable Greville, what woman could wish for more? Certainly not Emma Hart.

Whilst preparations were being made for her journey to the sea she said no word about the plan thus forming in her mind, but excelled herself in testifying her grateful love to Greville by the tenderest attentions to himself and to his guest. Sir William noted everything, daily becoming more enamoured. He was not without experience of ἑταῖραι, but he had seen none like this; she was εκλεκτοάτων ἐκλεκτοτέρα—*pulcherrima Dido*—peerless among women. He treated her with courtly gallantry, which grew gradually into the playful affectionateness so often subsisting between old and young relatives. He constituted himself her guardian and counsellor what time she displeased Charles by her liveliness or levity. He dubbed his nephew 'Pliny the Younger.' It was Pliny the Elder who was ever at hand with service and succour if the other were unduly severe.

There was no doubt Mr. Greville knew the way affairs were tending. There was little that escaped him when his own interests were involved. His uncle's anxiety when Emma fell into ill-health was far greater than his own, and the offer to bear the expense if her child were permitted to accompany her came unsolicited from Sir William Hamilton. Sir

William wished the proposal to appear to emanate from his nephew, and not from himself, for he had a great regard for Mistress Hart's delicacy, and would not for the world that she became aware of his knowledge of her unlawful motherhood. He treated her throughout with a consideration and respect that betrayed his growing feeling. Already a plan was forming itself in Mr. Greville's mind. It was not his nature to act precipitately, or he might have forbidden the visits to the studio, which still continued up to the very day of her departure from Edgeware Row. Mr. Greville's jealousy was coldly discriminating, and without expression. He did not resent his uncle's growing infatuation and had no anxiety lest it be returned. But his imagination followed Emma to the dais where Mr. Romney enthroned and gazed upon the loveliness that undraped itself freely for his benefit. And ever grew the resentment that had so strange a climax.

No one who occupies a position on which the light of publicity is thrown can hope to escape the malice of detractors. Calumny had not passed by Sir William Hamilton, who was now in his fifty-fifth year. It protested that he had taken advantage of his office to make bargains in the antiquities discovered at Herculaneum and Pompeii, afterwards selling them to his own country at an exorbitant figure. It further suggested that he had added to the functions of an ambassador that of *cavaliere servente* to the Queen of Naples. Truth may have lurked in both these accusations. 'I am more a *ministre de famille* at this court,' he wrote, 'than ever were the ministers of France, Spain, and Vienna.' Yet his wife, between whom and himself there existed a mutual

131

affection and esteem, has left it on record that he had been ever 'faithful and affectionate' to her; and she proved her confidence by leaving him her entire estate. There is no doubt, nevertheless, that Sir William Hamilton possessed the qualities essential to diplomacy and he made full use of them during the tour which he made now with his nephew. He had become enamoured of the 'Fair tea-maker of Edge ware Row,' but a transfer to himself of his nephew's mistress was a difficult matter, and needed the most elaborate negotiation. He was much longer in perceiving the trend of Mr. Greville's mind than Mr. Greville had been in realising his. And when they were both aware of the transaction each was contemplating, there was sufficient of decency left in them to desire to cloak its nature. For what it amounted to was that Mr. Greville possessed a work of art which his uncle coveted. The elder man was in a position to compel the sale, and the younger only concerned as to the price. It was for this reason that Mr. Greville concealed the Romney incident and the interpretation he put upon it. It was not his province to point out a flaw in the objet d'art of which he was disposing; rather would he extol it as flawless, and exact the last shilling.

Mr. Greville's financial position was not the most comfortable. He was still encumbered with his fine house in Portman Square. Under the testament of the late Lord Warwick he had engagements requiring two thousand pounds, of which he had not more than one moiety at hand; and, apart from the expenses of his present establishment, he was harassed by those entailed in connection with the representation of his family borough, which necessitated an annual tour in Warwickshire, to say nothing of disbursements to a corrupt electorate. The prospect was gloomy, seeming to offer no alternative to comparative poverty but a *mariage de convenance.*

Sir William listened sympathetically when Mr. Greville discoursed upon his troubles, professing willingness to extend any assistance in his power. He regretted that he had very little money lying idle, certainly not one, far less the required sum of two, thousand guineas. But his credit was good, and he had no doubt that his bankers, Messrs. Ross and Ogilvie, would find the amount to discharge his nephew's Humberston engagements, accepting his security for Mr. Greville's bond.

As for the future, and the *mariage de convenance* at which his nephew hinted, what was that he had heard about Lord Middleton's youngest daughter? Mr. Greville was doubtful. He feared she was beyond the mark for a younger son, being not only admirable in beauty and disposition, but possessed of a fortune of twenty thousand pounds. Of course, an assurance that he was to be his uncle's heir might influence the decision of her guardians. Sir William acknowledged it had always been his intention to make Charles his residuary legatee, and the admission was at the disposal of his lawyers. But if pourparlers were exchanged with Lord Middleton, 'what of the fair tea-maker?'

This was the manner of their discourse, but it is proper to remark that the discussion was not carried on within the limits of one day. Sir William was too clever a diplomatist, and Mr. Greville too cautious an antagonist, for the matter to be brought to so plain an issue. They pursued their tour in the utmost harmony, each taking the highest pleasure in the cultivated companionship of the other, everything that concerned poor Emma and her future well understood between them long before anything definite had been said.

Meanwhile Emma, happy in ignorance of what was impending, devoted herself to the care of little Emma, employing her spare time in pouring out her heart in long letters to Greville. After several removals in search of a lodging that should not be too fashionable nor too dear, she had found suitable accommodation in Parkgate, at the mouth of the River Dee, over which her own father was wont to gaze so longingly in his last days at Great Nesse. Here, in the house of a lady whose husband was at sea, she procured board and lodging at a price which she deemed high, but was certainly not ruinous. She punctually and faithfully reported all her movements and expenses, requesting Greville's free and unrestrained opinion upon them.

'I bathe and find the water very soult' [she wrote]. 'Here is a good many laidys batheing, but I have no society with them, as it is best not. So pray, my dearest Greville, write soon, and tell me what to do, as I will do just what you think proper; and tell me what to do with the child. For she is a great romp, and I can hardly master her. She is tall, good eys and brows, and as to lashes, she will be passible; but she has overgrown all her cloaths. I am makeing and mending all as I can for her. Pray, my dear Greville, do lett me come home as soon as you can; for I am all most broken-hearted being from you. ... I say nothing abbout this guidy, wild girl of mine. What shall we do with her, Greville? Wou'd you believe, on Satterday we had a little quarrel and I did slap her on her hands, and when she came to kiss me and make it up, I took her on my lap and cried. Pray, do you blame me or not? Pray tell

134

me. Oh, Greville, you don't know how I love her. Endead I do. When she comes and looks in my face and calls me "mother," endead I then truly am a mother, for all the mother's feelings rise at once, and tels me I am or ought to be a mother, for she has a wright to my protection; and she shall have it as long as I can, and I will do all in my power to prevent her falling into the error her poor miserable mother fell into. But why do I say miserable? Am I not happy abbove any of my sex, at least in my situation? Does not Greville love me, or at least like me? Does not he protect me? Does not he provide for me? Is not he a father to my child? Why do I call myself miserable? No, it was a mistake, and I will be happy, cheerful, and kind, and do all my poor ability will lett me, to return the fatherly goodness and protection he has shewn. Again, my dear Greville, the recollection of past scenes brings tears to my eyes. But they are tears of happiness. To think of your goodness is too much. But once for all, Greville, I will be grateful, adue. It is near bathing time, and I must lay down my pen, and I won't finish till I see when the post comes, whether there is a letter. He comes in about one o'clock. I hope I have a letter to-day. Emma is crying because I won't come and bathe. So, Greville, adue till after I have dipt. May God bless you, my dearest Greville, and believe me faithfully, affectionately, and truly yours only.'

Permission to take her child back to Edgeware Row was what Emma was seeking chiefly at this time, and in all her letters she sought to create a favourable impression of her daughter in her Greville's mind. But he, planning already how to reduce his present encumbrances, had no intention of adding to their number. He replied diplomatically, advising that the little Emma should be sent to some good school, and thus trained under better influences than can obtain in any irregularly established home. Emma was grateful for so much concession, and, it may be, agreed with the opinion that withheld more; for the child that

135

later proved of a bad disposition had already taxed her feeble maternal instinct beyond its strength.

'You don't know, my dearest Greville '[she answered], 'what a pleasure I have to think my poor Emma will be comfortable and happy, and if she does but turn out well, what a happyness it will be. I hope she will for your sake. I will teach her to pray for you as long as she lives; and if she is not grateful and good it wont be my fault. But what you say is very true; a bad disposition may be made good by good example, and Greville would not put her anywhere to have a bad one. I come into your whay of athinking; hollidays spoils children. It takes there attention from there scool, and gives them a bad habit. When they have been a month, and goes back it does not pleas them, and that is not wright, and the do nothing but thingk when the shall go back again. Now Emma will never expect what she never had. But I wont think. All my happiness is Greville, and to think that he loves me. I have said all I have to say abbout Emma, yet she only gives her duty. ... I have no society with anybody but the mistress of the house, and her mother and sister. The latter is a very genteel young lady, good-nattured, and does everything to pleas me. But still I woud rather be at home, if you was there. I follow the old saying, home is home though 'tis ever so homely. . . . I bathe Emma, and she is very well and grows. Her hair will grow very well on her forehead, and I don't think her nose will be very snub. Her eys is blue and pretty. She dont speak through her nose, but she speaks countryfied, but she will forget it. We squabble sometimes; still

136

she is fond of me, and endead I love her. For she is sensible. So much for Beauty. Adue, I long to see you.'

Emma's health having been at length completely restored by the sea-bathing, she returned to Edgeware Row, where she was soon joined by Mr. Greville and his uncle. Sir William had now to prepare for the resumption of his duties at the Court of Naples. He had come to an amiable arrangement with his nephew by which he assisted the latter in his pecuniary embarrassments. The transference of Emma was an unwritten clause in the contract between them. Sir William had his vanity, the vanity of a man to whom women's favour had been easy; he wished to woo and win her for himself. Mr. Greville thought secretly the task would prove to be beyond his matured powers, and that it was he who would have to arrange matters so that there should be no scene such as he knew Emma was capable of making. Mr. Greville was now quite decided to give up Emma. Her extravagant fondness over their reunion made no difference in his sentiments. Had she not owned that she visited Mr. Romney the very day of her return, and that he said she had 'improved in colour, and was growing buxom'?

But when Sir William had left England and was once more settled in his Neapolitan home, Mr. Greville set about to bring the matter to an issue without doing too great violence to Emma's sensibility. The acute student of human character will have no difficulty in following the operations of his mind, and will be prepared to admit that in the case of so pedagogic a nature there was more of the grammarian than of the hypocrite in his recognition of the difference between φαίνομαι εἶναι and φαίνομαί ωτ.

Mr. Greville's plan, which he had communicated to his uncle, and with which that gentleman was completely satisfied, was to dislodge Emma from Edgeware Row and separate her from himself under the pretext that such dislodgment and separation were only temporary, and for Mr. Greville's interest. A bantering suggestion from Sir William had been so ill received as to persuade him that for the moment at least her fondness for Mr. Greville was sufficiently great that she recoiled from the idea of having traffic with any other man. Mr. Greville had prevised this result; for although she had exposed herself to Mr. Romney, and thus lost her value in his eyes, he did her the justice to admit that she had no desire to transfer that which she was never averse from exhibiting.

It was incumbent upon him, therefore, as the first step toward his plan, to tell her of his necessity now to fulfil engagements where she could not conveniently accompany him. Later, he intended to plead financial distress as an excuse for closing the house in Edgeware Row. The question of her accommodation in the interval would then arise, and in dealing with this Mr. Greville proposed to avail himself of Emma's often-expressed desire for self-improvement. Italy offered advantages of education in music and languages beyond those of any other country. In Naples, Sir William Hamilton, Pliny the Elder, his own *fidus Achates*, and her true friend, would assist her in obtaining masters and all facilities for studying. So much of the problem having been thus set forth, the old process of *solvitur ambulando* might be relied upon to bring the parties to a point when *quod erat faciendum* could be written at the end of the proposition. Such was Mr. Greville's considered scheme.

It is tremendous to reflect upon the power to blind the conscience which is inherent in immoral desire. Satan, the cleverest of fallen angels, has the key to every locked heart. In tempting clever men he instils the most specious arguments into their minds, knowing how the subtlety of logic will titillate their intellects until they delude themselves into a belief that it is reason alone that moves them. As he considered and developed his plan for accomplishing his design, Greville entirely lost sight of the nature of the transaction in which he was engaged. Neither Mr. Romney nor his own pecuniary advantage loomed large, and he could even regard himself as a man sacrificing his own happiness for the happiness and welfare of others. He sincerely wished to gratify his uncle, who had ever been his very good friend, and he knew that Emma and her mother would enjoy a greater consequence in a larger establishment. All this and more he showed in letters written to Sir William, and at last put the proposal in its simplest terms.

'If you could form a plan' [he wrote], 'by which you could have a trial, and could invite her and tell her I ought not to leave England, and that I cannot afford to go on, and state it as a kindness to me if she would accept your invitation, she would go with pleasure. When you write an answer to this, inclose a letter to her, and I will manage to persuade her to it; and either by land, by coach to Geneva, and from thence by Veturine forward her, or else by sea. I must add that I could not manage

139

it so well later. After a month and absent from me, she would consider the whole more calmly. If there was in the world a person she loved so well as yourself, after me, I could not arrange with so much *sang-froid*; and I am sure I would not let her go to you if there were any risque of the usual coquetry of the sex being likely to give uneasiness.'

Stripped of all external decoration of verbiage Mr. Greville's action appears extremely sordid, even if a harsher word may not be more aptly applied to it. He may well have hesitated to throw himself so open even to the uncle whose good opinion he valued. But having brought himself to do so, he awaited the result with philosophic calm, employing the interval in making more perfect the yet not quite satisfactory arrangement of his collection of minerals.

When Sir William's invitation arrived, Mr. Greville feigned surprise, but after pretending a little consideration, he told Emma that he wished her to accept it. He explained that if he was to have enough to live upon, and to pay the interest of his debts without parting with his collection, he must reduce every expense, and as he would be obliged to absent himself for some months in Scotland, he would have no objection to her going to Naples for six or eight months; that she need not fear being troublesome, as he was sure she would be perfectly satisfied with the degree of attention Sir William would from choice give her, while she would be very happy in learning music and Italian.

Thus suddenly confronted with a scheme of which every detail seemed to be fixed already, Emma found herself without effective defence. She could only urge, with tears, that six months was an eternity, that she would be so miserable apart from her Greville she could not profit from studies to be substituted for conversation with him; and that she did not want to go. She met his reasons with a woman's lack of reason, and essayed to defeat his logic with her emotion. She said she did not mind going again to the sea, to Weymouth or to Exeter, whilst he was absent in Scotland. But she vowed she could not, would not, separate herself from him by such a distance as he proposed. At first it seemed nothing would move her from this determination. It was then Mr. Greville used the last weapon in his armoury.

'Emma, you must listen to what I have to say.' For she was crying and asseverating that she would not be parted from him. 'I am leaving London, and can no longer afford to support you and your mother here. Be reasonable; I have suggested a method which would relieve me until such time as I have paid off my liabilities, and can look forward to my prospects as my uncle's heir. In Italy, in Naples, you would be perfecting your voice, learning French and Italian, fitting yourself for my altered position.'

He paused; he meant her to understand the implication that it was because he wanted her to be more to him, and not less, that he was sending her away. A sudden flush of colour and immediate cessation of her tears told him she accepted the inference. She was to fit herself to be a better companion to her Greville, perhaps more than a companion! Hope told its ever flattering tale.

'But how can I live all these months without seeing you?' she exclaimed. 'No, no, let me stay; I will be more diligent, dear, dear Greville, and will apply myself better. I will indeed. You shall have no more cause to complain of my idleness. Your dear presence . . .'

'Is it mine, Emma? Is it my company that you fear to miss? I have told you that I am leaving London, that you cannot accompany me.

Yet you urge me to let you remain in town. Can it be that it is not me, but Mr. Romney, from whom you dread to part? . . .'

'Oh, Greville!'

Yet she hung her head. For the hours in the studio, where Mr. Romney was never tired of telling of her beauty and dilating upon its variety and perfection, were very dear to her. She had forgotten that Mr. Greville honoured, or dishonoured her by jealousy and she wished to be quite candid with him.

'I see I have hit upon the truth,' Mr. Greville went on, astounded nevertheless at the effect of his words. His suspicions were reinforced by her attitude. 'It is then Mr. Romney, and not I,' he repeated, 'who binds you to England?'

A spasm of genuine anger interrupted his speech, and momentarily crossed his intention, for none of his interests would be served if she took him at his word. 'It is then to Mr. Romney and his studio you would wish to transfer yourself when I leave town? '

She burst again into tears.

'Oh, Greville, how unkind! You cannot say, or think, such a thing. I only live to please you; indeed I have no other thought. I should be sorry to leave Mr. Romney because he paints so beautifully. I am so proud to be of use to him, and he has finished so few of the pictures. But only my Greville holds me. . . .'

'Then obey your Greville,' he put in quickly.

She could not combat his casuistry, nor his peremptoriness. Under his direction she presently wrote a letter accepting Sir William Hamilton's invitation. She wrote that Mr. Greville was going to places where she could not with propriety attend him, and she had too great a regard for his interests to hinder him from pursuing those plans which it was right to follow. She desired to be a little more improved, and since Greville out of his kindness had given his permission, she would be flattered if Sir William would assist her in this project. She would start the following 1st of March, when Greville went to Scotland, and she would remain at Naples until Greville came to fetch her back in October or November. She looked to find the pleasure of Sir William Hamilton's company and conversation the most agreeable thing in Italy. 'I shall be perfectly happy,' she assured him, 'in any arrangements you will make, as I have full confidence in your kindness and attention to me.'

So she signed the docket to her own disposal by Greville, and although not yet with open eyes, took the first steps towards the embraces of another man.

CHAPTER X

Emma, neglected and abandoned by Greville, solicited by the King of Italy, and pursued by the gentlemen of his Court, yields at length to Sir William Hamilton.

SIR WILLIAM HAMILTON'S satisfaction was unbounded when Emma's missive, enclosed in one from his nephew, assured him that the first part of this delicate transaction was accomplished. He had not so small an opinion of his power to please the fair sex as to believe that he would fail eventually in winning Emma's compliance to his wishes, when she should have grown accustomed to the loss of her Greville. He had but to follow the recommendation of Suetonius, and make haste slowly, to accomplish his design on what remained of Emma's virtue. He had no vision of how far his infatuation for her would lead, and what would be the end of their connection. He did not see himself at all in the rôle of *mari* to his nephew's mistress, far less in that of *mari complaisant*. Mr. Greville's sight was no clearer. No sooner had Sir William promised to make him his heir than the possibility of a second marriage had occurred to him. Since such an event might easily be the antecedent of his own disinheritance, it was plainly to his interest to avert it if he could. And, revolving the matter, he perceived quickly that the same obstacle that stood between himself and matrimony, to wit, a mistress, might well be set between Sir William Hamilton and the holy estate. It was this that settled him in parting with Emma.

'To sup with the devil, one needs a long spoon.' The devil was in Emma's charm, and soon began to urge her forward. Her story may seem to proceed slowly, but it never really halts, nor time stand still.

Mr. Gavin Hamilton, the painter, escorted Emma and her mother to Italy. After a journey occupying two months in time, they reached their destination, as chance would have it, on Emma's twenty-first birthday. Very soon after her arrival, and before Sir William Hamilton had exhibited himself in any other light than that of one who wished to make her stay agreeable, she began to pour out her heart to Greville.

'It was my birthday '[she said in one of her earliest letters],' and I was very low-spirited. Oh God! that day you used to smile on me and stay at home, and be kind to me—that that day I should be at such a distance from you! But my comfort is that I rely upon your promise, and September or October, I shall see you!'

She told him that she was sure to cry the moment she thought of him, and dreaded sitting down to write, as she wanted to show a cheerful face to Sir William. Although ruin depend on it, she vowed she must and would see him at the summer's end. After protestations of devotion that should have caused some uneasiness to him who was actually engaged in trafficking her, she concluded her letter in a manner which showed how simple and unsophisticated she was, despite her varied experience of the other sex:

'You have a true friend in Sir William, and he will be happy to see you, and do all he can to make you happy; and for me I will be everything you can wish for. I find it is not either a fine house or a fine coach, or a pack of servants, or plays or operas, can make happy. It is you that as in your power either to make me very happy or very miserable. I respect Sir William, I have a great regard for him, as the uncle and friend of you, and he loves me, Greville. But he can never be anything nearer to me than your uncle and my sincere friend, he never can be my lover.'

The ambassador certainly would not have subscribed his name to any such forecast of the future. He was exerting the whole of his very considerable powers to distract the fair creature's thoughts from his nephew, and to reconcile her to his own advances. At Up Park Mr. Greville had not been lacking in perception of Emma's capabilities, but he had not gauged them nearly so fully as did Sir William Hamilton in Naples. He saw that she would rise to every occasion, it was but a matter of giving her larger opportunities. The wider horizon, the brilliant colours, the warm climate of this subtropical region quickly expanded and matured her talents. She was pouring out her soul in love and longing to Greville, but she was growing all the time in beauty and realisation of power and was possibly neither so unhappy, nor so lost without him, as she expressed herself.

Italy quickly cast its glamour over her, and vivified her into the extraordinary fascination to which her intelligence conduced.

At first Sir William essayed to dazzle her with the power and the luxury he could put at her disposal. He had taken for her a suite of rooms furnished in the English taste, and commanding a view of the beautiful Bay of Naples. In the distance Capri gleamed like a gem in the sea, Novo, and Nuovo, and San Elmo, seeming to sleep in the sunshine, were ready to burst into thunder of guns in defence of the beauty entrusted to them. The splendour of the sun, reflected in the sea,

146

gave light so intense that it deadened the otherwise too brilliant colouring of flowers and trees—the garish tints, orange, madder, and carmine, that sprang from the fertile soil. Vesuvius dominated all. By day the long smoke stream was drawn menacingly against the blue sky; at night the moon sank palely behind its glowing lava. Emma could turn her eyes from these magical and natural beauties to look upon the crowded streets, all brilliant animation and moving kaleidoscopic sights. Gaudy handkerchiefs and ribbons, fluttering flags and gay plumes of feathers decorated the hats of the men; scarlet bodices and petticoats, banded with gold and silver, adorned the women's figures; artificial flowers, scarlet fringes and tassels, and gold tinsel bedecked the horses that drew calèches striped with bright red, and rich with gilt carving. Each detail in the ever-changing scene was a new point of interest to hold Emma's attention, and keep it from the one figure that Sir William desired her to forget.

To the distractions thus presented by her environment Sir William added all the others that his invention could devise, or his resources provide. He was lavishly extravagant in his expenditure of money on any object that pleased him, although he resembled his nephew in parsimony where other matters were concerned. Emma pleased him vastly, and he set no limits to his generosity towards her, trusting her consequent gratification would incline her quickly to his wishes. He showered presents upon her, quaint trifles purchased in the public market, costly trinkets chosen in the shops of fashionable jewellers. He bought her a camel shawl to take the place of some she had left in

London, until Greville should forward these. He escorted her on expeditions to Pompeii and Herculaneum, and fascinated her with stories he told of the life of the anonymous owners of these disinterred treasures, which had been the first object of his studies for so many years. He introduced her to his intimates, Sir Thomas Rumbold, the plutocrat from the East Indies, Prince Dietrichstein from Vienna, Mr. Acton, his successor in the Queen of Naples' affections, and to half the fashionable world, from the Duke of Gloucester downwards. Princes and nobles, ambassadors and ministers, the entire brilliant company that thronged the court of Ferdinand and Maria Carolina, all consented in paying court to the English girl, this 'modern antique,' that the well-known connoisseur in female loveliness was exhibiting to them; this 'counterpart and acme of Art and Nature,' with the apple-blossom complexion, and fine figure, so cunningly hinted at beneath the loose muslin gown, lace trimmed, blue ribanded. Sir William saw that she had not a moment's solitude in which to waft one thought to his nephew, Mr. Charles Greville, who was supposed to be economising in North Britain, trying to satisfy his love of the classical and antique with the prospect of Modern Athens seen from King Arthur's seat.

Her time was no less occupied within doors than without. She was given lessons in singing by Galluci, and in French and Italian, history and drawing by other masters of the first repute. She cultivated her own natural gift for dancing, and shared Sir William's studies in botany. To all these pursuits she applied herself with a zeal and concentration that were not more remarkable than her success. Until her first association with Greville an almost entirely uneducated and ignorant girl, she now amazed every one by the quickness of her natural understanding and the variety of the accomplishments she so easily acquired.

Emma permitted nothing to interfere with her studies which it was within her power to control. But she soon became aware of one source of interruption which she was unable either to dam or to divert. *Quis custodiet ipsos custodes?* is a question, like Pilate's 'What is truth?' to which no answer has been put on record. Emma needed guarding from her guardian. Soon the purpose of his attentions became unmistakable. The warmth of the embraces with which he regarded it as his avuncular privilege to salute her would have warned any young female of peril, even if she had not been, like Emma, *haud ignara mali*. She wrote and wrote again to Greville. She explained to him the predicament in which she was placed, the attentions to which she was exposed, his uncle's growing fondness. She implored a word of love, of counsel, she vowed her fidelity. There came no answer. She urged her youth, her loneliness, the temptations around her. . . . Silence, always silence, was Greville's persistent diplomacy, by which, in time, he hoped to succeed in gaining his freedom, and with it the price for which he had bartered what some men would have held dearer.

Now it was high summer. Emma's vitality and courage, waning under Greville's cruel neglect to answer her wild appeals, were further sapped by the damp Neapolitan heat. She was disspirited also by her mother's doubts of Greville's intentions, confirming her own increasing

149

uneasiness. She wrote again to beg for a letter, if only of farewell. Surely she deserved this for the sake of the love he once bore her.

'I have been from you going of six months, and you have wrote one letter to me, instead of which I have sent fourteen to you. So pray let me beg of you, my much-loved Greville, only one line from your dear, dear hands. You don't know how thankful I shall be for it. . . . If I dont hear from you and that you are coming according to promise, I shall be in England at Cristmass at farthest. Don't be unhappy at that, I will see you once more for the last time. I find life is insupportable without you. . . . I tel you give me one guiney a week for everything, and live with me, and I will be contented. . . .'

But whilst waiting for the reply that tarried so long in its coming, she plunged for distraction into the amusements and entertainments provided for her by Sir William.

Prosperity, it has often been pointed out, is a severer test of character than adversity. History has many instances to furnish of men who have risen from low origin to high place, making their way with steady perseverance to the predetermined goal, without dallying by the roadside to pluck the pleasant fruits, or to snatch an hour of the indolent ease offered by the grassy banks lining the dusty track. Yet when they have arrived at their journey's end, when success has crowned their unremitting effort, and they have attained a position where the virtuous qualities developed by long self-denial might have the greatest moral influence over their fellows, too often have they forsaken the principles, adherence to which brought them where they are, and rushing to a violent extreme, abused their position to secure

150

self-gratification, betrayed their trust, disappointed their well-wishers, and, it may be, damned their souls. The historian, contemplating the melancholy spectacle, must condemn, but his heart need not be steeled against pity. He may consider all the circumstances, and though naught extenuating, naught set down in malice, leaving hope that mercy may co-operate with justice.

And if this is permissible in the case of men who have hewed their own way through obstacles and over mountain barriers, it is an incumbent duty in the case of a girl who, with no contributory effort on her part, was lifted from a mud cabin to dwell in intimacy with a queen, and occupy a palace in the most frivolous capital in the world. This was the destiny of Emma Hamilton—to call her by the name which soon became hers, and by which she will be long remembered.

Born in a smithy, reared in a three-roomed cottage, and at thirteen years of age the little nursemaid to a country squire, she was now, only eight years later, the cynosure of every eye in a corrupt and brilliant court.

Sir William Hamilton knew his milieu perfectly, knew to a fraction how far he could go beyond the limits of propriety without imperilling his position as representative of his sovereign. He also knew the temptations that would assail the lovely creature in his charge, how to meet them, and how to turn them to his own advantage. He knew, moreover, exactly what he wanted, a precise knowledge, lacking which many a man fails to get anything at all, and took the straightest way towards it. He conveyed Emma everywhere with him, taking care to make it generally known that her kind favour was already pre-empted. Amongst the first, he showed her to the King and Queen, sauntering in the royal gardens in the cool of the evening. Prince Dietrichstein escorted her, and by the Queen's command led her nearer that Her Majesty might see the vaunted beauty more clearly. The Queen gazed at her, but not so ardently as did the King.

'The King as eyes,' was Emma's report, 'he as a heart and I have made an impression on it. I told the Prince, Hamilton is my friend, but I belong to his nephew, and all our friends know it.'

But what was Hamilton's nephew to Ferdinand, or he to Hamilton's nephew? The King did not give a fico for Hamilton's nephew. Hamilton's friend was a very different matter, and Ferdinand desired to know her more intimately. He shortly made his intentions obvious. The ambassador was entertaining a diplomatic party in his Casino at Posilippo, with Emma playing the role of hostess. At the conclusion of the entertainment, when she and her escort entered their felucca, they found the royal boat moored beside it. As they were being rowed away, His Majesty, in a loud voice, bade his band of French horns 'serenade the English beauty.' Sir William as in duty bound, stopped the boatmen. The King doffed his hat and bowed, he spoke to Sir William and looked at Emma. He asked Sir William to convey to her his regret that he could not speak English. She replied, herself, in her newly-acquired broken Italian, thus charming him afresh. After that the King's music serenaded and accompanied her frequently and His Majesty sought her company as often as was possible. It was in the royal gardens that the last interview between them took place. By this time he was completely enamoured and pressing his suit with Southern ardour. He was not accustomed to be rebuffed, but to Emma he was less a king than a boor, in comparison with whom she was able to appreciate Sir William's more courtly and agreeable wooing. Emma said 'No' to King Ferdinand and 'No' again. He made to take what she refused to give. She forgot his prerogatives and the sacredness of his person, and . . . boxed his ears. She was immediately abashed and terrified at her temerity, but King Ferdinand roared out laughing, and vowed she ought to have been the queen, for oftentimes she too had treated him so. The scene was ended for the moment by the appearance of the courtiers. But Ferdinand renewed his suit on every public and private occasion. There was no doubt Emma's presence provoked him, although when he did not see her she escaped his memory, for he was devoted to the pleasures of the chase, and had the mind of a child, unstable and forgetful.

Emma told Sir William of the attacks to which she was subjected, and it was he who devised the way not only to end them, but to turn them to her advantage.

Emma was advised to ask the King what he would give her for her compliance. Once instructed in her role she played it to perfection, teasing and inflaming him, until he would have promised her half his kingdom. She was satisfied with a little less, but must have it from him in writing, given under 'his hand and seal.' With the laughing eyes and tempting lips so near, King Ferdinand could refuse nothing. She dictated, and he wrote—laboriously, for he was no scholar, and the art of spelling was one that neither of them had mastered. But the purport of his writing was clear. Emma was to have Capri and a patent of nobility.

Once the King had signed, however, turning to her with a great guffaw as he flung down the pen and opened his arms for the reward, she seized the paper, and again eluded him as she ran off, laughing. 'Wait, wait, wait,' he heard her say as she danced away, curls floating, and eyes alight with pleasure at the trick she was playing. 'She'll be wanting my crown next,' he grumbled. But secretly he was not displeased at her lightness; it was in so great contrast to Maria Carolina's methods. He thought she would have come back, but it was to his wife she danced, to Maria Carolina herself! Sir William had found a means to introduce her to the palace.

Emma was a picture of Modesty Outraged, Innocence in Distress, when she obtained her audience. Sir William had had his in advance. What was between him and the Queen before he was ousted by Acton made her anxious to oblige him, even if she had not had her own interests with Ferdinand to protect.

With every sign of genuine distress written upon her lovely countenance, Emma besought Her Majesty's protection. She produced her paper, and now it appeared it was unexpected and unsolicited. What should she do? She was but a 'pore girl': always Emma's plea. She was in Italy to learn singing and dancing, but if the King gave her no peace. . . .

It was a *coup de théâtre*, admirably executed. The Queen was moved, impressed, greatly touched. She embraced Emma, promised her protection and countenance, and that she should have uninterrupted leisure for her studies. As for the King, she undertook he should pursue her no more. Maria Carolina knew how to deal with her spouse, how, and when, to influence him. The paper was torn up, Emma heard no more of it. And the King went boar-hunting. The whole incident redounded to the credit of our heroine, and the Queen was not slow in so regarding it. A more remarkable effort of Sir William's diplomacy is not on record. Recognition by the Queen was of the first importance if Emma was to be accepted in society. Whereas the King's mortification was evanescent, and the manner of it could not contribute to Sir William's nor Emma's disadvantage.

Where the King lead the way, however, it was the fashion to follow, and Emma had many admirers. Sir William Hamilton saw how things stood and redoubled his gifts, wooing her with the practised persuasiveness of his amorous experiences. The Queen, although she loved Acton, trusted Sir William Hamilton and was ever anxious to stand well with the only power that she saw between her and French aggression. Now she showed as much favour as was possible to his fair countrywoman whom he was understood to be educating for the stage. Any further pressure that was needed came in the shape of tardy letters from Greville. Of these two are extant, the one a chill epistle to Emma recommending her to oblige Sir William—a Delphic utterance capable of interpretation to suit any event; the other a candid expression to his uncle of the little value he set on Emma's protestations of fidelity. With this he enclosed all her fond letters written to himself, a heartless exposure of a woman's loving weakness, attaching to them a comment marking his cynic philosophy: *'L'oublie de l'inclus est volant, fixez-le; si on admet le ton de la vertu sans la vérité, on est la dupe, et je place naturellement tout sur le pied wai, come fai toujours fait, et je constate Vetat actuel sans me reporter d vous.'*

Whilst Sir William Hamilton was reading her letters to Greville, Emma, torn by emotions, was writing him yet another:

'Nothing shall ever do for me but going home to you. If that is not to be, I will accept of nothing. I will go to London, their go into every excess of vice till I dye, a miserable, broken-hearted wretch, and leave my fate as a warning to young whomen never to be two good; for now you have made me love you, you have abbandoned me; and some violent end shall finish our connexion, if it is to finish. ... I always knew, I had a foreboding since first I began to love you, that I was not destined to be happy; for their is not a King or Prince on hearth that cou'd make me happy without you.'

Thus did Emma subscribe her testimony to the case urged by every moralist, that happiness is only for the virtuous. Immoral relations between the sexes have the seeds of decay in them. Illicit love born of passion, nurtured in artificiality, ends with violence. 'If I was with you I wou'd murder you and myself boath.' In that threat did her indignation find expression and her association with Charles Greville come to an end.

When at length Emma could no longer conceal from herself or from her mother the knowledge that the separation from Greville was to be permanent, the greater part of the conspiracy against her had been successful. That which she had given to Captain Willett Payne out of ignorance, and to Sir Henry Featherstonehaugh in her extremity, but which Greville alone had received in love, she was persuaded at last to surrender to Sir William Hamilton from motives of self-interest, and these alone. In accepting his embraces neither ignorantly, in desperation, nor affection, our excuses for her must come to an end. She gave herself voluntarily to this elderly voluptuary in exchange for the benefits he could bestow. She had become the courtesan, selling her wares in the best market. And even yet she had not realised to where that sale would lead. She was satisfied to be Sir William Hamilton's mistress, not yet aspiring to become his *wife*.

She had her own suite of rooms at the Embassy, where Mrs. Cadogan was also installed in state. The servants called her *Eccellenza*, little guessing how recently she had been but a servant herself. And now her head began to rule her mistreated and cooling heart. She developed ambition, and studied passionately in order to be the equal, if not the superior, of the dissolute ladies that the habits of the Court made prominent in Neapolitan society. She was not long at the Embassy before the entire polite world sought the entree to her receptions, the 'receptions,' save the mark, of 'Frail Emma of Edgeware Row'! She sang, Sir William accompanying her on the viola, revealing miraculous powers of expression, at least so her admirers told her, and those who

157

had favours to expect from the British Ambassador. From others there were comments about the correctness of her ear. But prosperity inevitably brings envy, and Emma's detractors were few at this period, which preceded her zenith by some months. She danced the tarantella with a lightness almost incredible, and exhibited her 'Attitudes,' a form of *tableau vivant* devised by herself and quite unique at that time. Clad in flowing draperies, she took up her position before a pair of screens, where, illumined by torches, she showed by change of posture, by gesture and expression, every mood and emotion known to human nature. She was in turn the incarnation of Dignity, Supplication, Indolence, Gravity, Distress, Playfulness, Pleasing Torment, Abandonment, Remorse, Temptation, Doom, Agony. She held her audience spell-bound, and they justly called her 'inimitable,' and 'incomparable.'

Nor was her success confined within the limits where propriety might well have held her. As the mistress, not the wife, of the English Ambassador, Emma could not be received openly at Court. But the Queen was already on terms of private friendship with her, and held up her domestic behaviour as an example to the Neapolitan ladies. It was, however, Her Grace of Argyll, famous as 'the beautiful Miss Gunning,' who turned Emma's head entirely. The daughter of a poor Irish gentleman, of no estate or consequence, the Duchess of Argyll saw no reason why Emma should not aspire to equal rank with her own. She was a generous and emotional creature, sweet-natured and impulsive, but lacking education, and of an almost abnormal stupidity. It was she who had lisped gushingly to King George, already apprehensive about his health, how she and her sister 'longed to witness a coronation.' Many another *bêtise* about them was rife in society. Neither prudence nor fitness dictated to her why Sir William should hesitate to regulate Emma's position by marriage, and she not only encouraged Emma to this ambition, but employed her own high social influence to further the same object.

Emma had not mixed with the beauties admitted into the cosmopolitan society of Naples without learning something of the pressure that can be exercised upon an elderly lover by a young, lovely, and accomplished woman. The idea for which the Duchess of Argyll was primarily responsible began to germinate. Sir William commenced by laughing at it. He knew the rigid principles of his Sovereign, and that his consort was intolerant of the least impropriety. Such a marriage, instead of minimizing the evil of a guilty liaison, might give offence in high places, and perhaps ruin and terminate his own career. The suggestion nevertheless had its allurement, marriage would bind to him for ever this much-sought-after, young, and beautiful creature. But at first he laughed, and turned it away lightly, telling her he could not love her better, nor she have more consequence. It is not all at once that such affairs are settled. Emma was happy, proud of her salon, her large circle of friends, and Sir William's patent devotion. She might have abandoned her ill-advised attempt to rise any higher, notwithstanding the duchess, had not an incident occurred that drove her position home to her, and made her resolute.

159

An old acquaintance, Mr. Heneage Legge, whom Greville had admitted to the house in Edgeware Row when that establishment was first set up, arrived in Naples with his wife, who was momentarily awaiting her first confinement. Sir William waited upon him, and, willing to endorse and supplement such friendliness, Emma offered her company and services to the lady in her interesting situation. She was deeply mortified by the prompt and unhesitating refusal of her proffered attention. Mr. Legge, on the part of his wife, acknowledged the kindness of the intention, but said Mrs. Legge was in no need of company. Such company was the implication; but he had no wish to offend the ambassador, of whose conduct in the whole matter, however, he wrote home in no measured terms.

Emma was furious. The temper that 'nearly burst her girdle,' to use her own vivid expression, the tears of anger, tears of shame, passion of invective, passion of pleading, certainly moved Sir William. Gifts and caresses provided no remedy. There was but one way to save her from such humiliation, and to that point Sir William was all the time being led, or driven.

CHAPTER XI

Sir William Hamilton brings Emma to London to ask the consent of the King to his marriage. But in an interview with Greville she offers to give up all her prospects if he will restore her to her old place in his heart. Mr. Greville rejects the proposal and accuses her of having been unfaithful to him with Mr. Romney. She seeks Mr. Romney, whose mind is already clouded, and who dreams that she has been his mistress, and not only his inspiration. She marries Sir William Hamilton.

IT is a frequent experience in human life that, contrary to its first seeming, a check in an upward progress is in reality an advantage to the climber, since it provokes an access of energy on his part which carries him to the summit with a speed which otherwise he might not have attained. This was Emma's experience in her present march to the goal of matrimony.

She had come to acquiesce in her existing situation as Sir William's mistress, different as it was from the situation of other men's mistresses, in that she was smiled upon by a queen, and admitted into the society of such irreproachable great ladies as the Duchess of Argyll. Emma's salon at the Embassy was thronged nightly by English and Neapolitans of the highest rank, and, had she wished to change her position, or vary it, the opportunity would have been afforded her. But Emma, although frail, was temperate, that is to say she was instinctively a monogamist. Her present protector sufficed for the moment both her ambitions and her emotions. She professed, perhaps she felt, a great affection for him. Her footing, such as it was, in Italian society was secure. Marriage could give her little she did not already possess, and her native common sense and knowledge of the world did not allow her to ignore, when it was put before her, that such a marriage might entail consequences upon Sir William Hamilton for which she, too, would have to suffer.

All these considerations, however, were swept away by the torrent of mortification and anger let loose in her mind by the affront offered to her by the wife of the Honourable Heneage Legge. Marriage was the only possible way to avert its repetition. Now she began to importune Sir William; anon she hastened to Her Grace of Argyll and besought her to bring all her great influence upon the ambassador to this effect. The duchess was perfectly willing, and enlisted as an ally Lord Bristol, with whom Sir William had been on terms of peculiar intimacy since boyhood. Lord Bristol, after a few interviews with Emma, proved himself a single-hearted partisan. He was ever a man of eccentric conduct and insisted upon privacy for these interviews. As the Lord Bishop of Derry he might have adduced spiritual and ecclesiastical reasons for urging his old friend to renounce the life in sin which he was leading and causing Emma to lead. But, knowing his man and, it may be, attaching little importance to the rigid morality required of its sons by the Church, he preferred to make a different appeal. What inducement Emma offered Lord Bristol for his argument may be easily conceived. Certainly the correspondence between them, that came to light later, gives reason to suppose that Sir William Hamilton was not to be blamed for inconsistency when he accepted the advice and discarded the friendship that proffered it.

Thus reinforced, Emma pressed the siege closer, and had the satisfaction of seeing Sir William's resistance growing daily weaker. There were, indeed, only two persons whose disapproval he actually feared—his foster-brother and master, the King of England, and his nephew, Mr. Charles Greville. It was indeed necessary to obtain the consent of the former, and he made this clear to Emma when at length he gave her the conditional promise which so exalted her.

With regard to Mr. Greville, he stipulated for secrecy until the King's consent should have been obtained. And Emma was glad to oblige him in this matter. In spite of the terms on which she was living with Sir William, and all her distractions, she could not deceive herself into believing that she had forgotten Greville. She was not a little apprehensive of the manner and the temper in which he might receive the surprising intelligence of her approaching marriage to Sir William. But that she should see him once again, and soon, threw into the background even the new state that was to be hers.

The idea that in advancing age and amorousness his uncle might be persuaded to a marriage with Emma had presented itself to Mr. Greville's mind only to be discarded. But Mr. Greville did not know the new Emma. His knowledge was of a wild, emotional girl whose every action he could direct. He took no account of what effect his own conduct might have had upon her character, the conduct of the man she loved and believed in, and who had trafficked with and tricked her. For by now she knew the nature of the agreement between him and his uncle.

Mr. Legge wrote again to Mr. Greville at some length, recording his impressions of the establishment at the Embassy, of which, indeed, he had not hesitated to express an opinion to the ambassador himself.

'Her influence over him'[he told Greville], 'exceeds all belief. . . . The language of both parties, who always spoke in the plural number—we, us, and ours—staggered me at first, but soon made me determined to speak only to him on the subject, when he assured me, what I confess I was most happy to hear, that he was not married; but flung out some hints of doing justice to her good behaviour, if his public situation did not forbid him to consider himself an independent man. She gives every one to understand that he is going to England to solicit the King's consent to marry her. . . . I am confident she will gain her point, against which it is the duty of every friend to strengthen his mind as much as possible. And she will be satisfied with no argument but the King's absolute refusal of his approbation. ... I have all along told her that she could never change her situation, and that she was a happier woman as Mrs. H. than she would be as Lady H., when more reserved behaviour being necessary, she would be deprived of half her amusements.'

Mr. Greville was very ready to believe that Emma was not the woman to disagree with Mr. Legge's opinion of the advantages of mistress over wife, notwithstanding that she might do her utmost to persuade everybody that Sir William meant to make an honest woman of her. But as he did not believe that his *alter ego* would depart so far from the usages of the polite world, and that even if he wanted to, the royal consent would not be forthcoming to so scandal-provoking an alliance, he was not mightily disturbed by Mr. Legge's *communique*. He deemed that his uncle, no less than himself, was incapable of violating the unwritten laws of good society, although he might conceivably disregard the Decalogue on the ground of its being *vieux jeu*.

Nevertheless, the impossible was now in process of being accomplished. Bracing himself to meet the ordeal of his Sovereign's cold disapproval, or perhaps his warm displeasure, Sir William Hamilton took leave for a while of their Sicilian Majesties, and after a journey broken by short stays at Florence, at Venice and other centres of European fashion, brought Emma back to London after an absence of more than five years.

Had it been possible for her when she so reluctantly left her Greville to foresee the manner and the purpose of her return, she might not have been so despairing and broken-hearted as we have seen her. Then exile might have been welcomed in its true colour as a necessary and salutary break to all old associations. For the discarded mistress returned to London as an expectant bride; the modest 'Tea-maker' as the Ambassadress-elect.

Once installed in that mansion in Piccadilly where Sir William set up an establishment only a degree less splendid than that he maintained in Naples, the great and the wealthy—His Grace of Queensberry, my Lord Abercorn, Mr. Beckford of Fonthill, and many others—were quick to pay their *devoirs* to the beauty, *poseuse*, and songstress whose fame had travelled from Naples more quickly than herself; to whom were attributed all the talents, not only in the profession from which she was to emerge through the doors of Marylebone Church, but those that

165

would have fitted her to shine upon the stage. Emma was feted in London little less than she had been in Naples.

But the heart is a homing bird, and her thoughts dwelt ever upon the delayed interview with Greville. It was his welcome for which she longed, his praise on her improvement which she coveted, his good wishes she needed for the occasion. Mr. Greville was in Scotland when his uncle and former pupil arrived in London. She had to conceal her impatience whilst he tarried there. She did not yet know how he would receive the news of the approaching marriage, nor what difference he might deem it would make to his own prospects. She feared, she hoped, but above all she longed, to see his face, to hear his voice, knowing that was the goal to which all her hard work and desire for self-improvement had tended, that it was indeed he who had coloured her dreams and impelled her actions.

By this time she had excused his treatment of her, in the way loving women have, and was willing to believe he had had only her benefit at heart, sometimes going so far as to think that even this marriage had been in his contemplation. Having so greatly benefited by her sojourn in Italy, she deemed it not unreasonable to suppose he had foreseen it.

When at length she was advised of Mr. Greville's return to town, and Sir William announced to her that his nephew proposed to pay his respects that very afternoon, Emma flew to her mirror. Everything else faded from her mercurial mind—the importance of the interview with the King that was even now on the point of being accomplished, the dukes and marquises who had sought her favours, even Sir William

166

Hamilton himself. Greville, her dear, dear Greville, was coming this afternoon, and he would see the difference five years had made in her. No one had touched her heart since he had won it. The connection with Sir William had been forced upon her. If she had but recently been too complaisant with my Lord Bristol, 'twas but an incident that made little impression on one to whom sin ever presented itself under euphemistic name. She had bought Lord Bristol's advocacy of her claims to the married state by proving to him her accessibility as his friend's mistress. But Greville was a different matter.

Her heart beat high at the expectation of meeting him; she was all in a flutter, bewildered by her feelings, one moment thinking it possible he might ask her to give up his uncle and return to his embraces, another fearing lest he should find her altered but not improved. She had grown a little stouter, and Greville admired slender women. It was a radiant vision, nevertheless, that presented itself to him, a little paler than of old, the blue eyes soft and the exquisite mouth tremulous.

When he bowed over her hand he could note her emotion. His own voice was quite under control and his eyes only critical.

'Would you have recognised her?'Sir William asked Charles; he was proud of the transformation that had been achieved. 'She has an air of fashion, eh?'

'Sir William ever over-praises me,' Emma said blushingly.

'Would it be possible, madam, to over-praise where Perfection itself appears to confirm the charge?" answered Greville, surveying her with interest. But still her eyes were downcast, and presently her modish clothes could not disguise from him that beneath the frills upon her bodice her heart was beating tumultuously, and that the tumult was for him. He was secretly amused and completely reassured.

'I am enchanted by the sight of such beauty,' he ejaculated.

'Oh, Greville, do not, I pray you, make fun of me,' she murmured.

Sir William intervened before she had time to say more.

'You will excuse me if I withdraw; I stayed but to receive you, and hear what you might say of our fair one. Now the audience with the King awaits me. Wait, Charles, wait my return; Emma will have much to tell you. I am asking the King's permission to our marriage. If he grant it, yours, I am sure, will not be lacking. *Au revoir*, Charles; Emma, I charge you with his entertainment.'

If Charles Greville was taken aback by the intelligence that Sir William Hamilton really contemplated marriage with his mistress, that he was even now on his way to ask the King's permission, he made no immediate demonstration of his chagrin or astonishment. Emma's beauty had indeed increased, so apparently had her ambitions. He waited to be alone with her to discover them and decide upon his action. If she was to be his aunt, if he had blundered in his intentions, he did not intend to make another false step. But first he must know her mind.

Sir William Hamilton was satisfied with Mr. Greville's attitude. Charles's imperturbability was rarely ruffled, and if he were less eloquent than usual on this occasion, Sir William attributed it to Emma's appearance. His fine connoisseurship had used him to the admiration his specimens ever excited. An honourable gentleman himself, and accustomed to look upon his nephew as his counterpart, he had no fear lest he should seek to rob him. He was, on the other hand, pleased that Charles should see what lustre the treasure they had exchanged had acquired in his keeping. Sir William Hamilton knew the coldness of Charles Greville's temperament, whilst Emma in the old days, notwithstanding how frequently she had flung herself against its limitations, had never truly realised them.

Emma, after the departure of Sir William, was at first all in a tumult finding herself alone with Greville, and found words difficult. Greville's manner was perhaps less respectful after his uncle left the room. He continued to pay her compliments, but there was a touch of cynicism in them. Although she parried them with more wit than he had known she had at her command, yet was she less at ease with him than she had been with any man these last five years. Perceiving her embarrassment, but not quite understanding its genesis, he asked:

'So gossip spoke truly when it said you are contemplating marriage with my esteemed uncle?'

'It is for that he even now waits upon His Majesty; to secure permission and his confirmation in the Embassy.'

'And then Emma will have achieved the height of her ambition.'

'No, Greville, no'; her voice was low.

'You are not in earnest, then, in pressing this marriage?"

'I have the countenance of the Duchess of Argyll.'

'And of His Grace of Bristol.' For there was little concerning his uncle of which Mr. Greville failed to hear.

169

Emma coloured violently. 'Lord Bristol has great influence with Sir William,' she answered quickly, but with some embarrassment.

Mr. Greville laughed, observing her closely, and thinking his shot had gone home. He rallied her lightly upon her conquest of the eccentric roué, for, in truth, the term applied to Lord Bristol. Emma became confused, and her wit left her. Every minute she was in the company of Mr. Greville her feeling for him revived. She scarce heeded his word, so taken up was she with his voice and handsome person. No other man regarded her so coldly, yet for none other her heart could beat so fast. They talked a little longer, then her rising flush betrayed a new impulse, and quite abruptly she said,

'Greville, Greville, have you forgot everything? How you comforted me at Up Park, and taught me in Edgeware Row? Greville, have you forgot how I sat on your knee to learn my writing? '

She was desperate for a word of kindness from him, to know he had not forgotten. This, this was her man; not the elderly Sir William, nor the brutal Lord Bristol, nor any of the fiery Neapolitans who had begged her favours. It was only Greville who could reach her depths.

She had come near to him, and if her beauty tempted him—as indeed it might, being of such rare calibre—the knowledge that he had parted with it, and his honour now stood pledged, made him not fond, but cruel. He looked at her, and before his look her own fell, the lovely colour flushing, and her eyes filling with tears. She made as if she would find shelter in his arms against the blushes that burned her and satisfaction there for the hunger that consumed her. Once he had loved her, and seeing now she was more worthy of him, she pleaded again:

'Greville, you have not forgotten? '

'No, no, I have forgotten nothing.'

'You love me still? '

At that he laughed—Mr. Greville's low, well-bred laugh. 'The old Emma,' he exclaimed, 'the unchanged, unchangeable Emma! '

'She for whom her Greville once cared.'

'And misunderstood.'

'Never, Greville, never; you alone have known me.'

Perhaps she stirred his tepid blood unpleasantly, perhaps he was only angered by the knowledge how far she had succeeded with Sir William Hamilton. It is difficult to know what possessed him. He stood there in his knee breeches and lace ruffles, hat in hand, the most handsome and elegant of figures, opposite one whom everyone acknowledged to be the loveliest of her sex. And all that was in his logical mind was how he could hurt her. All that was in hers was how much she loved him still, this dear, dear Greville, his cold blue eyes, which she had seen half-closed, but with a gleam in them, his thin lips, on which she had felt warmth and seeking, his clear, fair skin, which she had seen flush. . . .

'Greville,' she burst forth again, 'you don't know how I have longed for this hour.'

'The hour in which you would announce to me your approaching marriage to my uncle?' he asked calmly.

171

'The hour in which I would tell you riches was nothing, nor honour, nor greatness, if my Greville loves me still,' she got out, the warm colour flushing in her cheeks and her eyes shining. At that moment she would have given up everything. 'Love is the greatest of all,' Emma cried. And again Greville laughed. The laugh misled her, and now she was babbling to him of how she had thought and dreamed of him for weeks and months after she had left him, and even after he had ceased to write; and of how other men had wooed her, but none had effaced his dear image. When he answered her lightly, but with a question, she admitted she had yielded to his uncle, but only in his interests. She swore it was only in his interests. Mr. Greville listened, watching the glow of her beautiful eyes, the rise and fall of her bosom, noting every curve and line. He was not unmoved, but, mysteriously enough, he was moved to anger. Perhaps the knowledge of how impossible it was to take what she offered him, to put back the hands of the clock, was what impelled him. For she was enough to tempt any man to his own dishonour, but Mr. Greville's must remain immaculate before the world, justified before himself.

'Greville'—she was very near to him, and her eyes pleaded—'will you take me back?'

'Always my impulsive Emma,' his pale lips murmured.

'But you will, Greville, you will . . .'

'Maintain a model for Mr. Romney?' Greville completed the sentence. 'No, my dear Emma, no. I will leave that for my uncle. If indeed he

172

choose it, when I advise him of my real reason for parting with one so fair and so frail.' He was still facing her with that smile.

It was as if he struck her; the colour that flushed painfully in her cheeks had that aspect, and so had her filled eyes. She shrank back from him all at once; then said, in a low voice:

'You don't mean that, Greville; you never really thought I deceived you with Mr. Romney?'

He had hurt her through and through, though as yet she could hardly feel the pain for the shock. A moment before her heart had been warm and quick for him, and leaped at his regard; now it felt cold and heavy, as if it would stop beating altogether.

'You cannot mean it,' she repeated. 'You said 'twas for my improvement. . . . 'Her beautiful eyes were full of tears, and it was all the best and finest of her they flooded. 'It was not because you believed I trafficked with Mr. Romney you sent me to Italy? Say it is not true. You don't think that Mr. Romney . . .'

'Although an artist, was nevertheless a man?' he finished her hesitant speech quite coolly. He never forgot his courtliness of manner. 'I did, I do. You must forgive me, my dear Emma, for my knowledge of human nature. I believe that as soon as I shared one of my privileges with Mr. Romney, I shared them all. I had forgiven you Captain Willet Payne, and perhaps Dr. Graham, Sir Henry Featherstonehaugh. . . .' Mr. Greville's snuff-box had been made in Paris, it was jewelled, and decorated with a miniature of Marie Antoinette. He helped himself from it delicately, and continued: 'But Mr. Romney! A mere countryman, of

173

little breeding and less manners. And after I had flattered myself that I had at least succeeded in refining your tastes. . . . 'He gave a little shudder.' From Charles Greville to George Romney! Oh! Emma, you disappointed me there.' A further recourse to his snuff-box showed his indifference; he was still smiling.

She burst forth:

'Say no more, Greville, say no more; you have said too much already. You affected then belief in my innocence . . .' Her anger was beginning to rise.

'You will do me the justice to believe that I acted upon that affected belief, guarding your best interest in transferring you to my uncle.'

'And wronged me all these years, wronged me, Greville.'

He shrugged his shoulders:

'Constancy, my dear Emma, constancy is the prerogative of the incurious; and you were ever of an adventurous disposition.'

'You are trying to anger me. You are going to tell this wicked story to Sir William.'

'A gentleman should be fully informed about the lady he intends to make his wife.'

'I had no intercourse with Mr. Romney; you know it. You want to stop my marriage with your uncle. But you shan't. I will marry him whatever you say. Sir William loves me truly. . . .'

The smile never left his countenance:

'And knows you so little. Think, Emma, think! Will this marriage be for your happiness any more than for his? Will you be true to him? You

174

know you will not. Do not think I am reproaching you for this; you will ever act in accordance with your charming and impulsive temperament, one which I have had the opportunity of studying, and which I have no hesitation in describing as characteristic of the true daughter of pleasure. What have you offered me this moment, whilst my uncle is even now in quest of the wedding ring? Once you found enjoyment in my embraces, and you would essay the gratification again. Mr. Romney tempted you with the thought of posterity, and Lord Bristol with his advocacy. So will you yield again, and yet again, to him who most cleverly flatters your vanity or appeals to what I now perceive to be a most excellent understanding.'

Again he had recourse to the snuff-box.

'You will not place me in the unpleasant position of having to tell my uncle how you posed to Mr. Romney, and that only recently he has boasted of your goodness to him. You will abandon the idea of this marriage . . . it is absurd, inadequate, there are no heights to which you cannot aspire. The young Prince . . . he has but to see you. Be reasonable, Emma; you jeopardise not only my interests but your own if you go on with this mad scheme. You force me to the truth; my uncle will listen to me. . . . '

In the days gone by Emma had listened to many orations proceeding from the lips of her idolized protector, orations lengthier perhaps, but little less polished in form or less suavely delivered. Never had she listened to one that so powerfully affected her as did this declaration of the light in which she had so long been regarded by the man with the belief in whose love she had deluded herself. She realised now to the full that those whom the gods would destroy they first make blind. Her love for Greville was disinterested and sincere, and it was he who wounded her.

She gazed on him with wide eyes and parted lips, and the heaving of her bosom betrayed the distress her pride urged her to conceal. She knew that it was Greville alone for whom she had ever cared, Greville alone whom she loved, or ever could love. In every cold syllable that fell from his lips she heard the metallic ring of scorn, and at last she knew that what he felt for her was not love but derision. The self-respect which he had once been so careful to instil into her, so attentive in nurturing, quivered and died. All her dreams turned nightmares. She might not fail in confronting the world with a proud mien, yet the memory of this moment, and the knowledge of Greville's contempt, and that he had never believed in the innocence of her friendship with Mr. Romney, was to remain with her, proving the incentive to all it forfended.

Man's vision is purged with euphrasy and rue, a sour herb, albeit a herb of grace.

Emma at last saw Mr. Greville as he was; a man without a heart, one who could be deluded by his own sophistry into misapprehending meanness for magnanimity. Was he not threatening her now with a revelation of what she had offered to him because she loved him? Was he even honest in his accusation of her with Mr. Romney? Was this her hero? She fell with his fall, for the only pedestal on which she had ever aspired to stand was his esteem.

'It is not to your interest, Greville, to disoblige me,' she began, when she had in a measure collected herself. 'You do not know what power I have. If I marry Sir William Hamilton, notwithstanding what you may tell him, will it not prove I can do as I will with him? Then what of your affairs? He has told me you are still in debt.'

Greville was not easy, but affected to dismiss the suggestion with indifference.

'I shall accept your ladyship's ruling,' he answered. The title on his lips was a sneer, and his bow was ironical. Yet when she spoke thus of reprisal, he could not but admire an ingenuity so kin to his own spirit.

'You shall put your wit against my wit, and the encounter prove us.' He took her hand, he kissed it. At the touch of his lips on her hand her courage failed again.

'But why does Emma speak of revenge in the same breath with you? Was not you good to my child, and was not you the cause of making me what I am?' She was hurried in her speech and a little incoherent. Perhaps he had not meant to repulse and threaten her. 'Greville, can we not be friends?' She was looking pleadingly into his eyes, and he was reconsidering his position, when the door opened to admit Sir William Hamilton. Not behind his nephew in correctness of behaviour, he evidenced no annoyance at the familiarity revealed by their attitude.

'Congratulate me, my dear nephew; congratulate me, Emma; the King consents. My love, we can be married at your convenience.' Mr.

177

Greville drew himself up and said all that the occasion required. Emma expressed herself as transported. She gave a side glance from her eyes to Mr. Greville when she exclaimed that she would like Mr. Romney to be the first to hear the news. She had recovered herself so quickly that Mr. Greville might well have believed the whole interview a dream, her tears and appeals to him for reinstatement in Edgeware Row but a farce she had played for his benefit.

'You know Mr. Romney and I was always such friends,' she went on to Sir William.

'Impudent' was perhaps the word Mr. Greville would have used to describe her manner. He could not, however, withhold his tribute to her cleverness.

'Mr. Romney must paint me as The Ambassadress.' Then, quite roguishly, she added, 'Will Mr. Greville attend his future aunt to Cavendish Square?'

Mr. Greville might have consented, and taken the opportunity to make his peace with her. But Sir William, a little pompous, although secure in the knowledge of all he was giving, interposed with, 'My love, it is I who will escort you to Mr. Romney's studio. The coach is even now at the door. You wish to surprise him, and you shall. But do not forget that the Duke of Queensberry entertains us to-night; I hear the Prince of Wales is to be there. Your old friend shall not be neglected; you show your good heart by the desire to acquaint him early with the change in your prospects. But our time is limited.'

178

Touched by Sir William's chivalry, for she saw he was wishful Mr. Greville should know how, and by whom, she was being received, Emma's eyes filled again. Taking leave of Mr. Greville with an easy grace, she followed her elderly cavalier downstairs, and allowed him to hand her into the carriage. She would get from Mr. Romney's own lips a refutation of the scandal Mr. Greville had started. He himself should tell Sir William how she had posed for him and why. Sir William would understand. He had often said there had been no figure like hers since the Greek.

In the carriage, *en route* for Cavendish Square, Sir William used the occasion to say a warning word about Greville. Emma avowed that all her affections were given to her future husband. If her heart was heavy, her vanity suffering from its first severe wound and her self-respect a torn and ragged garment that could never again cover her, her coquetry at least never failed. She so cajoled him that he believed her regard for Mr. Greville to be dead, and for him permanent. He left her at Mr. Romney's door, promising to return when he had visited his tailor and arrange how she was to be painted. Sir William knew that Mr. Romney was a great artist. There was a sob in her throat as she mounted the stairs. How could Greville have said that Romney boasted of her favours! He would himself tell Sir William he was only her friend. It was wicked to have slandered him.

Throwing open the door of the studio in her own dramatic manner, she stood before Mr. Romney, an unexpected apparition of beauty, ravishingly set off by her white embroidered organdie and straw bonnet with the blue ribbons. The artist was lying back in a great arm-chair, an expression of settled melancholy on his features, which were sunk and attenuated by long ill-health. At sight of her he first stared incredulous, then sprang to his feet with the liveliest joy reanimating his face and figure.

'Emma! Emma!' he cried. 'Heaven, I thank thee! Incarnation of beauty, source of all inspiration, dearest object of my affections, do I indeed behold thee again, or is this apparition but the figment of a brain weakened by sickness? Speak to me, speak; and let thy voice confirm what my eyes scarce dare believe.'

It took long for Emma to realise what had already become patent to Mr. Hayley and the other intimates of the painter. For if Mr. Romney's mind had become disordered the only immediate manifestation was an exaggerated pleasure in this unexpected visit, and an almost incoherent excitement that, whilst it touched her heart, gave her at first little clue to his condition.

She told him of her approaching marriage with Sir William Hamilton, and was satisfied with the transports her words evoked. No father could have shown greater joy in the brilliant marriage of a favourite daughter than Mr. Romney exhibited now. The gratification of the soothsayer who sees his prophecies fulfilled was his, for he had formed the highest opinion of Emma's capabilities at the very beginning of his acquaintance with her, and had never ceased to predict that she would rise some day to a secure and exalted position.

'How will you paint me now, Romney?' Emma asked artlessly, 'as The Ambassadress, as Campania smiling on Vesuvius to drive the clouds from his brow?'

Mr. Romney's enthusiasm was unbounded. He walked from easel to easel, placing new canvases here and there, and even making rough sketches in charcoal.

'I will paint you now, as you are, in that white dress and bonnet. I will paint you as Mirth, as you also are now. And then you must be my model for Joan of Arc; that is one idea I brought back with me from France. And as Cassandra. There is Constance, too. I am to paint a picture of Constance for the Shakespeare Gallery. But Joan of Arc first. Emma, you will be Joan of Arc?'

'And rout all my enemies? Yes, yes, indeed.' And she threw herself into a spirited attitude. 'But Joan of Arc was put to death. See, Romney, see!' She changed the pose; now she was the very spirit of humility. 'I am betrayed, I suffer meekly.'

'Wonderful, wonderful!' he cried. 'Do not move, I pray you; do not move. You are the Maid, the saintly Maid herself. . . .'

Again she flung up her head, and her eyes flashed courage. 'Look, I am borne in fire to Heaven, and my memory remains to encourage every maid to rise superior to her lowly origin. Paint me holding a kingdom in the hollow of my hand. For, Romney, I mean to hold Naples so. I am in the Queen's confidence.' She wanted to tell him all that happened to her.

181

A sudden despondency seized Romney the instant she had left off posing, and he sank back again into his chair with a groan. 'But you are going away again; you will leave me.'

'Not yet, not for a long time. And I will come to you every day I am in England.'

'This marriage will estrange us. Never, never again will you be my Emma, mine.' His head sank on his breast, he began to mutter to himself.

She stood perplexed, bewildered; then went over to him, and knelt by his chair.

'I am not altered, I shall not alter, Romney,' she cried. 'I will always be your inspiration, your "Divine Lady." Look up and tell me what I am to be. See! I have so many new attitudes.' She was still far from understanding what ailed him.

He went on talking to himself, and then, indeed, doubt and apprehension touched her. For what was it he was saying?

'Never again *my* Emma, mine; the goddess who gave herself to me, Venus, with the golden apple, to whose temptation I succumbed; Andromeda to my Perseus, or Helen. . . .' The next sentence that came from him must remain unchronicled.

Her heart went cold as she listened to him. Was he not voicing Mr. Greville's accusation? She rose from her knees and stood spellbound, her pallor increasing, and nothing but dismay in her heart or head. He went on as one who talks in dream:

'I see you still; your red gold hair falling almost to your feet. I feel your ivory shoulders, see the blue vein beneath your upraised arm as you throw back a curl that seeks to hide the invitation in your eyes, your sweet eyes. I feel your miracle of a mouth, that clung again and again to mine. You gave me love, and I conferred Immortality upon you. Immortal Emma! you are going from me. My arms will be empty and your figure refuse to come when I invoke it. Shadows to haunt me instead, clouds to gather, dark, and ever darker. . . .'

His mutterings grew louder and more incoherent. And now at last Emma understood with a chill that touched her spine and curdled her blood, that he knew not she was there before him in the flesh, the exquisite flesh. He was dreaming of that which she had never been, could never have been to him. She brushed her hands before her eyes. What was it he was saying? What had Mr. Greville said? She was more than unhappy, she was terrified! Could it have been true, had she forgotten? Had Mr. Romney gone mad, or was she mad? She turned and fled, never heeding her appointment with Sir William, nor what complexion would be put upon her flight. She fled from the unknown, from this destroyed genius who accused her, from herself, and all the memories of the studio. . . .

Fortunately, it was into Sir William's arms that she precipitated herself. He was already awaiting her at the foot of the stairs. 'My dear Emma, you have been alarmed, you are uneasy. Collect yourself. Let me convey you to the carriage. You will not forget, I am sure, that His Grace of Queensberry awaits us.'

Emma began to pour out an incoherent account of Mr. Greville's accusations, Mr. Romney's madness, her own fears. Sir William Hamilton found little difficulty in tracing the source of her emotion to the great news, the approaching assembly, to her affection for him, and the excitement the day had brought forth. He set himself to soothing her, and with success. She soon recovered her composure as she realised the strength of her position with him. Greville could not harm her, she was too deeply entrenched in this strong heart for any shots to reach her. *Il passato e morto.* The past was all behind her, and the future radiant with promise.

At the Duke of Queensberry's reception her glowing and lovely face eclipsed all the ladies of fashion. Her Grace of Devonshire looked old and faded in comparison. The duke told her so himself, and the smile with which she regarded the compliment was like sunshine in the room. It was impossible she had ever been 'Emma of Mrs. Kelly's,' or 'Frail Emma of Edgeware Row.' She was at this brilliant reception in her proper person, the affianced wife of the King's brother, the future Ambassadress! Everything else had been a dream, a nightmare; only now she was awake, to find the world at her feet and Greville's threats negligible and absurd. A beautiful woman is an irresistible power.

On September 6th, anno domini 1790, ætatis suæ xxv., Emma Hart was married at Marylebone Church, by the Reverend Doctor Edward Barry, to Sir William Hamilton, K.C.B., in the presence of Lord Abercorn and Mr. Dutens.

The first volume of Emma's life-story is completed. The next is concerned with Lady Hamilton.

CHAPTER XII

Explains the political position at the Court of Naples when Emma returns as the
wife of the British Ambassador. The Queen uses Emma as one of the pawns in
the game she is playing with the Powers. Emma imagines herself the Bishop, the
Castle, and all the larger pieces.

HISTORY has its fictions, no less than the law, and amongst these is
one that the world's affairs are shaped by men. In the King's Council
reverend seigniors wag wise heads ere promulgating his decrees; grave
elders codify his laws and administer his justice; brave captains wage
his battles by land or sea. Women, these declare, lack judgment to
decide matters of statecraft, as they lack strength to enforce decision by
arms. For their part, women are not greatly concerned to argue the
thesis. They have not failed to perceive that the influence exerted
without ostentation commonly escapes opposition by eluding
observation, and that the most effective forces, like those of nature, ever
operate silently. They are content to leave action to men born of them,
while they themselves, behind their silken curtains, breed the ideas
from which alone action springs. Through long ages the story of men's
deeds, which have made history, is in its essence but the epitome of
women's thoughts. Her pride, her vanity, her lust, her ambition—it is to
gratify one or all of these that man has intrigued, fought, and died ever
since the sons of God saw the daughters of men that they were fair.

One of the innumerable examples of the truth of this proposition is
furnished by the illustrious lady into the closest personal relations with

186

whom Emma was brought on her return to Naples as Lady Hamilton. Calumny has been ever busy with Maria Carolina, Queen of the Two Sicilies, but fairness must admit that, whatever her private pleasures or predispositions, it was she who shaped the affairs of the country of which her royal consort was the nominal ruler.

The eldest daughter of Maria Theresa, that woman of heroic parts, she inherited from her mother pride of race, a tenacious attachment to the Roman Catholic Church, and an unalterable belief in her own intellectual capacity. Bred in an atmosphere of cosmopolitan politics, and imbibing statecraft with her mother's milk, Maria Carolina grew up to watch with an observant eye the trend of the world's thoughts. Soon after her marriage she perceived how, throughout the continent of Europe, this was in the direction of freedom. Too intelligent to suppose that the advancing spirit of the age could be withstood by government— whether invested in a corporation aggregate or a corporation sole—she considered only how she could so guide its direction among the populace of her own country as to preserve her monarchy by the introduction of reforms, and thus avert the ruder shock of revolution.

Had she been mated to a consort the equal of herself in political sagacity, in ambition, and in application to the due discharge of a prince's high responsibilities, Maria Carolina might have had the happiness of seeing her country ranked among the European Powers. For it is not by the number of its population nor the extent of its superficies that the greatness of a country is computed; else Greece had not broken the pride of Persia, nor Alva hammered in vain upon the iron courage of the Netherlands.

But King Ferdinand had no inclinations towards the graver duties of the royal state. Content to reign, he did not choose to rule, accepting the privileges of the throne, whilst ignoring its responsibilities. Easy pleasures, sport, wine, and woman sufficed him; he was only serious about the chase; everything else he took lightly. If he resented, whilst he admired, his spouse's strength of character, he was yet fitfully willing to leave the government of his kingdom in her more able, and far more ambitious, hands. His was the life that commended itself to the most part of his subjects, a thoughtless, reckless, superstitious crew, hot-blooded, and indolent under the Southern sun. With the *lazzaroni* he was popular and his rough despotism safe. He concerned himself but little with the feudal lords, grimly tenacious of their ancient rights, or for those others to whom the spirit of the new age was making its resistless appeal, and who clamoured they hardly knew for what. He preferred to leave them and their affairs to his Queen and Ministers. Whilst she perfected and experimented with her schemes, some visionary, few practicable, all of them well-intentioned, not all of them well-approved, he interested himself more particularly with the size of his bags.

Until the storm of revolution, thundering appallingly in France, rolled in lowering clouds towards Italy, Maria Carolina, too, found time for entertainment. A woman of intellect, she gathered around her men and women eminent in literature and science. But she was lacking in

188

neither vivacity nor feeling and she permitted herself certain indulgences which gossip exaggerated into the most scandalous excesses.

Into this lighter side of her life the whole world could not have produced a better companion than the one ready to her hand in Lady Hamilton. When the famous beauty returned to Naples, whitewashed and made respectable by marriage, the Queen was more than ready to receive her into favour. Sir William had brought her back to Naples by way of Paris, where they had had audience of the Queen of Naples' sister, the ill-fated Marie Antoinette, already standing under the shadow of the scaffold. That poor lady, entrusting the Ambassadress with a letter to her sister, gave a passport which Maria Carolina was not the one to challenge.

'I have been received with open arms by all the Neapolitans of both sexes' Lady Hamilton wrote to Romney a few weeks after her arrival], 'by all the foreigners of every distinction. I have been presented to the Queen of Naples by her own desire, she as shown me all sort of kind and affectionate attentions; in short, I am the happiest woman in the world. Sir William is fonder of me every day, and I hope I will have no cause to repent of what he as done, for I feel so grateful to him that I think I shall never be able to make amends for his goodness to me.'

Sir William, too, had the gratification of being able to write that Emma had succeeded wonderfully, and by having no pretensions had gained the appreciation of all the English ladies, besides being received by the Queen, who treated her like any other travelling lady of distinction.

The metamorphosis was indeed complete; and Mr. Greville was fain to admit that Emma had more than made good her assurance that he did not know what power she had in Naples even before her threatened marriage to his uncle had become an accomplished fact. That power was doubly reinforced now, and nobody was so unwise as not to make a point of being civil to Charles Greville's discarded mistress.

The Queen made her home at Caserta during the summer solstice, and thither Sir William Hamilton moved his establishment for political reasons.

'Our house has been like an inn' [Emma wrote]. 'We had the Duchess of Ancaster several days. It is but three days since the Devonshire family has left; and we had fifty in our family for four days at Caserta. 'Tis true we dined every day at court, or at some casino of the King; for you cannot imagine how good our King and Queen as been to the principal English who have been here—particularly to Lord and Lady Palmerston, Cholmondeley, Devonshire, Lady Spencer, Lady Bessborough, Lady Plymouth, Sir George and Lady Webster. And I have carried the ladies to the Queen very often, as she as permitted me to go very often in private, which I do. ... In the evenings I go to her and we fire *tête-à-tête* 2 or 3 hours. Sometimes we sing. Yesterday the King and me sang duetts 3 hours. It was but bad. . . . To-day the Princess Royal of Sweden comes to court to take leave of Their Majesties. Sir William and me are invited to dinner with her. She is an amiable Princess and as lived very much with us. The other ministers' wives have not shown her the least attention because she did not pay them the first visit, as she travels under the name of the Countess of Wasa. . . . Her Majesty told me I had done very well in waiting on her Royal Highness the moment she arrived. However, the ministers' wives are very fond of me, as they see I have no pretensions nor do I abuse Her Majesty's goodness, and she observed the other night at court at Naples we had a drawing-room in honner of the Empress having brought a son. I had been with the Queen the night before alone, *en famille*, laughing and singing, etc., etc., but at the drawing-room I kept my distance and payd the Queen as much respect as tho' I had never seen her before, which pleased her very much. But she showed me great distinction that night, and told me several times how she admired my good conduct. . . . You may imagine how happy my dear, dear Sir William is. We live more like lovers than husband and wife, as husbands and wives go nowadays. Lord deliver me! and the English are as bad as the Italians some few excepted. . . . I study very hard, and I have had all my songs set for the viola, so that Sir William may accompany me, which as pleased him very much so that we study together. The English garden is going on very fast. The King and Queen go there every day. Sir William and me are there every morning at seven o'clock, sometimes dine there, and all ways drink tea there. . . .'

A like tale of familiarity with the greatness of the world, and even of conscious superiority to it, is told in the letters which her husband wrote to Emma on his occasional absences from her side, when he accompanied the royal sportsman on his expeditions.

'You did admirably, my dear Em., in not inviting Lady A. H. to dine with the Prince, and still better in telling her honestly the reason. I have always found that going straight is the best method, though not the way of the world. You also did very well in asking Madame Skamouski, and not taking upon you to present her without leave. . . . As the Prince asked you, you did right to send for a song of Douglas's, but in general you will do right only to sing at home.'

That Emma's new prudery was shocked by the behaviour of some of the friends of royalty, and found it more fitted for the stables or kitchen than her own gilded drawing-rooms, is suggested by her husband's light rejoinder to some criticism she passed:

191

'Let them all roll on the carpet, provided you are not of the party. My trust is in you alone.'

Calumny, we have said, has been busy with the name of Maria Carolina, not hesitating to describe her as a modern Cytherea, who lent herself to orgies of extravagance and riotous pleasure, indulging in vices of which one cannot even write the names. The truth can certainly never be known by any mortal until that final awful day when the secrets of all hearts shall be laid bare. But it is more charitable, and probably it is far nearer to the truth, to say that much of her conduct at this critical juncture in her country's history was actuated solely by reasons of high policy.

She gave the extravagant entertainments which were the talk of the fashionable world because they were congenial to her courtiers, and, by amusing, kept them from playing at politics, and dabbling in revolutionary intrigues. They were also agreeable to her husband, and checked any possible inclination on his part to interfere with her exercise of power; and they drew to the capital a throng of fashionable and influential visitors from the centres of civilisation, among whom it was possible to disseminate ideas that might lead to action beneficial to the cause of royalty when those lowering thunder-clouds of revolution should envelop Italy, too, in storm.

The Queen was far-sighted in her statecraft. From the beginning of the happenings in France she foresaw that a day might arise when the active sympathy and offensive and defensive alliance of Great Britain would be necessary to save her own kingdom of the Two Sicilies from rapine, and her throne from extinction.

In bestowing unlimited favour on Lady Hamilton, and in encouraging her consort's familiarity with Sir William, already for twenty years a personal friend, the Queen truly believed she was diplomatically securing the influence of the British Ambassador for her own political schemes, and thus laying the foundation for an Anglo-Sicilian alliance. Whatever pleasures for herself she may have gathered by the way—and for our part we have no belief that her intimacy with Emma was other than the natural inclination of one woman of temperament with another—there is no doubt that in her negotiations with Sir William Hamilton, and through him with his Government, Maria Carolina wrought better and more surely than many a man whose name has been inscribed upon the roll of the great statesmen of the world.

Diplomacy is the science, or art, of conducting negotiations between nations, and differs essentially from politics, which treats of the distribution of power in a country. An undeniable talent for diplomacy rendered the Queen of Naples competent to deal ably and successfully with foreign affairs. But in the domestic equivalent she was less successful. Dictatorial by native temper, she scorned conciliation as unbeseeming to her dignity, and, whilst undoubtedly inspired by a sincere desire to inaugurate wise reforms, she alienated the loyalty of one class of her subjects, without freeing the other from a feudal system long odious to it. In her anxiety to detect the earliest germination in her dominions of the seeds of anarchy, she irritated to a dangerous point

193

the easy *lazzaroni* by establishing a kind of secret inquisition particularly hateful to their Bohemian temper.

This is not the history of Maria Carolina, except in so far as it impinges upon that of our heroine. It is enough to say that she loved licence, but feared anarchy, and was late in learning that in Italy, and in these times, the one presaged the other. England was the land of freedom, and upon England she concentrated her strength.

Lady Hamilton was the recipient of her complicated and halting confidences. Seeing how her countrymen were regarded, and how she herself stood *facile princeps* in the Queen's regard amongst the distinguished English colony then in Naples, it is not, perhaps, surprising that Emma, Lady Hamilton, came in time to imagine she had been the pivot upon which all history revolved. It was she who was the medium of communication between the Queen and the British Ambassador, and between the Queen and the unofficial, but no less powerful, representatives of the British people. Those of the Neapolitans whose sympathies were French would have been wiser had they contemned her less as a *parvenue*, so frivolous as to be negligible as a factor in political affairs.

Both Sir William Hamilton and Acton had a more accurate perception of her real utility. It was of the first importance that they should obtain and transmit to their Government the earliest intelligence of the intentions of the other Powers, and this they were enabled to do by the confidence placed by the Queen in the Ambassadress. The Queen's fear and bitter hatred of France, both raised to the ultimate extremity by the execution of Louis and the even more horrible assassination of Marie Antoinette, led her to condescend to every device by which she might pave the way to vengeance on her sister's murderers, and combat the Jacobinism which had produced such bloody spawn.

With Spain wavering in her opposition to the National Convention, and the Austrian Bourbons paralysed by the increasing power of the Corsican, Napoleon Buonaparte, she was more than ever set upon a definite English alliance. She transmitted, through Emma, every scrap of information that she thought might be useful to the English Ambassador in persuading the Ministry in London to save Naples from the encroaching flood.

A signal instance occurred when a courier brought Ferdinand, whose inclinations were Spanish, a private letter from the King of Spain announcing his intention to withdraw from the Coalition and join the French against England. The Queen took it from the King's pocket unseen, and allowed Emma to make a copy of it. As it happened that Sir William lay dangerously ill at that moment. Lady Hamilton herself, acting under the Queen's instructions, dispatched a messenger with the letter to Lord Grenville in London, taking all necessary precautions for the safe arrival of this most important despatch, and spending near four hundred pounds out of her privy purse on this delicate affair. But there is reason to believe Maria Carolina gave her the requisite money! Emma was still reckless and extravagant and had no means of her own. Emma enjoyed playing at statecraft, but chiefly because it was a mark

195

of the Queen's confidence, and enabled her to report to Greville, with whom, strangely enough, she was again on corresponding terms.

'They ought to be gratfull to Sir William, and myself, in particular' [she wrote of the Government]; 'my situation in this court is very extraordinary, and what no person has yet arrived at.'

But it was many years before that situation, to which she alluded, attained an important political aspect in her eyes or warranted her claiming that what she did was in the nature of distinguished service to her country, deserving of large pecuniary recognition. She was satisfied now, and for a long time afterwards, to rely upon her voice and her figure, her complexion and the gaiety of her entertainments to maintain her position. Those entertainments waxed ever in importance and splendour. Emma danced, sang, and attitudinised herself into prominence, aided by the senile fondness of her husband, and the countenance and good graces of the Queen, who used her services, and confided in her . . . that which she wished her to know.

The letter which had been extracted from Ferdinand's pocket, and which Emma had despatched to London, bore the serious news that, under irresistible pressure, Spain had left the Coalition. Events marched henceforward with inconceivable rapidity; Buonaparte's progress acquired an ever-increasing momentum. Treaty after treaty bore signed and sealed testimony to his amazing triumphs. It seemed hopeless for the Neapolitan kingdom to hold out against the spirit of democracy of which his armed host was the incarnation. But Maria Carolina's spirit was unyielding; and even when she signed what was now urgently put before her, following the humiliating example of the other Powers, and seeking an armistice, she was secretly intriguing for the recovery of the position she had pretended to abandon.

What had Emma to do with these negotiations? She went to and fro, from the Palace to the house of the Ambassador, carrying letters of which she scarcely understood the significance, revelling in the importance she enjoyed, but knowing little what it portended. And had she realised it, and seen into the future as we know it to-day, it is doubtful but that she would have considered the discovery to Sir William Hamilton of Napoleon's designs on the Mediterranean second in importance to the advent of the English naval captain to which that news indirectly led. For, as Mr. Greville so truly said, Emma was always Emma, and already her elderly husband was becoming insufficient for her exuberance.

*　　*　　*　　*　　*　　*　　*

It was the Mediterranean upon which Buonaparte had set his eyes, the Mediterranean he meant to have. The English fleet was there. It would have to be removed or destroyed. So the Queen wrote to Sir William, and Emma carried the news. England must look to its navy; it was the English navy that was now threatened, she wrote. As a preliminary preparation, Buonaparte was closing as many ports against it as his arms, or his diplomacy, permitted. The clause in the treaty with the Neapolitan Court that no more than four English men of war should be provisioned in any Neapolitan or Sicilian port at one and the same time, was the one that alarmed Maria Carolina. Unless saved by

England, Naples, the Two Sicilies, would follow the rest of Italy into subjection to France, and she herself would be but the negligible wife of yet one more *roi prétendant*.

This was the *réveillon* that called Nelson to his fate, the fate that cost him more than the loss of an arm, or the obscuration of an eye, that was to outbalance his honour, and send him down to history, not the single-hearted patriot and hero that should have been his only title to fame, but as the victim to the wiles of a woman who had graduated in the school of vice whilst he was employing all his energies and powers in working for his country.

We have followed Emma's progress from innocence to misfortune, and from misfortune to prosperity. The retrogression of her character has been steady. Greville's hand precipitated the fall and the ultimate tragedy is in sight. Once the victim, we shall see her become the temptress. To her eternal shame, and his confusion, all the fascination of the education she had acquired, of the position to which Sir William Hamilton's weakness had raised her, of her beauty, now at its prime, and her natural talent, now at its meridian, was put forth for the seduction of the simple-minded sailor, Captain Horatio Nelson, whose victories at the Nile, and triumphs at Trafalgar, have been overshadowed for all time by the publicity of the intrigue in which he engaged with the wife of the English Ambassador at Naples.

But this is for the next and following chapters.

Meanwhile the Court comedy was being played on. The old barons might sulk in their castles, the *lazzaroni* gabble about revolution over their macaroni and *lacrime Christi*, but still the King must hunt, and still the Queen must be amused. The English Ambassador was the King's constant companion in his big battues. Sir William wrote his wife, 'The King has killed eighty-one animals of one sort or other to-day and amongst them a wolf and some stags. He fell asleep in the coach, and awaking told me he had been dreaming of shooting. One would have thought he would have shed blood enough.'

There was blood enough to be shed, and tears.

Nelson was on his way to Emma, but he had left a wife behind, a wife to whom up to now he had been loving and faithful, in whom he saw no fault, and of whom he imagined no unkindness.

CHAPTER XIII

Chronicles the appearance of Nelson on the scene. The destruction of the French Navy is followed by the surrender of the Hero of the Nile to the wife of the British Ambassador. He outwits Villeneuve, to be himself outwitted by Frail Emma of Edgeware Row.

THE splendid sinner never lacks apologists and not much reflection is needed to suggest an explanation. The sin that does not appeal to us is the one we deem unpardonable; we can find forgiveness for faults when we understand the antecedent temptation. It is commonly through excess of love, or of ambition, that the heroic and romantic figure errs, and those, in due degree, are generous and ennobling passions, to whose vitalising energy no soul is so dense as to be quite impervious. Nevertheless, we must not lose sight of proportions. 'Love and ambition draw the devil's coach,' said the poet wisely, and the house to whose courtyard they travel is the home of the devil—hell.

The reminder is not untimely at the point now reached in the narrative of our heroine's adventures. Her present situation as the central figure of a brilliant court is so dazzling, her influence in the impending collision of armed nations so amazing, her reputation as the virtuous wife of an old man so unblemished, that one on the level plain of life, turning wondering eyes from the pit whence she sprang to the peak she has won, has an inclination to disregard the weaknesses, the extravagances, the immoralities of her earlier years, and even to harbour for a moment the envious, dangerously wicked, thought that

200

such success may be justification of any fall from virtue, however frequent, however far. But wait, and count no man happy until he be dead. *'I myself have seen the ungodly in great power; and flourishing like a green bay tree. I went by, and lo, he was gone: I sought him, but his place could nowhere be found.'* When we shall write finis to this book, these are the words that will ring dominant in our ears.

Beyond doubt this was the moment of our Emma's zenith, and it presaged her great fall. Nelson was coming. Presently it was to seem that all her experience and all her powers were given her for this end: the subjugation of one who elsewhere proved himself unconquerable. To explain the situation we must, however, glance aside from Emma for the space of a paragraph.

Resenting the tyranny of the new Republican Government of France, the inhabitants of Toulon had recently made overtures to Lord Hood to take them under his protection, and, assisted perhaps by treachery on the part of Admiral Trogoff, the English admiral took possession of that place in the name of King Louis XVII. A military force being immediately necessary, Lord Hood resolved to apply to the Neapolitan Government. He despatched Captain Horatio Nelson of the Agamemnon on a special mission to Sir William Hamilton, asking him to use his influence to procure ten thousand troops upon the instant.

The reception of Captain Nelson by King Ferdinand was gracious in the extreme, His Majesty sailing out to meet him, and inviting him almost daily during his stay in the capital. At a banquet he was placed at the King's right hand, before the English Ambassador and all the nobles present; a gala was given at San Carlo in honour of his squadron and provisions were generously lavished on his crew, who for near nineteen weeks had not had a morsel of fresh meat or vegetables.

With such a preamble it is hardly necessary to add that Captain Nelson succeeded perfectly in his mission, and six thousand troops were despatched to Toulon. Whilst the purport of his visit was being achieved, he was free to enjoy all the hospitality that might be offered him. He was lodged in the Embassy, in the room prepared for Prince Augustus, and both there, and at the Court of Caserta, he had daily opportunities of consulting with the Ministers and informing himself of the state of affairs in that part of the Mediterranean.

But what is more especially relevant in this narrative, he was brought into relations of the closest personal intimacy with Sir William Hamilton, and incidentally his lady.

At the time of their first meeting, Nelson's genius had still to be proved to the world. What fired Emma was not his genius, but his denseness to what was required of him as a guest at the Embassy. The world was at Emma's feet, victim to her charms, either ravished with her singing, enraptured with her 'Attitudes,' or lost in admiration of her understanding. So they all told her, and she believed them all. That the fleshpots of Egypt—in other words, the boundless hospitality of the Embassy—had any share in the enthusiasm she excited was past her credence. Her head was completely turned with her position, the Queen's confidences, and Sir William's foolish fondness. It seemed inevitable that the much-sought-after English officer would follow in

202

the wake of his betters, and declare his passion. But Nelson was in Naples on business, and had no eyes for anything but his ten thousand troops. With him in his suite was his stepson, one Josiah Nisbet. Josiah would lounge willingly in Emma's boudoir whilst his captain was out on affairs of State, and it was to him that Emma must perforce exhibit her attractions.

'Lady Hamilton has been wonderfully kind and good to Josiah,' Nelson reported to his wife, to whom he wrote regularly. 'She is a young woman of amiable manners, and who does honour to the station to which she is raised.'

He had no presentiment of what this 'young woman of amiable manners' would become to him in the future. Amorous adventure was not for him; he was a faithful husband, and, young as he was made a good and careful stepfather. Josiah had been spoiled by his mother, as is the way of widows with only sons, and was something of a lout, with a greater taste for the bottle than for work. Nelson thought Lady Hamilton was having a good influence upon Josiah, and that those lounging hours in her boudoir would prove beneficial to his character. He told her so one day, quite simply and candidly. It was at a banquet he found the opportunity.

'I wanted to thank you for your kindness to my stepson, but occasion has not served me until now,' he began, almost as soon as they were seated.

'He is a dear boy,' she answered; 'a little wanting in manner, perhaps, and his education has halted, but I am learning him a little French.' She turned her lustrous eyes upon Nelson.

'The Queen desired the English officers should have every attention, but Captain Nelson is all taken up with business,' she went on, artlessly.

'Or he had given himself the pleasure of hearing Lady Hamilton sing. But I have found time to envy Josiah,' he added gallantly. She was quick to reply that she would sing for him presently, that very evening. She wanted him to talk about her amazing talents, but he spoke instead of his wife's anxiety for her son, and a little of politics. Then they both grew enthusiastic about the Queen: Emma, because next to herself, her royal friend was her favourite topic of conversation; Nelson, because to champion the Queen and her cause seemed to bring him nearer to the one object of his ambition. He wanted to engage with the French fleet, and to destroy it. Beyond the beautiful face of his hostess he saw the ships, his and theirs, and heard the sound of guns. Emma assumed a great knowledge of the Queen's views, and Nelson believed every word she said. That her vanity was piqued because he paid her so little attention is undoubted. After dinner it was for him she sang her songs and posed, but to no purpose. Nelson gave her a perfunctory attention; his best was given to Sir William, to whom he talked strategy, and of Napoleon's schemes.

When Sir William came into her bed-chamber that night he said, 'My love, that is a very remarkable young man.'

'Did he say anything to you about my "Sappho" or my "Eurydice"?' she asked eagerly.

'He had a complete plan of the ports, and a scheme to intercept the French ships. . . .'

But Emma was impatient. 'And my singing; did he think my voice was as good as Nella's? Count Pavlo says it is much stronger, and would have a greater success at the Opera House. . . .'

Sir William agreed with Count Pavlo, and said all and more than could be expected of the fondest and most uxorious husband, but he could not tell her that Captain Nelson had agreed or disagreed with him, he had talked only of the ships.

Emma's vanity was outraged. Again and again in the week that followed she essayed to provoke the little English captain, who had captured all hearts by his earnestness, into betraying some more personal interest in her, or her multiform accomplishments and charms. It was all in vain. War clouds were ever more lowering, and Nelson enwrapt in them. He was a patriot before he became a lover, and after. The wife of the English Ambassador was very beautiful and very winning, but his own heart was with the *Agamemnon*.

For twelve days Nelson remained in Naples, engaged with Sir William or the Queen, learning all they could tell him. The Queen openly admitted that she had 'fell in love with him.' Maria Carolina knew, and Sir William Hamilton knew, long before Emma or the world realised, that there was a great spirit enshrined in that little feeble body. It shone through his blue eyes, lingered round his sensitive mouth.

'The age has found its man,' Sir William told Emma. Emma pouted, and renewed her coquetries with the great little man's stepson. Before he sailed, Nelson spoke to her about it again.

'You have been the saving of him,' he told her, looking his gratitude. Then, because he found it in his, he kissed her hand.

' 'Twas only your stepson has cared for my company,' she answered in her softest and most cooing of voices.

'There is one who could not have had enough of it, if Duty had not called him elsewhere,' Nelson replied. For he was a sailor, and, although no squire of dames, alive to their charms.

'Would that I had been Duty,' sighed Emma.

'Then Nelson would never have been absent from his post,' he exclaimed, regarding her more attentively than ever before. He was bewildered by her sigh and pensive air, flattered; caught at the last moment, though he knew it not, in the toils that were to bind him.

'You and me would have been friends if you had not been over-occupied?' Emma asked, wistfully. It was then he seemed to see her for the first time. She was in a brocaded dress, her fine kerchief not whiter than the bosom it only half concealed. A long ringlet had escaped and fell over her shoulder. Her eyes were glistening and spelled forlornness at his going; her beautiful mouth trembled.

'I have wanted to be friends with you, but you have shut yourself up with the Queen and Sir William.' He was quite overcome that she should have wanted his friendship, and he not known it.

'I thought you were wrapt up in Lieutenant Nisbet,' he stammered.

'When Nelson was in the Embassy?' she exclaimed.

'If ever I come to Naples again . . .'

'Ah! then you *will* come to Naples again!'

Her smile was exquisite. And now it was she who took his hand and held it, exclaiming in her extravagant way:

'I know it, I feel it, this hand will save the Queen, and save the country. Then Emma will hold it, kiss it'—she suited the action to the word—'and call out that every one may hear: This is the hand of Horatio Nelson, the Saviour of Italy.'

She added more, so much more that he blushed to hear it. Her own eloquence had ever the power to rouse her to greater. She had caught the universal belief in him, and now she poured it forth. No man is insensible to flattery from a beautiful woman, and this one was peerless. Her speech inflamed him, their eyes met; hers were the colour of the Mediterranean; he was caught by their blue depths, held. She had her art, and let him see that as it was with him, so it was with her; there arose between them on the instant, impalpable, but unmistakable, that for which there is but one name. He turned a little pale; she grew a little red. There were steps outside, and the sound of voices; they had come to fetch him, the boats were waiting. She stepped

toward him impulsively, crying again: 'You will come back to Naples?
'She laid her hand upon his arm. Nelson was never a laggard.

'But I have been blind, blind,' he cried. 'How beautiful you are!'

'Oh, Nelson!' she fluttered in his arms.

That was all, then, for they were no longer alone. But she knew she
had won, and need not be jealous of the Queen, nor of the ships. When
her ringlets escaped, and she let the kerchief on her bosom slip, when
her eyes were bright and her voice soft, 'twas no man could resist her.
And if Nelson was, as Sir William said, 'the man for the hour,' it was
not to the Queen he looked any longer for encouragement.

The British squadron weighed anchor and Emma followed its captain
in her thoughts. As indeed did many another, although from different
reasons.

The Queen, desponding because of the growing unrest of the
populace and the serious encroachments of Buonaparte, heard from her
confidante there was no doubt that Captain Nelson would keep the
enemy engaged until Naples was safe. Emma could be more
enthusiastic for a man than for a cause. Nelson would secure the
command of the Mediterranean, Emma had never a doubt of it. The kiss
he had left upon her lips had sealed the promise of his return, for who
that had sipped could refrain from drinking? She talked of policy but
dreamed of love. She was young and Captain Nelson was young; Sir
William was growing old. She animated her royal mistress with her
optimism. They all believed in Captain Nelson. Emma had no doubt of
his prowess; Captain Nelson had no misgivings as to his fleet.

But at first, and for quite a long time, there was difficulty in persuading the Ministers in London to the same view. Many months were wasted, months of turbulence among the people and of ever-growing anxiety in the Court of Naples, ere Nelson was commissioned for that expedition which set the seal upon his glory.

Acton heard of Buonaparte's oath to set more kings apacking, and make the Sicilies republics also. Sedition had been sown broadcast over the Peninsula and the harvest was nearly ripe for the sickle. Naples might be at peace with France, but the latest communication from the Republic to the Kingdom was couched in precisely the language of a highwayman, 'Deliver up your money, or I will blow out your brains.' Only on payment of an exorbitant sum would the Directory guarantee immunity. Acton begged Sir William Hamilton to lay these facts before Lord St. Vincent, and plead for succour without an instant's delay. With the help of an English expedition the Kingdom could be saved; without it the Two Sicilies would follow the rest of Italy into French hands. Surely England could not contemplate that with indifference? But it was only after long delay Grenville and his fellow-ministers agreed that England could not.

Nelson eventually received his commission. Horatio Nelson, Saviour of Great Britain and the Continent, as he was soon to be acclaimed, was appointed Admiral of the Fleet and launched at length on that great adventure of which the fame will never die.

He arrived with fourteen sail on June 16th, and, himself proceeding in the *Vanguard* to Capri, sent Captain Troubridge of the *Mutine* to make certain requisitions from the British Ambassador at Naples. The situation was sufficiently delicate. Nelson had been provisioned for little more than three months. He had instructions to take in stores and water in any Mediterranean port, compelling acquiescence by arms if necessary. His Government had likewise instructed Sir William Hamilton to ask the free and unlimited admission of their ships into Sicilian ports and the provisions and supplies usually afforded by an ally.

The Neapolitan Government was thus placed on the horns of a dilemma. For the clause in their treaty with France still obtained, precluding the admission into any Sicilian harbour of more than four British men-of-war at one and the same time. Violation of this term of the compact, specifically provided by Buonaparte's astuteness, in anticipation of the very event that had now come to pass, might be justifiably regarded as an act of war against France, entailing not only war with that power, but final rupture of the tentative negotiations for an alliance now proceeding with the Austrian Government. On the other hand, to withhold this first necessary service would be to stultify their own action in bringing the British squadron to Neapolitan waters.

Then it was there happened one of those incidents upon which, although they are never officially known, and are never recorded in despatches, the history of a great campaign has turned more than once in the annals of war. Nelson sent Captain Troubridge to Naples to make the necessary requisition. The Ministers met and met again, debated, procrastinated, doubted. Captain Troubridge grew impatient. 'If there is

210

any difficulty, urge Sir William Hamilton to use his influence,' had been Nelson's instructions. Sir William was laid up with another attack of malarial fever. But it was an open secret that his beautiful wife had the ear of the Queen. Emma's inflammable heart had been full of Nelson ever since his departure; she was eager to do him a service and placed herself entirely at Captain Troubridge's disposal.

She sought her husband on his sick-bed and he approved and dictated her action. He himself wrote to Nelson, Emma supporting him whilst he held the pen, and she gave the missive afterwards to Troubridge. 'You will receive from Emma herself what will do the business and procure all you want.'

Then, hurrying to the Queen, to whose apartment she had access, Emma explained the needs of the British fleet, imploring her to use her own authority and write an autograph permit for Nelson's use. Her Majesty needed no urging, although Sir John Acton might. Now the women laid their heads together and found means to move him. The way of a man with a maid is not more secret nor more certain than the way of a Queen with her Minister.

Once things began to move, Captain Troubridge and Emma between them conducted matters with a quarter-deck directness of manner that ignored all diplomatic usage. With the Queen's secret authorisation, and God knows what of other consideration, they secured from Sir John Acton a General Order, written in that Minister's own hand, but in the name of His Sicilian Majesty, directed to the governors of every port in Sicily, to supply the English ships with all sorts of provisions, and, in case of an action, to permit the British seamen, sick or wounded, to be landed and taken proper care of in their ports. On the face of it, this was an order difficult of being explained away in the event of unpleasant complications. Acton was full of misgivings. He could consult no one, for Sir William Hamilton was hors de combat, and from everyone else the whole transaction was to be kept a profound secret.

Elated and happy, and deeming herself the prime mover in the intrigue, and certainly she was the medium for its furtherance, Emma wrote to Nelson:

'DEAR SIR,—I send you a letter I have received this moment from the Queen. Kiss it, and send it back by Bowen, as I am bound not to give any of her letters. Ever your   EMMA.'

This was the first time she had written him, and the signature must be taken to represent the potential rather than the actual state of affairs between them. She was excited and emotional, and ever impulsive. Nelson's permission to land and procure what he would for the fleet meant that she would see him again, and she was all agog for new experience, more particularly since Sir William was becoming enfeebled by his repeated illnesses.

'I only wish to get sight of Buonaparte and his army, for by God we shall lick them,' Troubridge boasted. And Nelson said no less of the French navy.

Nelson lost no time in replying to Emma's letter. He wrote:

'MY DEAR LADY HAMILTON,—I have kissed the Queen's letter; pray say I hope for the honour of kissing her hand when no fears will

212

intervene, assure her Majesty that no person has her felicity more at heart than myself, and that the sufferings of her family will be a Tower of Strength on the day of Battle. Fear not the event, God is with us, God bless you and Sir William, pray say I cannot stay to answer his letter. Ever yours faithfully,

HORATIO NELSON.'

An hour later the squadron weighed anchor for Syracuse.

At that historic spot everything had ever been conducted hitherto in accordance with the most rigid rules of precedent. But by the very circumstances of his arrival Nelson gave the Governor convincing evidence that he and precedent had nothing in common. For, in spite of the fact that for centuries no large ships had attempted the passage into the great port, owing to the channel having become silted up, Nelson determined to make the venture. Leading the way himself, and taking constant soundings as he moved, he brought his entire squadron to excellent anchorage abreast of the Marina, which would afford inimitable facilities for the later carrying of stores aboard. This achievement in navigation filled all who beheld it with amazement, and the bewilderment of the authorities was little less when the Admiral took no notice of the officials sent to remind him that the number of his ships exceeded that which they were permitted to entertain.

He waited until he was in comfortable possession of the place before consenting even to discuss his right of entry. Then, however, to the Governor's great astonishment and some fear, he produced Sir John

Acton's general instructions, over-riding all treaties, and authorising him to assist the British ships in every possible way.

Nelson was perhaps not surprised to find the order questioned and the Governor vacillating. Acton had endeavoured to save himself in the case of eventualities. The Governor declared a sentence in the despatch proved that admission was not intended to be thrown open to the entire squadron; and Nelson might yet have been compelled to go empty away had it not been for the 'private instructions' from the Queen which Lady Hamilton had forwarded to him. This letter, when produced, as it now was, had the full virtue of an 'open sesame,' and although the Governor of Syracuse made some protestations of having been overruled by show of force, and carried his protest so far as to decline to return the official visit on board ship, he made it plain that these protestations were merely formal and for the purpose of being reported to King Ferdinand, who was in entire ignorance of his royal consort's action in the matter. Privately he assured the English captains that he was delighted to see them. He made good his words by fulfilling Nelson's orders to the last orange, and by offering the whole fleet the warmest and most generous hospitality that his not unlimited resources permitted.

Two days later, with his wants amply supplied, and gratified by the attentions paid to him by everybody, Nelson set out to find the French fleet, having first written a confident and grateful note to the ambassador and his lady:

'MY DEAR FRIENDS,—Thanks to your exertions, we have victualled and watered; and surely watering at the fountains of Arethusa we must have victory. We shall

214

sail with the first breeze, and be assured I shall return either crowned with laurel, or covered with cypress.'

Another week, and Nelson found the French fleet—sixteen sail of the line and four frigates, besides a larger number of gunboats—lying anchored in Aboukir Bay, sheltered by the cape, and so strongly secured on the outside that the guns on the inner side were neither manned nor ready. Not expecting the English, the French ships were not cleared for action, and even when they saw their enemy's squadron, they looked to have until the following day to prepare. It was already late in the evening when Nelson caught sight of them, and they knew he could scarcely lay alongside before sundown, when, because of the latitude, darkness would fall instantly. But Nelson's way was swift as Nelson's touch was firm. He had discussed every possible position with his captains daily during the voyage, and only the signal to attack the van and centre was necessary. At once the English fleet stood in; five of the ships engaged the French on the inside, and five, including Nelson's ship, the *Vanguard*, on the outside, where the fire would be hottest.

Taken by surprise, the Frenchmen lost their opportunity of pounding the Englishmen while navigating for position, and by the time they really got to work the battle was half won. In the first ten minutes three French men-of-war were dismasted, and in less than a couple of hours five were taken. At ten o'clock the huge French flagship *L'Orient*, 120 guns, blew up, the magazines being reached by the fire that had been burning for some time, illuminating the whole awful scene, but which her crew had been prevented from extinguishing by Captains Hallewell

215

and Ball of the *Swiftsure* and *Alexander*, who, coming late into action—
having been some miles ahead of the others when the *Zealous* signalled
the enemy—trained their upper guns on the burning poop.

Awed by the tremendous explosion, both sides ceased firing, and
strenuous efforts were made by Nelson's sailors to save some of the
hundreds of Frenchmen who leaped into the sea from the blazing vessel.
But the battle was resumed again, and continued until after three in
the morning. By five o'clock only two French men-of-war were flying
their colours, and at the close of that second day, twenty-four hours
after the engagement began, the French fleet was wiped out.

'Almighty God having blessed His Majesty's arms with victory, the
Admiral intends returning public thanksgiving at two o'clock this day;
and he recommends every ship doing the same as soon as convenient.'

Such was the memorandum issued by Nelson to all his captains. He
was a God-fearing man, like most sailors, and the more so by reason of
his parentage and training. He issued this order whilst in the busiest
press of repairing the damage sustained by his ships in the late battle.
Although wounded he took his place on the quarter-deck whilst the Rev.
Mr. Comyn conducted the service, not a little to the surprise, and
something to the admiration, of the prisoners of war.

It was not until after prayers were over that he prepared his
despatches, not forgetting one to Sir William Hamilton, simply
announcing that the French fleet had been destroyed. To sink as many
of the French ships as were past salving and secure the rest as prizes
was his next step. After which he set sail for Naples, quietly

216

triumphant, a little expectant, anxious above all things to see how Lady Hamilton would take the news that he had justified her faith in him.

Emma's letters—one bearing the wishes of her heart and soul that victory might be his, the other sending the Queen's authorisation for supplies—had been the last to reach Nelson ere he left Aboukir Bay. Her letter of gratulation on his triumph was the first to reach him on his return.

'MY DEAR, DEAR SIR,—How shall I begin, what shall I say to you. 'Tis impossible I can write for since last Monday I am delerious with joy, and assure you I have a fevour caused by agitation and pleasure. God! what a victory! Never, never has there been anything half so glorious, so compleat. I fainted when I heard the joyfull news, and fell on my side and am hurt but am now well of that. I shou'd feil it a glory to die in such a cause. No, I wou'd not like to die till I see and embrace the Victor of the Nile! How shall I describe to you the transports of Maria Carolina, 'tis not possible. She fainted and kissed her husband, her children, walked about the room, cried kissed and embraced every person near her, exclaiming, Oh brave Nelson oh God bless and protect our brave deliverer, oh, Nelson Nelson what do we not owe to you, oh Victor Saviour of Italy, oh, that my swoln heart cou'd now tell him personally what we owe to him! You may judge, my dear Sir, of the rest, but my head will not permit me to tell you half of the rejoicing. The Neapolitans are mad with joy, and if you wos here now you wou'd be killed with kindness. Sonets on sonets, illuminations, rejoicings; not a French dog dare show his face. How I glory in the honner of my Country and my Countryman! I walk and tread in the air with pride, feiling I was born in the same land with the victor Nelson and his gallant band. I send you two letters from my adorable queen. One was written to me the day we received the glorious news, the other yesterday. Keep them, as they are in her own handwriting. I have kept copies only, but I feil that you ought to have

217

them. If you had seen our meeting after the battle, but I will keep it all for your arrival. I cou'd not do justice to her feiling nor to my own with writing it; and we are preparing your apartment against you come. I hope it will not be long for Sir William and I are so impatient to embrace you. I wish you cou'd have seen our house the 3 nights of illumination. 'Tis, 'twas covered with your glorious name. Their were three thousand lamps, and their should have been 3 millions if we had had time. All the English vie with each other in celebrating this most gallant and ever memorable victory. Sir William is ten years younger since the happy news, and he now only wishes to see his friend to be completely happy. How he glories in you when your name is mentioned. He cannot contain his joy. For God's sake come to Naples soon. We receive so many sonets and letters of congratulation. I send you some of them to show you how your success is felt here. How I felt for poor Troubridge. He must have been so angry on the sandbank, so brave an officer! In short, I pity those who were not in the battle. I wou'd have been rather an English powder monkey, or a swab in that great victory, than an Emperor out of it, but you will be so tired of all this. Write or come soon to Naples, and rejoice your ever sincere and oblidged friend   EMMA HAMILTON.

'The Queen at this moment sent a Dymond Ring to Captain Hoste, six buts of wine, 2 casks, for the offices, and every man on board a guinea each. Her letter is in English and comes as from an unknown person, but a well-wisher to our country and an admirer of our gallant Nelson. As war is not yet declared with France, she cou'd not show herself so openly as she wished, but she as done so much and rejoiced so very publickly, that all the world sees it. She bids me to say that she longs more to see you than any woman with child can long for anything she takes a fancy to, and she shall be for ever unhappy if you do not come. God bless you my dear, dear friend.

'My dress from head to foot is all Nelson; even my shawl is in Blue with gold anchors all over. My ear rings are Nelson's anchors; in short, we are be-Nelsoned all over. I send you some sonets but I must have taken a ship on purpose to send you

218

all written on you. Once more, God bless you. My mother desires her love to you. I am so sorry to write in such a hurry. I am afraid you will not be able to read this scrawl.'

In such torrent of broken and illiterate sentences did Emma give vent to the emotions that possessed her and warn Nelson of the nature of the public reception that awaited him.

Nelson, shaken by his wound and ensuing fever, simple and sincere in his affections, treasured the letter without seeing what its self-revelation portended.

It was indeed a royal reception he received in Naples. The royal barge, commanded, as ironical fate would have it, by that Caracciolo who, later, was to meet the Admiral in such very different circumstances, put out from the Bay, carrying the King and Princess Clementina, the Court, and Sir William and Lady Hamilton, and followed by a vast flotilla of small boats, joyous with music, gay with flags and flowers. But already it was neither King, nor Queen, nor people that counted first with him.

'Alongside came my honoured friends,' Nelson reported to his wife; 'the scene in the boat was terribly affecting: up flew her Ladyship, and exclaiming, "O God, is it possible!" she fell into my arms more dead than alive. Tears, however, soon set matters to rights, and then came the King. The scene was, in its way, as interesting: he took me by the hand, calling me his deliverer and his preserver, with every other expression of kindness. In short, all Naples calls me *Nostro Liberatore*. My greeting from the lower classes was truly affecting. I hope some day to have the pleasure of introducing you to Lady Hamilton, she is one of the very best women in the world, she is an honour to her sex. Her kindness, with Sir William's to me, is more than I can express. I am in their house; and I may now tell you, it required all the kindness of my friends to set me up. . . . '

He was, indeed, in a state of health to occasion alarm. He had been struck in the head by a heavy splinter during the recent battle and had not only lost a great quantity of blood but suffered a slight concussion of the brain.

From the landing-stage near the Castel Nuovo he proceeded in a state coach to the Embassy at the lower end of the Strada S. Caterina, and there, supported by the arm of the British Ambassadress, he painfully ascended the great staircase, and was conducted to a suite of apartments commanding a magnificent prospect of the Bay.

He deemed it a very kindly thought of Lady Hamilton's, revealing more clearly than a more important matter might have done the wonderful knowledge she had of the workings of his mind that the bed was so placed that whilst lying in it he had the whole fleet under his eye, and thus was relieved of that nervous anxiety about his responsibilities which distresses so many invalids even though they know it without basis in reason. With his mind at rest about his fleet, Nelson's body could rest.

This was Emma's opportunity and one of which she had no scruple to avail herself. The great hero was entirely in her hands. He had been at first unconscious of her charms, unimpregnable to her arts, entrenched and safe in his devotion to duty. Now in his weakness she brought all her armoury to bear upon him, and he had no available defence. Constant headaches lowered his mentality, the fever played such havoc with his digestive organs that asses' milk was the only nourishment he was permitted to take for some days. But the magnetic current that passed through Emma's hand as she smoothed his long hair or cooled his hot forehead, worked a miracle of healing. In seven days from his landing he was sufficiently restored to be present at the superb entertainment given at the Embassy in honour of his birthday.

It was an entertainment which might have satisfied the vanity and extravagance of Heliogabalus himself. Covers were laid for eighty at the dinner with which the Ambassador's hospitality began and which was attended by the whole of the Royal Family. A ball followed, thronged by some eighteen hundred of the rank and fashion of Naples. A supper, almost as magnificent as the dinner, was set for the same number of persons. The most brilliant toilettes and jewels of the ladies, in conjunction with the naval, military, and diplomatic uniforms of the men, provided a spectacle of incomparable splendour. A rostral column displayed the names of all the hero's victories; an ode in his honour was delivered and a special verse, celebrating him by name, was added to the National Anthem. Every ribbon, every button bore the magic word 'Nelson'; the whole service was marked 'H. N.'

'Well might such a compliment fill me with vanity,' the Admiral wrote to his wife.

But that was all he wrote of what was to prove the most momentous incident in his life. Never again was Nelson to write with candour and simplicity to her who bore his name, to whom he owed fidelity and allegiance. Emma's armoury had been brought into requisition and the first breach that it made was in his candour. He related nothing to his wife of a scene in which her son figured but ill. Yet the scene itself was remarkable and what it presaged has become historical.

It will be remembered that Josiah Nisbet, a youth not ill-favoured, but wanting every quality that could commend him to the company among whom his stepfather's position brought him, had been used by Emma as a means of attracting Captain Nelson to her side. She had played with him the part most familiar to her, the part of 'The Enchantress,' and, unhappily, she had played it only too well. When Nelson's illness gave him the invalid's privileges and Lady Hamilton sat long in his bed-chamber in order to superintend the nursing, Josiah, at first was only impatient; then he grew sullen; at length, before the week was over, he had become suspicious. Suspicion breeds quickly in a mind like Josiah's.

Naples was not jealous of female reputation, yet although there was common knowledge of Lady Hamilton's past, none of the unhappy story, as unfolded in these pages, had then reached Lieutenant Nisbet's ears. The night of the ball he heard the matter spoken of openly, and coupled with that old story was light jest and prophecy of what would come of Emma's attentions to the Hero of the Nile. Josiah was already sullen and suspicious, to-night he became inflamed with jealousy. He drank more than was good for him at the banquet, and with lowering brows and gathering anger, watched how, whilst Royalty was almost unheeded, and the Italian noblemen openly flouted or ignored, Emma talked to Nelson, laughed with Nelson, sat so close beside him that her bare shoulders touched his epaulettes, made a show of nursing him, that she might direct his food and taste from his glass to see if his grog was mixed to his liking. The wrong done to him, Josiah Nisbet, by such conduct festered in him. Nelson was his mother's husband, and . . . just so had Lady Hamilton smiled on him. Now she seemed not to know he was there. The consciousness of her indifference embittered his remembrance of the past and made the present unbearable.

All through the evening Emma was solicitous of Nelson's health. He was the recipient of compliments and speeches, stood for some time before the King, and then the Queen gave him a long interview. Ferdinand and Carolina combined in praises of Emma, many allusions were made to her devotion to him and her emotion when she heard of the great victory. Nelson had hardly recovered from his wound; he was moved almost to tears by hearing of how the lovely Emma had been affected.

When the Royalties left, although the revelry was at its height, Emma persuaded Nelson to her ante-chamber, there to rest and recuperate for the further exertion of speech-making and handshaking that would be required of him when the company departed.

She had hardly settled him on the sofa, herself placing the cushion under his wounded head, bending over him to adjust it the better, when

Josiah burst in. Emma was leaning solicitously over the invalid; her wonderful shoulders, so cool and white, were near to his fevered lips.

Josiah was the worse for drink, rude and unmannerly at the best.

'Let him alone,' he cried; 'let him be, I tell you. I guessed what was going on. You're nothing more nor less than a . . . and he's my mother's husband.'

He advanced upon her threateningly. Emma shrank back startled, taken at disadvantage. Nelson himself was dumbfounded for the moment by the apparition, then he struggled to his feet. Josiah was pouring forth coarse invective and abuse, accusing them both of commerce and what not. Nelson seized his stepson by the scruff of the neck, but the hero was enfeebled by illness and rage whilst Josiah had the strength of French brandy in him. There was no saying how the scuffle might have gone; Emma had both hands to her ears, but was alternate scarlet and pale at hearing herself characterised in such terms. And to her credit be it said, she was really alarmed for Nelson's safety; his wound was like to burst out again, and in his anger he might be seized by an apoplexy.

Happily Captain Troubridge was aware of Josiah Nisbet's condition, and now, hearing a noise, broke in upon them even less ceremoniously than Josiah himself had done, although to a better end. Before Emma had time to be ashamed lest he, too, should hear what the drunken oaf was calling out about her, and whilst she was as yet only conscious of gladness at the interruption, Captain Troubridge seized hold of the graceless lieutenant and was carrying him from the room:

224

'You'll go back to your ship this very night; you're not fit to be ashore,' she heard the captain say, with much more not to be repeated, characterising Josiah's conduct and himself in language that savoured more of the forecastle than of the poop.

No sooner were they alone than Emma fell a-crying, and on her knees by the sofa. 'What must Nelson think of me, think of his Emma?' she said, and hid her face. He was touched by her tears and inflamed by her nearness to him. He vowed in a husky voice that he thought she was an angel.

She became even more angelic in his eyes when she pleaded for Josiah, who, Nelson swore, should be strung up and flogged, dismissed his ship, or court-martialled. Nelson, who had been beside himself with rage, was soon beside himself with something else. Emma was so distraught by what had occurred, and the accusations that had been brought against her, that she would have made any man compassionate. When he had cursed himself for having occasioned the scene, and she had cried out, between her sobs, that if all the world was to calumniate her because she had been in his room, she would still have nursed him, the end was in sight. She went on to say wildly, what did she care for her reputation compared to his health, but perhaps *he* feared what the world might think, and would rather be alone when in fever. . . . ? Nelson answered hastily, without stopping to reflect, that neither ill nor well did he care to be alone. . . . And then they both reddened, and surprised each other's eyes.

225

The two inflammables were in contact, the one on fire with chivalry, the other tinder to his touch. How long could it be before the conflagration should occur that would burn out everything between them save that which made them one? History deponeth it was that very night, the night long remembered for the grand ball at the Embassy, that Emma, going into Nelson's room to inquire after his wound, or to show how little she heeded Josiah, and the world's opinion, stayed first to be reassured, and afterward, at Nelson's request, because he was sleepless; that then they conversed, and she learnt his wife was older than himself and unsympathetic to him, and much more that led to intimacy.

In any case, from that night dates the change in their correspondence and the alteration in their manner to each other that set the tongues a-wagging that were never afterwards to be silenced.

CHAPTER XIV

Revolution spreads from France to Italy, and Nelson becomes anxious for the personal safety of the King and Queen. Emma assists him in persuading them to flight. They set sail for Palermo in the midst of a great storm, during which one of the royal children expires in Emma's arms. Her courage and capacity arouse Nelson to enthusiasm and rivet his chains for ever.

DURING the three following weeks in which the hero of the Nile continued to enjoy the hospitality of the British Embassy and the attentions of his hostess, he had every opportunity of ascertaining the precise nature of the malady from which the body politic of Naples was suffering. To the Englishman's hereditary hostility to the Frenchman, there was superadded the religious man's detestation of the revolutionary doctrines and pernicious Jacobinism of the new Government in Paris, which he believed to be antagonistic to the spirit of Christianity. Nelson refused to cry peace where there could be no peace. At this very time, recognising how little valuable to him was the assistance offered by the Neapolitan navy, and indeed by all our other allies in the Mediterranean, he wrote a declaration to the French commander at Malta characteristically candid, and untainted by malignity.

'In addressing to you this letter' [he wrote], 'containing my determination respecting the French now in Malta, I feel confident that you will not attribute it either to insolence, or impertinent curiosity, but to a wish of having my sentiments clearly understood. The present situation of Malta I am told is this, the inhabitants are in possession of all the Island except the town which is in your hands, and that

227

the port is blocked by a squadron belonging to His Britannick Majesty. My objects are to assist the people of Malta in forcing you to abandon the Island that it may be delivered into the hands of its lawful Sovereign, and to get possession of the Gme. Tell, Diana and Justice. To accomplish these objects as speedily as possible I offer that on the delivery of the French ships to me, that all troops and seamen now in Malta shall be landed in France without the condition of their being prisoners of war. If my offers are rejected, or the French ships make their escape, notwithstanding my vigilance, I declare I will not enter or join in any capitulation which the General may hereafter be forced to enter into with the inhabitants of Malta, nor will I ever permit any which may be like the present, much less will I intercede for the lives or forgiveness of those who have betrayed their country. I beg leave to assure you that this is the determination of a British Admiral.'

Reinforced by memories of what had happened so lately at Aboukir Bay—to which with native modesty this British Admiral made not the least allusion—these quiet words carried the menace of heavy guns and could not fail to awaken in any brave bosom a desire for retaliation and revenge. Maria Carolina might try to conceal the fact, but she *had* aided and abetted Nelson in the revictualling of his fleet and thereby precipitated the annihilation of the French one, over which event she and her husband were now publicly rejoicing so loudly that the echo thundered in the ears of Garat, scowling behind the windows in the French ministry at Naples. He reported everything to the Directory, and Buonaparte took a rod from pickle wherewith to scourge the arrogant Bourbon. He decreed that war should be carried to the heel of Italy, and all Italy brought to the heel of France. And until that actually occurred every excitation was to be applied to the smouldering sedition of the Neapolitan people in order that King Ferdinand might be further embarrassed by all the troubles and perils of civil disturbance. Napoleon intended that the Kingdom of the Two Sicilies should be absorbed in the Ligurian Republic, and that Ferdinand should lose his throne by revolution if not by defeat in war.

All this was clear to Nelson even before the event. He was now fully recovered of his fever and of his wounds, but not of the greatest that he had sustained. Emma was gloriously happy, and completely enamoured of her new lover. She gave herself magnificently to Nelson, and now he held her miraculous. Already she had persuaded him he owed his Syracusan supplies and the Queen's countenance entirely to her influence.

One may ask where was Sir William Hamilton while all this was going on? Emma was clever enough to hoodwink her husband into the belief that it was the politics, and not the person of Nelson, that enraptured her. Sir William was easily persuaded; he had never been vexed by jealousy, but only proud when his treasure was admired. And he, too, was absorbed in affairs of State, and in no humour for domestic altercation. If it pleased Emma to make herself conspicuous on all and every occasion with the English Admiral, it suited him, and the Court to which he was attached, to secure Nelson's allegiance to the Italian cause at any cost.

'Nelson, you must never forsake the Queen; I love the Queen,' Emma said solemnly.

And Nelson believed her, not knowing it was Emma's own consequence she loved above everything, and thought to secure by her loyalty. In the first few weeks of such an intrigue as this upon which he was engaged with Lady Hamilton a man is scarcely in possession of all his faculties. Of course he promised all she asked, and that he would safeguard Her Majesty's interests with his life.

But he pointed out the difficulty of helping those who will not help themselves, and urged her to bring pressure upon the King and his ministers to stir them from their lethargy. This was counsel very congenial to her temper, and it was given greater effect by the inclination manifested just now in Vienna to take advantage of the discomposure into which the defeat of their fleet had thrown the Directory. Austria made overtures to King Ferdinand to co-operate in a new war. With Emma influencing the Queen, and the Queen exerting all the pressure of which she was capable, the King, for once, displayed something approaching energy. He announced that he would put himself at the head of an army if one were provided for him. Forty thousand young men, the flower of the country, volunteered immediately; the poorest cities in Italy offered to contribute to the expenses of the campaign. With the standing army, and these volunteers, a force of near seventy thousand men formed camp under the command of General Mack, who came from Vienna for that purpose.

The hopes of Maria Carolina rose high; these were measures in consonance with her proud spirit. But her elation was short-lived. Mack was out-generalled, and further crippled by the inexperience of the volunteers. In the long desuetude from war of the regular troops the officers had become venal, and many of the men were cowards. The army entered Rome indeed, but not to hold it. The city was retaken and Ferdinand driven back to his own territories with the undignified rapidity of a rout.

Nelson's valuation of the fighting qualities of the Neapolitans was low, although that had not prevented him from recommending the Neapolitan King to put them to the test. He said bluntly that His Majesty had his choice. Either to advance, trusting to God for His blessing on a just cause and be prepared to die, sword in hand, or to be kicked out of his kingdom; for that one or the other of those things must happen. Ferdinand had tried the first alternative, but had neither conquered nor died. The moment was come now to contemplate the second. The routed army, the disaffected populace, Buonaparte's overpowering and continuous victories were enough to excite apprehension in the stoutest heart.

That strange trio, Sir William Hamilton, Nelson, and Emma, discussed the situation from every aspect. At the colloquy Sir William was discursive and irresolute:

'I am waiting despatches from England. There had better be nothing attempted until I receive them,' was the speech that represented his attitude. But Nelson was keen that the Royal Family should be persuaded to flight before the fate that befell Louis XVI. and Marie Antoinette was upon them. Emma was inflamed at the prospect of taking part in an historic adventure so marvellously dramatic.

'Nelson is right,' she exclaimed enthusiastically. For had he not always proved his prescience? The Royal Family must be persuaded away, forced away. Who so fitted for the task as Emma, with Nelson to help in the high enterprise? Sir William's feeble objections were overruled. And as for waiting for despatches from England, there was danger in every hour of delay. Emma was all on fire to seize an opportunity, incredible so short a time before, of playing a prominent part in royal drama.

'Together we will save the Queen, Nelson,' she cried. She saw herself the centre of the stage on which the limelight of the world was turned. Nelson would take the part of hero in the drama, and the world should applaud them together. If, in her eagerness and sparkling eyes, her deference to his opinions and adoring humility, might be found a clue to the state of her feelings, Sir William Hamilton at least gave no hint he observed anything unusual. Neither now, when the enterprise for conveying the Royal Family into safety was being discussed, nor for a long time afterwards. He had something of his nephew's reticence, although with a far greater generosity.

The Queen herself seemed likely to provide the first obstacle in the way of the projected flight. Emma knew every working of that proud spirit, and believed she would be immovable by entreaty from herself alone:

'Nelson, you must write a letter, and I will myself take it to the Queen; she believes in your opinion; she will do anything you advise her,' was her final decision. When Nelson said he thought 'twas to the

232

King he should address himself, she was quick to agree with him, but said he must send it by some other messenger. She blushed, and put on a pretty air, allowing Nelson to divine why a private interview with the King was an adventure she would rather not undertake. It was stale news to Sir William, but new to Nelson, who, far from exhibiting a husband's calm, had now, and always, a great inclination to jealousy. Emma was aware of it, and shrouded her past. She had no fear for the future, for one lover at a time had always sufficed her and Nelson's greatness was Nelson's safeguard.

But what she hinted, or what he read in her downcast eyes and blushing cheek when the King's name was mentioned, made him write with less sympathy than he might otherwise have done, albeit with no less frankness. The King had been unable to decide on action, once his army was defeated and himself stranded, and his ministers were in no better case. They had opened negotiations with this and the other Power, procrastinated, shuffled, and planned impossibilities. Nelson now saw nothing for it but flight:

'Should unfortunately this miserable Ruinous system of procrastination be persisted in I would recommend that all your property and persons are ready to embark at a very short notice. It will be my duty to look and provide for your safety, and with it (I am sorry to think it will be necessary) that of the amiable Queen of these kingdoms and her family. I have read with admiration her dignified and incomparable letter of September 1796. May the councils of this kingdom ever be guided by such sentiments of dignity, honour and justice. And may the words of the great Mr. Pitt be instilled into the ministry of this country—"*The boldest measures are the safest*," is the sincere wish of your etc. . . .'

The letter was sent to the King, but it was the Queen who had to decide how its recommendation should be treated. At first she was passionate in her opposition. To leave Naples was an admission of fear and failure, galling and intolerable to her high spirit. The rout of General Mack's army and the King's return to Naples, defeated and disconcerted, *roi fainéant* and futile, left the Queen the man's part to play. So she told Emma; and that she would play it where she was.

'The French is knocking at the gates of the Palace,' Emma urged. She had been well coached; and having conquered the Hero of the Nile, was prepared to do battle with such meaner foes as the beaten Bourbons. In truth, Revolution had raised its hydra head, and could not now be viewed without terror; it vomited blood and fire, belching fury and spreading dismay. No crowned head was safe within the monster's reach. Maria Carolina had more than a woman's courage, but Emma had the art to sap it. What of the Dauphin of France, and the Dauphiness? She had not herself to consider, but her children, was Emma's argument. This took the Queen from her balance; for whatever else may have been said of her and her morality, none has denied she was a good mother, and devoted to the interests of her offspring. Therefore, although she still believed that flight would be regarded, and justly regarded, by the people and the *lazzaroni* as desertion in the face of the enemy, and would alienate their loyalty to the King whilst increasing their hatred of herself, the Queen was brought at last to listen to Nelson's advice.

And once she was brought to listen, it was not long before Nelson completed his plan, and Emma was helping to its execution. No time must be lost, for a rumour being circulated in Naples that the British Ambassador had formed the project of driving the King away from his people, the fury of the Neapolitans rose to such a height that not only the Queen's party, but the Queen's person, was in direst peril. Then was established the value of Emma's bad reputation. Her intimacy with the Queen was known, and Lady Hamilton went backwards and forwards between the Palace and the Embassy without exciting attention or suspicion. She used her opportunities to collect jewels and treasure, conveying them first to the Embassy, and then, for safety, to the British ships. Everything had to be thought of, and all contingencies provided against. The courtesan turned conspirator proved her quality and rose to the occasion. Nelson would convey the King and Queen, their family and suite, to Palermo, and of course Emma would accompany them. Clothing and provisions must go, and as much else as could be carried. The Queen was obstinate in her refusal to depart, leaving the treasures of the palace as booty for the advancing French. Then, too, there were the King's vacillations to be reckoned with and combated. He clung to the hope that even so late the disturbances in Naples might die down, and Providence intervene on his behalf.

The delay was unfortunate, for it brought them into bad weather. Had Nelson been permitted to weigh anchor earlier, the fatal incident we must soon chronicle might perhaps have been averted. The wind that was then blowing fresh from the north-east would have carried the

235

refugees safe to Palermo before the storm broke over the fleet. But the King was irresolute to the last, even when his consort's scruples had all been overcome. Emma was actively engaged in conveying and superintending the secret removal of money and goods to the extraordinary value of two and a half million pounds sterling. Meantime the excitement of the mob was waxing higher and more fierce, and their Majesties were compelled to make frequent appearances on the balcony of the royal palace in order to satisfy the people that they had not deserted their capital.

On December 18th, however, General Mack writing that he had no prospect of stopping the progress of the French, and adding his entreaties to the others that the Royal Family should retire from Naples as expeditiously as possible, the King at length signified his approval of the arrangements concerted by Nelson and Lady Hamilton for the embarkation. A secret passage led from the royal apartments to the little quay, and here it was agreed that the refugees should be met by the Admiral, and conveyed to the Vanguard, which lay at about the distance of an hour's hard rowing.

The Kilien Effendi, who had been sent by the Grand Seignior to Naples to present Nelson with the Plume of Triumph, was holding a reception that night, and, in order to raise no suspicion, the British Ambassador attended the entertainment. Emma, too, was there, the loveliest and most animated figure of them all. The great enterprise before her only served to make her spirits more ebullient. She and Nelson exchanged glances and were conscious of the double secret they were sharing. They had grown quickly into intimacy and every hour made it clearer to them that there was nothing they could not adventure together. To carry off the King and Queen, their entire family and the treasures of the Crown was only the beginning. All was arranged, and well arranged. The embassy carriage was standing before Kilien Effendi's front door when the British Ambassador walked away unobserved from the back. Emma had stepped hurriedly out of her fine clothes and into those more suitable to the voyage before her. When the time appointed for the rendezvous arrived, Emma met the Queen at the secret entrance to the palace, supporting her through the darkness of the tortuous passage to the hardly lighter quay. She then committed her to Nelson's safe custody, and, rejoining her husband and mother in Sir William Hamilton's private boat, followed the royal party to the ship.

The night was horribly dark, with a strong wind blowing off the shore, raising a heavy ocean swell that made the voyage extremely hazardous. The *Vanguard* stood out to sea under a sky whose threatening aspect was borne out the next morning by a storm more terrible than any Nelson had experienced in the whole of the thirty years he had known the sea. All the sails were blown to tatters, and sailors stood by with axes ready to cut away the masts. The terrific violence of the tempest shattered the nerves of many of the refugees, already strung to the point of snapping by the excitements and anxieties of the past weeks. They crowded into the captain's cabin as if Neptune would not dare to strike them there, and their prayers and cries of fear rose louder with each deeper roll of the labouring vessel. It was now that Emma for the first time really merits our reader's admiration and showed the qualities that not only palliate her shortcomings, but might well prove our excuse for having selected such a heroine for our memoir. She forgot all her consequence remembering only that she was a better sailor than the rest. She gave up her cabin to the Queen and devoted herself to the care of the royal children, who were in the last extremity of fear, and suffering terribly from sea-sickness. All the mother-love she had in her, cheated by circumstance, rose in full flood, and spent itself upon these frightened little ones.

To one of them, Prince Albert, now but six years old, she was especially attached, and it was he whom death reft from her protecting arms. For, after being tortured by the most violent seasickness, making a brave effort to take food, his stomach rebelled against his will, and, falling into a succession of convulsive fits, he died in the late afternoon of Christmas Day, adding by his untimely death the last drop to the brimming cup of the Queen's distress. Nelson was present at the prince's demise, and, watching Lady Hamilton as she held the dying child—for all the women in attendance on the Queen were incapable of assistance, and there was not another soul to be of service—his admiration of her womanliness and sweetness overcharged his heart. His own longing for fatherhood swelled to the point of pain, and was distilled in the tears he hurried away to hide. When he left the pitiful scene, the image of Emma with the child in her arms was the one he carried with him. He would it were a child of his she cradled there; the wish haunted him for many days.

It was not until two of the clock the morning following the death of the prince that the Vanguard was enabled to anchor in the harbour of Palermo. For close upon twelve hours, ever since three in the afternoon of Christmas Day, she had been detained outside, with the Royal Standard flying in full view of the capital. For once the Queen's spirit was not equal to the burden imposed upon it. She left Naples still full of Bourbon pride, although bowing to the force of circumstances. She reached Palermo a despoiled mother, a woman with an unbearable pain in her heart, craving only solitude and obscurity in which to hide her grief from the world. But queens may not weep for their children like common folk. Sicily was waiting to acclaim Ferdinand and his consort with passionate shouts of loyalty and unalterable devotion. She could not, however, bear to go on shore in a public manner. At five o'clock in the morning Nelson himself escorted her thither with the royal princesses, returning to the *Vanguard* afterwards to attend the disembarkation of the King, for the satisfaction of the shouting Sicilians, in all the ceremony of State.

In the swing of the pendulum are pictured all the natural operations. Night follows day, ebb, flow, reaction succeeds to action. Emma had had her hour, had worked like a man, wept like a woman, won Nelson's heart truly and completely as she never could have won it through all the splendid gift to him of her beauty, or the love she laid so lavishly at his feet. It was the Emma of the *Vanguard* to whom he made complete

239

surrender; she who met stress and storm with smile and succour, who had been lovely in helpfulness, undaunted in danger. She had met his conception of all womanhood; his spirit leaped to hers, and called her mate. This was no creature for dalliance, she was wife and mother, palpitating and alive to all demands. 'Incomparable,' she had been called, 'Peerless 'and 'Divine.' But Nelson saw her human, and the beauty of her soul held him more securely than would ever the beauty of her body. To him her great heart was visible in those twelve awful days. Whomever else it had held, it held Nelson now, and as far as he was concerned it was for all time. For twelve days and twelve nights she had toiled incessantly, had faced every danger fearlessly, and hardships without a murmur.

After the landing at Palermo the Queen fell ill. At the same time Sir William Hamilton developed a bilious fever. Both of them leaned on Emma's vitality and wearied for her company. Nelson was lost in admiration of the strength that held through such fatigues and the spirit that survived them. His admiration and tenderness were the food on which Emma flourished, and the knowledge that she was a heroine. She and Nelson were thrown daily and hourly together, for Sir William kept his room, complaining of this and the other, querulous, and beginning to show the weakness of his years. He was for ever urging Emma to look after Nelson, to devote herself to his entertainment; he had in his illness a weak and unreasonable fear lest Nelson and his ships should depart, leaving them stranded.

Nelson made his quarters in their house, and there, among an alien populace, alone save for the invalid husband, in the lax hours that follow great exertion, we see him taking for his own that which had heretofore been only borrowed. Sir William was nearing three score years and ten, Emma was less than half his age, and in the full perfection of her beauty. The ambassador's powers were failing, but he had ever been a man of experience with woman; he knew now that if he were to hold the choicest of his collection, it must be by an appeal to her compassion, or perhaps to her self-interest, not by a claim which he was incapable of enforcing and to which she had lately been indifferent.

'As I wax old,' he said, 'it has been hard upon me having had both bilious and rheumatic complaints.' This is not to excuse his conduct, but only to explain it. He wanted Nelson's friendship and the enjoyment of his society; he had to keep Emma by his side, even if only as a nurse. There was a decent veil thrown over the position. The word friendship served well for what we must henceforward call the 'triple alliance.' Nelson would have shared Emma with no one after that voyage in the *Vanguard: Quod habeo teneo* was his motto. But what Sir William Hamilton wanted from the woman to whom he had given his name, and some estate, years of kindness and protection, was what no man could grudge him. Here in this veracious history shall be no attempt at judgment on the case of Horatio Nelson and Emma Hamilton, or Sir William Hamilton's part in it, here is only to be found a plain statement of the facts. Let a verdict be arrived at by a jury of their peers—if such exist.

What is to be chronicled is how, notwithstanding Emma, Nelson soon found himself fretting at his inactivity in Palermo. The news was all of the French irruption in Naples, and of the growth of Jacobinism. He itched to mow it all down with the sword, and as for the men who sowed it, to scare them with the thunder of his guns beyond the farthest barriers of the Alps. He ached to deal another hammer blow at the French, for whom his hatred was always growing. Aboukir Bay had been good, but it seemed a long time ago. He must soon find vent for his inexhaustible energy; waiting was the hardest form of service. He was shut up in Palermo, whilst a hundred things might be happening, things of vital consequence. Duty tied him here in Sicily to cover the blockade of Naples, and preserve Sicily in case of an attack. If only he could see the King safe again on his throne in Naples with every rascally Jacobin hanged as high as Haman, with what joy would he leave the Mediterranean for good and all! But would he? Was it really only duty tied him there? A sigh that was almost a groan escaped him, audible in the stillness of the night.

'What is it, Nelson?'

The dear voice reached him, deep, and soft, and musical, soothing his fretted nerves, and bringing a sense of exquisite peace. He had not expected her to-night, for it was very late; but it seemed right that she should come to him just then, and he turned his tired, grave face to her, not smiling, but welcoming her by thevery quietness with which he accepted her presence.

242

'Sir William has been worse than ever to-night,' she said, coming in and joining him by the window, 'fevered and restless, in some pain. I don't think he has had one day of real health since we came to this miserable house. He has only just fallen asleep.'

'Cannot you do the same?' he asked.

'I? No, I'm too tired to sleep.' There were tears in her voice.

'My poor Emma,' he said, and drew her into the shelter of his arms, 'would that I could take all your burdens from you.'

'I heard you sigh when I was at the door; Nelson has his troubles too.'

'Not when Emma is in his arms,' he whispered. She had the power to make him forget all beside herself.

*　　*　　*　　*　　*　　*

'It grows late, and you are ever more fatigued,' he said presently. 'I am but selfish in my desire to keep you with me.'

She shook her head and the movement freed her loosened hair which shone like a red gold sun-mist and made an aureole for her beautiful face.

'I want you most when I am most tired,' she told him. 'No one but you has ever rested me. It has always seemed I must give and give, and be what they want, but you think of me.' She found it difficult to explain herself.

'What do I do for you?' he asked tenderly. 'Whatever it is, I would that I could do more.'

'You make me know you care for me as if . . . as if we was real husband and real wife.' He drew her closer to him, and she went on. 'Sir

243

William has been good to me, and wanted me to dress handsome and look well. Other men have told me I'm beautiful, but you, Nelson, you tell me something different. I feel it, and it makes me so happy, so proud. I have never had a lover but you. . . .'

Emma meant the phrase metaphorically, Nelson in his simplicity accepted it as fact. Ever his love for her grew, and it is no doubt she was a great mitigation to the tedium of the days at Palermo. But Nelson was essentially a man of action, and although his heart was anchored, his mind was restless.

History was made quickly in these closing years of the eighteenth century. In Naples it was being written at double speed. Deserted by their King and army, the *lazzaroni* had been left to defend their homes and institutions against the French invasion. They fought irregularly, but with a desperate courage; they were eventually borne down by the weight of the French arms, reinforced by the Revolutionists among their own fellow citizens. A Republic was declared, the French occupied the fortress of St. Elmo, the Neapolitan Revolutionists garrisoned the castle of Uovo and Nuovo; the capital lay at the mercy of the enemy. In addition to this a powerful French fleet was cruising somewhere in the Mediterranean. It was knowledge of this last fact that held Nelson at Palermo.

King Ferdinand, before he fled from Naples, had given his royal commission to Cardinal Ruffo to rouse the Calabrese, and His Eminence was so successful in stimulating the martial spirit of this proud and patriotic people that in a short time the invaders and the Revolutionists were in a mood to discuss terms. News of this now reached Palermo and some uneasiness was felt by the King as to the lengths to which the Cardinal's unfettered action might carry him. Nelson, in particular, was ill content to leave His Eminence in the full power of a plenipotentiary; the ardent desire of his whole career had been to crush and stamp out this damnable Jacobinism, not to make terms with it.

Even Emma's arms could not hold Nelson when rumour after rumour reached Palermo of what was occurring.

'Don't leave me, Nelson,' Emma pleaded.

'Don't hold me, Emma. I am ill to hold when duty calls. Help me rather.'

'How can I help you? '

'Seek the King. I have wearied him and now he will no longer grant me audience, but pleads illness, and vexes me with delays. I ought to be in Naples; it is working in me His Eminence has been won over.'

'But how am I to live here without you? And, Nelson . . .' Then her colour heightened, and she whispered in his ear what she thought, or feared. He flushed too. The breach of his marriage vows had been followed by no perceptible moral deterioration. Since he had felt it was not the flesh, but the spirit, speaking when it told him this was his true mate and wife that should have been, and might be yet, he had been quite deliberate in his assumption that their union, although irregular, was for all time. What she whispered to him as a possibility was something for which he had ever longed. His wife had borne him no child; it was Emma who should give him that pride and fulfilment of

245

manhood. He told her now that her news filled him with joy, if with some apprehension for her.

'And now you won't leave me, you won't want to go.'

But he could not be made to see that the circumstance should alter his plans; and all Emma's pleadings left his view unaltered. All that it effected was to hasten his movements. For suddenly Emma said:

'Why not carry me and Sir William with you to Naples? You will want an intermediary between you and the Cardinal. . . .'

It was an inspiration. Nelson was transported at the idea that she would accompany him, and nothing remained but to secure the King's permission. With Emma at work, this was only an affair of hours.

Before it seemed possible they were on board the *Foudroyant*, sail set, flags flying, and the populace cheering them to the water's edge.

'My love, it was good of you to persuade Nelson to let us embark with him. I am sure I shall recover quickly once I am out of this uncongenial town,' Sir William said, from the couch that had been rigged out for him on deck.

'Oh, Emma! how quickly you got the King's permission; what a diplomatist you would have made! And now we have the voyage before us, and the wind in our favour. Dear one, but we will make the journey memorable,' was Nelson's comment ere he hurried to the quarterdeck.

Arrived at Naples, Nelson for once found rumour had not exaggerated. The Cardinal had agreed to a truce; he had promised security of their persons and property to the Revolutionists, and to the French garrison permission to march out of the fortress with all the

246

honours of war, prior to being conveyed to their own land at King Ferdinand's expense! And to this astonishingly liberal proposal the representatives of the other Powers had already affixed their signatures.

Nelson made short work of the convention. He annulled the amnesty, declaring that whoever had served the Republic was a traitor, and that kings do not capitulate with rebels. Ruffo's protestations were overruled, and himself dismissed into obscurity. The army was quickly reorganised, St. Elmo retaken, and the rebels forced to submit to what clemency the King might show. Sharp diseases call for sharp remedies, and the knife was not spared now in cutting this gangrene of revolution out of the heart of the country. Disloyalty had spread like the plague, the most signal instance of all being supplied by that same Caracciolo, who so few months before had brought the King in his barge to meet Nelson when returning victorious from the Nile.

It was only a few weeks ago that Caracciolo had left the King at Palermo, to all appearance a faithful loyalist. Yet he had no sooner reached Naples than he joined the rebels, and even commanded their fleet. In Nelson's eye the case was simple as it was black. He held his King's commission, and he had fired on his King's flag. That spelt death. Caracciolo must hang. Emma pleaded for him, but it was of no avail. About five of the clock on a glorious June afternoon all Naples turned its eyes to the yardarm of the *Minerva*, the frigate that had been the target for Caracciolo's rebel guns. There swayed and swung the lifeless form of Prince Francesco Caracciolo, Admiral of the Neapolitan

Navy, a warning to all traitors. At sunset the rope was cut, and the heavy-shotted corpse dropped into the sea.

Emma played no part in the reprisals; she was wholly occupied in making herself indispensable to her lover, whilst not neglecting her duties to Sir William, whose rapid recovery enabled him to take up again the reins of his authority. Acting for one and both of them, and with the full concurrence of the Ministers, it was Lady Hamilton who received the Royalists on behalf of the Queen, supplied the *lazzaroni* with new arms, and so conducted matters with the feudal lords and others whose affection Her Majesty had alienated, that her praises were heard on all sides. Nelson was transported by her tact and intelligence. It seemed to him that she bore prosperity and adversity equally well. For instance, a bomb burst in Sir William's new apartment, an echo of the storming of St. Elmo; the damage done was estimated at thirty thousand pounds. Emma said stoutly it was well lost if it ended the Revolution. Nelson heard her; Sir William fortunately was out of earshot.

'You care nothing for money,' he exclaimed. 'Peerless and incomparable woman. It is enough for you that the revolution is ended, that the Queen will be restored. A restoration to which you have contributed so much.'

'Not so much as my Nelson.'

'Nelson and Emma are one,' he answered soberly. 'I have done no more for Italy than you.'

248

And she came to believe him, which is perhaps the strangest thing in her strange history. The English Ministry later on had much ado in disillusioning her, and Grenville and others have been blamed for their action. But after the publication of these memoirs the whole matter will be better understood.

CHAPTER XV

The Hamiltons, with Nelson in their train, make a triumphant progress through the capitals of Europe, but on arriving in England are cold-shouldered by the Court. Lady Nelson becomes a factor in the situation and further estranges her husband by her conduct to Emma. The pressing attentions of the Prince of Wales excite the jealousy of the Admiral, but the birth of Horatia is a signal for the renewal of his ardour. The purchase of a country house is decided upon, and a selection made of Merton in Surrey.

WITH the restoration of King Ferdinand to his Neapolitan throne, the repression of the forces of Jacobinism in the southern regions of the Italian peninsula, and the raising of the blockade of Malta, Nelson's work in Italy was practically accomplished. As ever in times of inactivity his physical health suffered and in the phantasmagoria of fevered nights he saw life out of proportion; facts and fancies became interwoven and indistinguishable. Now he was possessed of the idea that he was held in disfavour by the Admiralty, and this in despite of the magnitude of his services to England and Europe. Emma tried in vain to rouse him from the depression into which he fell; indeed she became part of it.

'They have done nothing for you,' he complained, 'though you were the cause of all my victories. They send no answer to my letters.'

'They will be glad enough of your services when Napoleon is again active. Don't fret, Nelson; they know there is no one but you if ever they should need a commander. And meanwhile we are together, and as happy as the day is long.'

'You are a sweet comforter, but it is hard to be neglected and passed over. . . .'

Nelson was neither neglected nor passed over, but he was fain to believe himself ill-used, and, in a condition that in one less great would be called bad temper, he asked for and obtained leave. Thus it came about that he struck flag and set out for home at the same time as Sir William Hamilton put into execution what had long been in his mind, and sent in his resignation.

Emma assuredly believed that in leaving Italy for England she was but altering the scene of her triumphs, and that St. James's Palace would be as accessible to her as had been the Court of Ferdinand and Maria Carolina. She had some excuse for her blindness or folly, for she had really forgotten or found excuses for all that had happened to her before she became the wife of Sir William Hamilton. And if such a past as hers could be effaced, the present, that gave a husband's countenance to her intimacy with Nelson, might easily appear to her as nothing to debar her from enjoying the consideration and the company of virtuous women.

She had quite come to believe that Nelson owed his victories, and Italy its freedom, to her exertions, and confidently expected the plaudits of the world. It was an elate and confident Emma who bade farewell to Italy, and, with her complaisant husband, accompanied Nelson on his almost royal progress across Europe. Maria Carolina went with them as

251

far as Vienna, travelling by Leghorn, Florence, and Trieste, each of which towns sought to eclipse the other in the magnificence and honour of its welcome to the distinguished party. In Vienna the noble houses of Esterhazy and Bathyani spread their most splendid hospitality before the Queen and her favourite, and fireworks, balls, hunting parties, concerts were the order of the day. Prague, Dresden, and Hamburg were only more places where Emma's pride and vanity were fed. It is surely no matter for wonder that a woman before whom a whole continent bowed down should have looked for a cordial reception in her native land.

That which she had omitted to reckon with was the virtue which is inherent in the English character. Although in every age and under every king a class may emerge, profligate, extravagant, heedless of the public weal so long as it may indulge every selfish wish and satisfy every carnal appetite, yet the people as a whole do inherently believe that their national greatness is built upon the purity of home life.

The English Court epitomised the English people. A narrow and pietistic dogmatism characterised the Queen and was incidentally responsible for the breaking away of the young princes. George III. in his intervals of comparative sanity subscribed to the doctrines held by his consort.

The trouble began with the arrival of Sir William Hamilton and his party at Yarmouth. Nelson was greeted, as it seemed, by all England excepting only his wife. Her son Josiah had supplied her with sufficient information to poison her mind, and the accounts of the receptions at the various foreign Courts inflamed it further. She had had no part in Nelson's triumphs, no share in his glory; that lot being reserved for Lady Hamilton. Even if her affection for her second husband had been greater than there is reason to suppose was the case, her forbearance would have been strained beyond the point of endurance at the publicity of the affront now put upon her by his conduct towards another woman. For his infatuation was patent to all the world. It was Lady Hamilton who shared his triumphant entry into England as she had been one with his triumphant progress through Europe. The carriage that drove him from the quay held also Lady Hamilton, Sir William following almost unobserved. The people acclaimed and shouted; to them Nelson was 'the Hero of the Nile,' the one figure to scare away the bogey Buonaparte. But to his wife, remaining in London, silent and solitary, he was a husband who insulted her dignity, no more and no less.

Satirists up in London were quickly busy with pen and graving tool. The scandal was well disseminated before the Hamiltons arrived in the house in Piccadilly, facing the Green Park, which had been prepared in anticipation of their coming.

Because of the lampoons, prints, and all the gossip set afloat by Josiah, it seemed an audacity truly amazing on Emma's part, and a compliance and lack of tact hardly less astonishing on that of Sir William, that the Hamiltons not only elected to accompany Nelson on his journey from Yarmouth to the capital, but actually persuaded him to take up his residence in their house. It was as if they had all three blindfolded themselves, and now imagined no one else could see.

253

They were astonished by the news quickly conveyed to them, that whilst the King would give Sir William audience, the Queen refused to receive Lady Hamilton! Nelson stormed and swore the Court should not see him either; Sir William nursed his gout; Emma sent for Greville.

'She has heard something against me, some rival must have spoken or wrote ill of me. Women is all such jealous creatures!' was what Emma said to Greville. She was quite naive and unconscious of offence. 'You must get it to the Queen's ears that I am all discretion now. I am no longer giddy and frivolous like I used to be. I have been in high affairs. . . . ' She appealed to Sir William, and he confirmed her warmly. He was weary of ambition, strife, and politics, vexed that the question of Emma's standing should be questioned, and anxious she should be satisfied. It was a long time before she was brought to realise the true state of affairs and the share Nelson's wife had in bringing it about. She had expected to be courted, and behold she was practically, if not entirely, ostracised—a parlous state of affairs for one who, in her own opinion, had made Nelson, released Italy, and proved the closest friend and confidante of the proudest of the Bourbons. We could regard her amazement and disappointment with less wonder if it were not that she was already six months gone with child.

If this was not known, it was at least more than suspected, and the effrontery of the whole affair appeared always more incredible. If Emma had actually been as much the nation's benefactress as she imagined herself, her public merit would not have weighed in English eyes against her private indiscretions. In such a matter England differed completely from Italy.

The private arrangement, if one existed, was the affair of nobody but the three persons concerned. Sir William Hamilton was not the first, and would not be the last elderly husband of a beautiful young woman to accept a pair of horns. That he should wear them openly and as an ornament was the offence, and one that rankled. And even if there had been no Nelson, and no Lady Nelson, with her cold aloofness and bitter tongue, it is doubtful whether the royal attitude towards Sir William Hamilton's wife would have been very different. In truth, Emma was too exotic, too ebullient, too self-conscious and flamboyant to be to the taste of Queen Caroline and the ladies of the Court. The gayer her manner, the brighter her smiles, the sweeter her singing, and the more captivating her Attitudes, the less was the likelihood she should be accepted as one of themselves by those who could not compete, and would not admire.

The Queen definitely ignored Emma's existence, and society followed the example she set them. Invitations to the big house in Piccadilly were either left unanswered or met by curt refusal. Emma was first incredulous, then indignant, but finally, when the Duke of Queensberry and others of his kidney came around her, as they began to do very soon, she became indifferent. Her sensibilities were so blunted that she could not see that the world had a grievance against her. And that grievance became accentuated by her blindness to it. Never, perhaps, did Emma display so clearly the wantonness from which her character had not altered as in the first few weeks of her return to England. Nelson and Sir William Hamilton were perhaps as much responsible as she for the state of her mind. The sense of guilt, which a man naturally so religious as Nelson should have felt in his adulterous connection, was all obliterated by Lady Nelson's attitude towards his 'sweet Emma.' Coldly contemptuous she was, and self-righteous, lacking in sympathy and understanding of the indignant and warm-hearted sailor. She insulted and ignored Lady Hamilton, and wanted to make Nelson's breaking off his intimacy with her a prelude to their own better agreement. She stood out for her rights and privileges, confronting him with lawyers, whom he hated next to Popery and the French, when he would have approached her with kindness. She really drove him back to Emma, who had experience in men's ways, and knew how to soothe him. Then there was the sense of joy in his approaching fatherhood and his gratitude to her who promised it him. Everything combined in Emma's favour to excite Nelson's chivalry and deepen his attachment. He was a religious man, and because his wife was Josiah Nisbet's mother, and to him inflexible and rigid, whilst Emma was about to bear him a child and was ever warm and loving, yet never forgetting his greatness and superiority, he was confirmed in his decision that it was indeed she who was his 'wife before God.'

We must in his extenuation remember that he was unaware of all her history, so familiar now to us. He had heard, for thus far Emma's ingenuous confession admitted, that in an unsheltered youth her innocence had been betrayed. But that was all. Of Sir William, all that

256

can be said is that he was in ill-health and valued Emma's nursing, and having set so high a value on Nelson, he had no stomach to refuse him that which he no longer required for his own gratification. Sir William Hamilton was of so autocratic a temper he thought he could carry any situation. Had not Greville been in the way, there is little doubt he would have fathered the coming child. As it was, some little circumspection was necessary; the more so, perhaps, as the matter of his pension was not yet settled, and difficulties about it were already being raised. Secrecy as to Emma's condition was further rendered advisable by the attitude of the Prince of Wales. It is well known that not only did the Prince fail in subscribing to his parents' doctrines, but was on ill terms with them on account of the licentiousness of his own conduct and the debauchery of his days. To him, nevertheless, Sir William began to look to repair his broken fortunes. The King's health was already a matter of concern to his loyal subjects, but there were those of the Prince's set who built hopes upon it. When no influence that he could himself bring to bear moved the inflexibility of the Court towards Emma, it was not perhaps unnatural that Sir William's thoughts should turn to the heir to the throne. Already the Prince had honoured Emma with his regard, had been particular in his attentions when he met her at the Duke of Queensberry's house, where he conversed with her for a long time. But that Nelson was there also, always inclined to jealousy, fiery, and capable of making a scene, Emma's encouragement might have been more marked. She was aware of Sir William's mind, and would not have thwarted him in an

257

enterprise so suitable to her talents. At His Grace's ball the Prince handed her through a quadrille; when he was sober and willed it, his manners had an elegance that caused him sometimes to be named as 'the First Gentleman in Europe.' Emma has put it on record that he had a pretty leg and looked at her 'approvingly.' That she looked back again may be gathered from Nelson's letters to her, letters written after he was recalled to his ship.

The summons came all too soon. Nelson left his Emma in the midst of temptations, from which it seemed that only her condition protected her. And about that condition it was finally agreed the utmost discretion must be observed. Greville was at the back of all the arrangements; to him alone Emma was completely open. Their interests were again opposed, and again it was Mr. Greville who carried the day. The charge of pregnancy must be denied at all hazards, Emma must be seen everywhere, the Prince's attentions must be encouraged. These were Mr. Greville's instructions; all his prospects would be jeopardised if a child were openly born in wedlock. This was not the argument he used to Emma. He urged that the most distinguished career can be injured and checked in England by open scandal, and that whatever Nelson had done in the past he was capable of greater things in the future if he were not hampered. Generous-hearted Emma was moved by this argument. He went on to point out Lady Nelson might elect to sue for a divorce, although, on the other hand, her temper was such that it might incline her to punish her husband's infidelity by refraining from taking action, and so, even in the event of Sir William's death, prevent him from making her whom he called his 'wife before God 'also his wife before man.

Sir William was brought to declare publicly that the friendship between his wife and Nelson was platonic. An acknowledged accouchement would confute him, or force him to a claim his state of health made untenable. Mr. Greville had been shocked by the want of reticence and tact already exhibited. Now, in view of the Prince of Wales's attentions, and all to which it might lead, he exerted himself to the adjustment of the position. Emma was ever clay in Mr. Greville's hands and plastic to his moulding. She was proud when Greville said the Prince was attracted by her, and listened with avidity when he told her that she had been the toast of the evening at Mr. Fox's. Her vanity was all agog, and Mr. Greville's knowledge how she was appreciated was the healing salve for the wound which Queen Caroline inflicted.

Nelson was recalled to his ship, and Emma took leave of him with many tears and protestations.

'How can I leave you to bear your pains and apprehensions alone?'

'How can I part with my hero?' was the burden of their talk in that interview so overladen with emotion.

'You will never let me be without news?' he begged.

'I will write by every opportunity,' she asseverated. 'What pleasure shall I have in life save writing to him who makes my entire happiness?'

'And keep all men at a distance until your Nelson returns to guard you.'

'You do not doubt me, Nelson, you do not doubt your Emma? 'she asked tenderly.

' 'Tis your innocence I fear, and the damnable rascality of the Prince and his crew,' he answered gloomily.

Emma promised all and more than Nelson asked. Since it made him uneasy, she said she would not speak to the Prince, nor accept the banquet he had already offered her; she would not let him come at all to Piccadilly.

But for themselves they must keep all they were to each other a secret, an inviolable, absolute secret, else Lady Nelson would make trouble, and his enemies, always on the alert, would have a lever to move the Admiralty against him. Emma's tongue spoke Greville's words. She proceeded to tell Nelson she had thought out a plan for their correspondence, in case it should be intercepted or come into unfriendly hands. The plan was Greville's invention, but it became Emma's in the telling. Nelson was slow to subscribe to it, but could refuse his Emma nothing in taking leave of her at such a time.

Greville's plan was that they were to pretend the existence of a Mr. and Mrs. Thomson, of whom the former was supposed to be serving under Nelson and on his ship, while the latter, hourly expecting her confinement, was committed to the kind-hearted care of Lady Hamilton. Under pretext of committing news of the mother and child to the anxious naval officer, Lady Hamilton was to address all letters bearing upon this interesting subject to Mr. Thomson 'by favour of the Admiral,' who in return would address his replies to Mrs. Thomson 'under the

260

care of Lady Hamilton.' These letters, should they happen to be perused by any other party, would thus be capable of an explanation which would make up in plausibility what it lacked in truth, and meanwhile the guilty lovers could carry on their habitual correspondence under their proper names.

Nelson agreed with difficulty. He hated subterfuge, and, had not his hand been forced by cajolery and argument, would have been bold in acknowledging the true state of affairs. The price of his complaisance was Emma's promise that she would not see or speak to the 'first gentleman in Europe,' Prince George of Wales. We shall see how she kept her promise.

After Admiral Nelson left London to sail once more against the French, Emma retired to her room and gave herself up to tears. She was disconsolate at the departure of one whose championship was her greatest claim to consideration. She was also dismayed at what lay before her, although it was so much less strange or new to her than Nelson supposed. Nevertheless, that very evening, to revive her spirits, she went to the Opera to hear Banti. Before many hours had elapsed, whilst still her vows to Nelson were hot on her lips, sealed there by his kisses, she not only gave audience to the Prince but met his attentions in so engaging a manner, that nothing would serve him but that the meeting should be quickly repeated. She excused herself easily for her misfeasance:

'Sir William's pension depends on it,' she told Mr. Greville; 'he is himself writing to Nelson that we have no choice.' And Sir William actually did write of the 'absolute necessity 'of giving a dinner to the Prince of Wales! It appeared that he had expressed a desire to hear Emma sing a duet with the famous cantatrice, and afterwards witness some of her incomparable Attitudes. Sir William was pressing his application for additional pension, and he dared not offend the Prince.

Before the admiral's furious answer arrived, events had moved rapidly. The Prince was no laggard in love-making, if every other offence could be brought to his charge. He was of catholic tastes in that regard and there is no doubt Nelson had reason for his vehemence. The Prince was quite untrammelled by those conscientious scruples which distinguished his august parents. He had been for some time enamoured of Emma's beauty, of which he had acquired several counterfeit presentments, notably Mr. Romney's pictures of her as 'Joan of Arc 'and 'The Magdalene.' He knew more about her history than Nelson himself, and there is little doubt he now proposed to enjoy charms which by the proved consent of so many polite people were of quite superlative excellence. He accordingly honoured Sir William by inviting himself to his house. Up to this moment Emma had been flattered, and by no means unwilling to listen to the Prince's compliments. Now she found herself embarrassed.

Again Greville was consulted; we see his hand in the entertainment that was so quickly arranged. Emma must sing, laugh, talk, and lead the Prince on. He, Mr. Greville, would charge himself with the rest. It was but a matter of postponement, of a 'promise to pay,' that could be cancelled or contrived against after the matter of the pension had been concluded.

Nelson got wind of the affair, and was wrought to the highest pitch of nervous excitement by the prospect of his adored one, who was so soon to be the mother of his child, being placed in circumstances in which she might be compelled to yield to a royal seducer.

'You are too beautiful not to have enemies,' he wrote to Emma, 'and even one visit will stamp you. He is without one spark of honour in these matters, and would leave you to bewail your folly. But I know you too well not to be convinced that you cannot be seduced by any Prince in Europe.'

The conviction did not allay his anxiety when he heard that the entertainment could not be avoided.

'I am so agitated that I can write nothing. I knew it would be so and you can't help it. Do not sit long at table. Good God! he will be next you, and telling you soft things. If he does, tell it out at table, and turn him out of the house. Oh God! that I was dead! But I do not, my dearest Emma, blame you, nor do I fear your constancy. I am gone almost mad, but you cannot help it. If I was in town nothing should make me dine with you that damned day. I have read your resolution never to go where the fellow is, but you must have him at home. Oh God! but you cannot, I suppose, help it, you cannot turn him out of your own house. If you cannot get rid of this, I hope you will tell Sir William never to bring the fellow again.'

Again, and in still greater heat of passion, he wrote:

'I cannot help saying a few words on that fellow's dining with you, for you do not believe it to be out of love for Sir William. I knew that he would visit you, and that you could not help coming downstairs when the Prince was there. His words are so charming that, I am told, no person can withstand them. If I had been worth ten

263

millions I would have betted every farthing that you would not have stayed in the house knowing that he was there, and if you did, which I would not have believed, that you would have sent him a proper message by Sir William, and sent him to hell. And knowing your determined courage when you had got down, I would have laid my head upon the block with the axe uplifted, and said "strike" if Emma does not say to Sir William before the fellow "my character cannot, shall not suffer by permitting him to visit." . . . You cannot now help the villain's dining with you. Get rid of it as well as you can. Do not let him come downstairs with you, or hand you up. If you do, tell me, and then . . .'

All this heat and anxiety might have been avoided. The Prince of Wales did dine with Sir William, but fate intervened to prevent the contamination Nelson dreaded for his lady. To entertain royalty necessitates a certain amount of preparation and delay. It was January before Banti could be secured. La Banti was at the banquet, and the Prince, but the hostess was on a bed of sickness! Her excuses had to be made; they were accepted with ill-humour, a show of incivility, and want of credence. But Mr. Greville was again at hand to smooth down matters. He had seen to it that all the guests were to the Prince's mind, his own boon companions, there were ladies present almost as fair as Emma, certainly as frail; there was wine and song, Mr. Fox and Lord Barrymore. After the first hour the fun waxed fast and furious and the absence of its prime incentive hardly considered.

Meanwhile Emma, in the solitude of her own apartments, attended only by her ever faithful mother, went through her tribulation with the courage we are unable to deny her. Sir William sent the report to Nelson at sea. Emma was not well, she was troubled with 'convulsive complaints in the stomach, and vomitings, which required some confinement, and required her to take a little tartar emetic.'

Shortly afterwards he was able to announce that she was 'certainly much better, but not quite free from bile.' Those two communications contain the sum of Sir William's acknowledgment of the event that now occurred in his house. But by means of the Thomson device Nelson was kept better informed. He poured out in return all the emotions that rent his bosom, although not failing to couch his letters in a form that was consistent with the fiction of his anxious subordinate.

'I delivered poor Mrs. Thomson's note; her friend is truly thankful for her kindness and your goodness. Who does not admire your benevolent heart? Poor man, he is very anxious, and begs you will, if she is not able, write a line just to comfort him. He appears to feel very much her situation. He is so agitated, and will be so for 2 or 3 days, that he says he cannot write, and that I must send his kind love and affectionate regards.'

'Pray tell Mrs. Thomson,' he wrote again, 'her kind friend is very uneasy about her, and prays most fervently for her safety—and he says he can only depend on your goodness.'

These letters antedated the birth for which they were all waiting. When at last that happy news reached him, the enthusiasm of his letter was too ardent to appear truly vicarious.

'I believe dear Mrs. Thomson's friend will go mad with joy. He cries, prays, and performs all tricks, yet dares not show all or any of his feelings, but he has only me to consult with. He swears he will drink your health this day in a bumper, and damn me if I don't join him in spite of all the doctors in Europe, for none regard you with truer affection than myself. You are a dear good creature, and your kindness

265

and attention to poor Mrs. T. stamps you higher than ever in my mind. I cannot write, I am so agitated by this young man at my elbow. I believe he is foolish, he does nothing but rave about you and her. I own I participate in his joy and cannot write anything.'

And yet once more he wrote to say how good a soul and how full of feeling was that friend of dear Mrs. Thomson, how much he wished to see her and her little one. That

'good and dear friend does not think it proper at present to write with his own hand, but hopes the day may not be far distant when he may be united for ever to the object of his wishes, his only, only love. He swears before Heaven that he will marry her as soon as possible, which he fervently prays may be soon.'

By many other spontaneous ebullitions of joy Nelson's contribution to the correspondence between imaginary persons was spoiled of verisimilitude. He certainly did not share Emma's aptitude for dissimulation. He sent Emma an order on his agents for a hundred pounds to be distributed among those who had been useful on the recent occasion, and he told Emma how dear she was to him, how she was to kiss and bless for him his dear little girl, which he wished to be called Emma, 'out of gratitude to dear, good Lady Hamilton.'

On the other hand, the resolution with which Emma carried through this matter may well have astonished even those who have witnessed her courage on less notable occasions. To within a few days of her confinement, she never omitted to write to the father of the expected child, nor spared any precaution to prevent a mischance that might

266

have acquainted her household with the nature of her condition, or even have aroused suspicion.

In the last days of January her child was born, in a period of storm such as marked more than one of its father's great adventures—the voyage from Naples to Palermo with the royal fugitives, for example, and his first arrival at Yarmouth after the victory of the Nile. Once more did Emma's magnificent health stand her in good stead. Her recovery was extraordinarily rapid, so much so indeed, that in less than a week from the date of the birth she was able to rise and make her appearance in public, thus confirming the story, assiduously circulated by Greville, that it was but a bilious fever had prevented her meeting the Prince.

Emma's first objective was to get rid of the living evidence of her recent illness. Concealing the infant in a large muff, and taking with her Mr. Oliver, whom she had provided with his present situation as confidential agent to Lord Nelson, she drove in her own carriage to a house in Little Titchfield Street, where she committed the babe to the custody of Mrs. Gilson, with whom she had previously concluded arrangements to this end. What her feelings were in thus being compelled to part with her offspring it is idle to surmise. Although this was the third time she had brought into the world one of those unhappy innocents who, until the coming of the merciful new dispensation, were debarred from entering the congregation of the Lord, we have nowhere evidence of repentance, nor even of acknowledgment, other than pecuniary, of the awful responsibility she incurred.

Her next anxiety was to meet the Prince again. Sir William had not failed to keep her informed of how ill his own affairs progressed. He had thought, in the event of his request for an increased pension being refused or referred, he would have been allowed to retract his resignation and return to Naples. But Paget had already been sent out and his application was practically ignored. Sir William, like Emma, deemed his services had been great, and but ill rewarded. He had spent lavishly and was now in debt. Emma had been extravagant also. He was querulous, which is not to be wondered at in his situation. But Emma met him with unfailing good-humour and good spirits, and bade him be not anxious, for now that her health was restored she had little doubt she could work upon the Prince of Wales. She was in ignorance of the fact that she had missed her opportunity for ever. The Prince was engrossed with the young widow, Mrs. Fitzherbert, and his desire for the wife of the whilom ambassador died a natural death.

Emma was not one to grieve long over the Prince's defection. Nelson still held all of her large heart that was not filled by vanity or Greville, and Nelson wrote her differently from what she anticipated about the child. Emma could abandon an infant as lightly as she could discard a lover. But to Nelson the event was of overmastering importance; and it was fame and honour he would give up rather than the little Horatia should want a father. He wrote that he was ready to resign his command, leave England and his post, and return with Emma to Bronte, to the Sicilian estate granted him by the grateful Ferdinand. There, with her and the child, he could build up a new life, even without the divorce for which he now saw his wife would never apply. He called Emma his 'own dear wife.'

'I never did love any one else. I never had a dear pledge of love till you gave me one, and you, thank my God, never gave one to anybody else.'

Emma had no mind to leave England at this juncture. She pleaded that Sir William Hamilton was 'old and feeble,' 'needing her company and ministration,' and owned that she 'dreaded the outcry 'such a proceeding on Nelson's part would provoke. But when, as has been seen, the Prince disappointed her, and she became aware that he had abandoned the pursuit, it needed all Greville's wit to save her from changing her determination.

Nelson offered to abandon everything for her sake. She might have said 'yes 'to his request, and the course of the world's history been changed. The Prince's defection had been followed by a slackening of the attentions of the Duke of Queensberry. The birth of this third child, and the want of professional tendance with which the event had been met, had destroyed her figure, and the duke was ever *gourmet* rather than *gourmand*. Everything combined to make London insupportable to her. She *might* have left Sir William Hamilton, and thus forced a scandal even greater than that she had already evoked, had not Greville decreed otherwise. At all hazards Charles Greville had to prevent her acknowledging that she had given birth to a child, for that child, of whatever paternity, had been born in wedlock, and therefore, in law, to Sir William Hamilton.

Mr. Greville was conscious Emma's character had retrograded, although always oblivious of his own share in its despoilment. He had no illusion about her, he could even see that her beauty was becoming somewhat overblown and her complexion thickened. It was time she settled down, not at Bronte with Nelson, in open defiance of society, but in the country, somewhere near town, where he could keep in touch with her, and charge himself with the comparative decorousness of her conduct.

This was Greville's decision; he wanted to get Emma out of London, where already her presence had brought him inconvenience, and was likely to bring him more. That Nelson should have had the same idea at the same time was not wonderful. War, long protracted, had depreciated the value of every form of property. This was a good time to buy land. Nelson wrote again that, if Emma had no mind to join him at Bronte, what did she say to joining him in a home in England? Sir William could live with them, she could manage it in her own way. She was to write him openly, fully. He had 'nothing but her welfare in his mind.' But when he came back and the war was over, they must 'be all together, you and I, and Mrs. Thomson's little one.'

Greville seized the occasion of the letter and turned it to his own advantage. Before Emma had time to wonder if she could abandon the delights of London and give herself up to country pursuits, a pleasant residential estate had been found at Merton in Surrey. Negotiations were entered into hurriedly and Nelson was soon transported by the news that, if he wished it, Merton could be his on easy terms. A

270

description followed. Nelson wrote that if his Emma was satisfied he was, he had no doubt Merton was all she described. She was to buy and furnish it for him. It was Sir William who wrote in answer to that; he was still the figure-head, although Greville pulled the strings:

'I have lived with our dear Emma several years, I know her merit, I have a great opinion of the head and heart God Almighty has been pleased to give her, but a seaman alone could have given a fine woman full powers to choose and fit up a residence for him without seeing it for himself. You are in luck, for on my conscience I verily believe that a place so suitable to your views could not have been found and at so cheap a rate. And if you stay away three days longer I do not think you can have any wish but you will find it completed here. . . . I never saw so many conveniences united in so small a compass. You have nothing but to come and enjoy immediately.'

Once the house had been secured Emma became enthusiastic at the idea of being its mistress. She began to find happiness in seeing herself as chatelaine, with Nelson by her side. Sir William had ceased to interest and his talks with Greville about pictures and *virtu* frankly bored her. She needed a fresh *entourage*. From London's neglect and the Prince's she turned to Nelson's warm and passionate love-letters and the future he was always picturing when he might spend his life in worshipping her. She wanted to be worshipped. Her youth was on the wane, although that she would not confess even to herself. Nelson was right; it was a home she needed; and Merton could be made into a very paradise.

Now she threw herself into the furnishing and embellishing of the house and grounds with all and more than her old impetuosity, and the greater zest because Nelson declared his intention to bequeath the estate to her at his death, and meanwhile to regard her as its sole mistress. Nelson was becoming more desirable; fresh glory was already his. Copenhagen had been added to his laurels and his fame was ever increasing. He wrote he thought he saw the beginning of the end of the long war in which he had rendered such signal service. He yearned for 'home, Wife, and child.' By now he had forgotten he ever had any wife but Emma! God alone knows for what Emma yearned, perhaps she persuaded herself it was Nelson. In any case she occupied herself in making the new house worthy of him, and of them both.

Nelson, when at length he was free to take a short leave, found her already installed at Merton. Of all forms and manners of life, that of the English country gentleman is the gentlest and most agreeable, and here, at Merton Place, Nelson enjoyed it for a brief period. He made friends with his neighbours, who, less sophisticated than the people in London, accepted the position that the frequent presence of Sir William Hamilton at Merton made reasonable. He went regularly to church, and gave liberally to all the charities of the neighbourhood. He made a pretence of farming, and took interest in his dairy. 'Mrs. Thomson's baby,' the infant Horatia, was brought there, and on her was lavished all the love Nelson could spare from Emma.

The house, the small farmery and projected improvements, Emma and Horatia, his wide charities and quick friendships, filled his days. He belonged to his country, but all this belonged to him. So he conceived, his blind eye turned towards Lady Nelson and her claims, and the other bright with short-sighted happiness.

CHAPTER XVI

Clouds gather and the sky is overcast. The death of Sir William Hamilton is followed by Arnodeo Gibilmanna's successful attempts to blackmail his widow. He has obtained possession of Lord Bristol's letters, and threatens to show them to Nelson. Emma impoverishes herself to meet his demands, and then enjoys a brief period of respite with Nelson at Merton. But the battle of Trafalgar ends her happiness, and henceforth all is gloom. Gibilmanna returns to the attack, and when Emma can no longer satisfy his cupidity, sells her correspondence to Lovewell, a publisher of the Barbican. Emma cannot face the gossip that ensues, and retires to Calais, where her troubles end.

DEATH has many henchmen but none more trusty than Care. Physicians and chirurgeons, Health's bodyguard of gentlemen-at-arms, lack art and weapons to repel that insidious foe. The whole pharmacopoeia contains no antidote for Care's slow poison; the pathology of anxiety is as yet unprinted. That man's days are numbered whom Care effectively besets.

Sir William Hamilton was thus attacked. Serenity of temper, moderation in his habits, agreeable occupation, plenitude of intelligent interests had kept him younger than his years, but the end was in sight. He was harassed by the constant drain upon his resources, due to his wife's imprudence and his own. He had entertained lavishly, believing that money expended in hospitality to high and influential persons would prove to have been invested judiciously, and he had also expended large sums of money from his private purse in forwarding his country's public interests in the Mediterranean. Now he saw no hope of

274

reimbursement from a ministry who disregarded all his claims. The purchase of Merton by Nelson, and the removal there of a greater part of his household, mitigated his embarrassments for a time, but creditors, no less than age, will not tarry for ever. At this time, too, he began to discover that he had no longer the strength to hold even his undignified position in the triple alliance, and had sunk below his wife's consideration. He had looked to enjoy seclusion and peace at Merton, and perhaps economy. But Emma willed otherwise. As Greville truly said, she was 'ever the same Emma.' No sooner was Nelson at sea than her extravagances were renewed. She kept open house in Piccadilly and filled Merton with guests, employing the intervals in visits to which she dragged Sir William with or against his will. The waning of her charms, and another cause to be explained later, made her restless, and she sought admiration where erstwhile she would have disdained it. Sir William understood Nelson's temper better than she did and trembled lest her escapades should come to his ears. Peace was what Sir William Hamilton longed for in his old age. But where Emma was, there was no peace. Save when Nelson was by her side, enveloping her with such adoring love and single-hearted belief in her virtue that for lack of opportunity she deserved it.

Sir William Hamilton did not waver in his chivalrous loyalty to his wife, and there is indisputably something pathetic in the figure he presented in his endeavours to persuade Emma from the consequences of her new imprudences. Whilst Sir William Hamilton lived Nelson knew no anxiety about Emma, and by the time he was removed from caring for her, Nelson himself was within sight of his glorious end.

Greville viewed with no less alarm than his uncle the failure of the Merton plan as a means of economy. Greville never forgot that he was his uncle's expectant heir, and he contemplated the lavish expenditure with a good deal of concern as being sure to depreciate largely that residuary property of which he was the legatee. Remonstrance to Emma was useless. She twitted him with his parsimony and boasted that Nelson grudged her nothing. She said he would return laden with prize-money, and pour it all in her lap. Greville's criticisms, his coldness and ill-concealed contempt, his polished wit, and calm superiority, provoked her ever into fresh excesses. It was through him she had lost her self-respect, and it was but justice if his fortune should suffer from her lack of it. He turned his attention to his uncle and presently brought forward proofs that it was not only extravagance Emma was committing, but that already she was exciting comment on her conduct with a Neapolitan lawyer, one Arnodeo Gibilmanna, by whom she was attended whenever Nelson was absent from home and Sir William otherwise engaged. There was exaggeration in his allegations, but when did Greville wait for truth when subterfuge better answered his purpose? He succeeded in raising altercation between Emma and Sir William, and even led the septuagenarian to reconsider for a time his whole mode of life. His mind was preceding his body in the inevitable decay. The letter that he wrote to Emma is full of inconsistencies, and plaints that led to nowhere, yet exhibiting the result of Greville's handiwork.

'I am arrived at the age when some repose is really necessary. I promised myself a quiet home at Merton, and although I was sensible, and I said so when I married, that I should be superannuated when my wife would be in her full beauty and vigour of youth, I think you should show me some consideration. . . . There is no time for nonsense and trifling, I know and admire your talents and many qualities, but I am not blind to your defects, and confess having many myself; therefore let us bear and forbear, for God's sake.'

He had no longer the power to express himself, but what he was pleading for was that she should cease to squander Nelson's fortune and his own, that she should not show herself in public attended by Signor Arnodeo Gibilmanna, and should have some regard for her good name. In any case that she should let him have repose. He could not rest whilst he felt that Emma was betraying Nelson and all their lives hanging over a volcano. Emma could only have deceived Nelson once; he knew it, and she no less well. But what Sir William Hamilton did not know was that the man against whom he warned her was also aware of Nelson's idiosyncrasy and was using his knowledge in a way that accounted for much of her conduct which both Greville and Sir William found inexplicable. It was not what Greville hinted, and Sir William tried to disbelieve that made her accept Signor Gibilmanna's unwelcome attentions. She had told Nelson of her past, but that past had neither included her children nor . . . my Lord of Bristol!

Arnodeo Gibilmanna was from Sicily. He was a lawyer, settled in Girgenti, but with frequent engagements in the court-house at Palermo. He had been backwards and forwards whilst the King and Queen were sheltering there and so became acquainted with the Hamiltons. He had quickly fallen a victim to Emma's charms. But Emma was engrossed with Nelson, and at that period of her life would not have stooped to one of Gibilmanna's position. The lawyer bided his time, and found his opportunity when the Hamiltons sailed for Naples leaving the house vacant. Emma left many of her paraphernalia behind her, amongst them letters, clothes, and jewellery. The latter were restored to her; Gibilmanna charging himself with their care, and honestly restoring them, making indeed a journey to Naples for that purpose. Emma received him with kindness and gratitude, feeding alike his vanity and passion. He was really a low fellow and unworthy of what she bestowed on him.

It was two years later that Gibilmanna came to England, and, having good introductions as well as his acquaintanceship with the Hamiltons, he was received into society, and used every opportunity to press his suit. Emma was, as has been seen, less exclusive in London than she had been in Naples, and at first was flattered by the idea that the lawyer, of whom, however, she had but faint recollection, had followed her from Italy. But in the end his Sicilian methods failed to commend themselves to her. Nelson was on his way home to console her for the Prince's indifference, society's neglect. If she had been again imprudent, she was characteristically again repentant. She thought to flout the

Sicilian and rid herself of him easily, but reckoned without her man. He had strained his resources to follow her to England, and, after the favour she first showed him, had no mind to be balked of her possession. He began by pleading and playing the lover boldly.

'*Je suis avocat criminel, je comprends votre disposition amoureuse.* I, I am the man for you, not ze English sailor, who is besides away.'

His dark eyes could betray an immensity of feeling, and although he spoke bad French, broken English, and the Sicilian dialect, his voice was throughout low and musical. Emma was *amoureuse*, but for the moment Nelson held her heart. She said 'No' and 'No' again to Gibilmanna, and when he would have surprised her, forcing what she withheld, she let him see it was no assumed aversion she betrayed. Lust, but not love, as we have had occasion to remark before, knows no scruples. It was Nelson who stood in Gibilmanna's way. Well, *ce cher* Nelson should know what her life had been in Naples. He had letters . . .

Emma had forgotten her lost letters, and took quick alarm. What did he intend doing with them? Showing them to Nelson. Whose, for instance? Well, there was one from Lord Bristol. Emma crimsoned and her heart began to beat; her mind had ever been uneasy about Lord Bristol; he was at least as imprudent as herself, and if it came to Nelson's ears that she had had commerce with him, she knew not how she would explain the matter. Now she pleaded with Gibilmanna for the letter. And it is unsafe to turn suppliant when one has a favour to refuse. Emma paid dearly for the letter, which we reproduce for the better enlightenment of our readers.

'EVER DEAREST EMMA—Write me word, explicitly, how you are, what you are, and where you are; and be sure that, wheresoever I am, still I am your's, my dearest Emma.

'I went down to your Opera box two minutes after you left it; and should have seen you on the morning of my departure—but was detained in the arms of Murphy, as Lady Eden expresses it, and was too late.

'You say nothing of the adorable Queen; I hope, she has not forgot me; but, as Shakespeare says, "Who doats, must doubt "; and I verily deem her the very best edition of a woman I ever saw—I mean, of such as are not in folio, and are to be had in sheets.

'This moment I receive your billet-doux and very dulcet it is!

'I will frankly confess to you, that my health most seriously and urgently requires the balmy atmosphere of those I love and who love me.

'Sweet Emma, adieu! Remember me in the warmest and most enthusiastic stile, to your friend, to my friend, and the friend of human kind.'

The letter itself was not convincing evidence of misdemeanour, and Nelson would never so have regarded it. The allusion to the Queen was in bad taste, but the time had gone by when Emma would ruin herself to protect the reputation of the Queen of Naples.

Emma, however, never knew how to deal with scoundrels, and Gibilmanna profited greatly by working now on her fears, and now on her feelings. Her weakness proved her undoing. When he had ceased to value that which he had striven so violently to obtain, he began to persecute her with requests for money, and to render her life intolerable by his persistence.

We have seen at Up Park how despair made her reckless. She was no less despairing nor less reckless when she had been forced into establishing Arnodeo Gibilmanna as steward of the estate at Merton, and lived in dread of what else he might demand from her as the price of his continued silence.

This summer that was to prove the last of Sir William Hamilton's life saw Nelson again in England. Sir William wished to pay a farewell visit to his Milford property and Greville was ready to accompany him. Nothing would serve Emma but that she and Nelson should go too. She said she had never seen Milford and longed to know how it looked. In truth, by now she knew it was Greville's design to alter the provisions of his uncle's will in his own favour, and she did not care that uncle and nephew should long be out of her sight together. Sir William was falling into something like second childhood, and could be moved this way and that.

The journey was supposed to be for Sir William, but it resolved itself into a triumphant progress for the national hero. Nothing was more to Emma's liking. Huzzaing mobs and rocking steeples, flying flags and public orations—these made the wine of life for her, and with it her cup could not be filled too often. At Swansea, however, the whim took her to stay and take a course of sea-bathing, such as had been wont to benefit her in her early womanhood. Nelson was willing, but Greville impatient. She pretended she thought it was because Sir William could not brook the quiet of Swansea that he wanted her to move on.

'As I see it is pain to you to remain here, let me beg of you to fix your time for going. Whether I dye in Piccadilly or any other spot in England, 'tis the same to me; but I remember the time when you wished for tranquillity, and now all visiting and bustle is your liking. However, I will do what you please, being ever your affectionate and obedient E. H.'

The unfair charge pricked Sir William.

'I neither love bustle nor great company,' he replied. 'I am in no hurry, and am exceedingly glad to give every satisfaction to our best friend, our dear Lord Nelson. Sea-bathing is useful to your health; I see it is and wish you to continue a little longer; I care not a pin for the great world, and am attached to no one as much as you.'

But Emma still was piqued and would not yield gracefully. 'I go when you tell me, the coach is ready,' she answered. 'This is not a fair answer to a fair confession of mine,' wrote Sir William, with some reason.

Sir William only lived a few months more. He died in Piccadilly, in the presence of his wife and of Lord Nelson. At the last his mind seemed to be fully restored to him, and the knowledge of the position he had, if not created, at least accepted. His words are on record, and have been often used to the end he had in mind.

'Nelson, our friendship has been long, and I glory in my friend. I hope you will see justice done to Emma by ministers, for you know how great her services have been and what she has done for her country. Protect my dear wife; and may God bless you, and give you victory, and guard you in battle.' And to his wife he said:

'My incomparable Emma, you have never in thought, word, or deed offended me; and let me thank you again, and again, for your affectionate kindness to me, all the time of our ten years' happy union.'

In Sir William Hamilton Emma lost her truest friend, the bulwark that had protected her, at least as far as was possible, from the scorn and hostility of the world. Notwithstanding his intentions, but perhaps through Greville's vigilant and incessant endeavours, the provision made for her appeared inadequate to their friends—to the Queen of Naples, for example, and to Lord Nelson. But the unit by which the former measured wealth was not one to be accepted in this country, and the latter would have deemed any provision that was not limitless inadequate to the merits of his beloved. The actual amount was three hundred pounds in ready money, the contents of the house in Piccadilly, and an income of eight hundred pounds per annum. Inasmuch as to the last he counted upon his pension being continued to his widow, and some monetary compensation being made to her for her services to her country, Sir William's memory is surely not to be considered as sullied by parsimony in his ordering of Emma's affairs. Her origin and upbringing being taken into consideration, she might indeed be regarded as fortunate in the material position in which she was now confirmed. Moreover, there was still Nelson to protect and provide for her interests.

Nelson took immediate steps to repair what he deemed the shortcoming of Sir William Hamilton's will. Almost before the funeral of her husband had been accomplished with every mark of the royal recognition that had been denied to him in his lifetime, Nelson settled an annual income of twelve hundred pounds for her benefit. It was to be paid in monthly instalments. He further gave her unrestricted occupation of Merton Place and made a separate provision for Horatia. He took up his responsibilities eagerly, having no hesitation in making definite that which had long been obvious.

Emma's situation, in a word, would now appear both comfortable and secure even to persons accustomed by inheritance to luxury and freedom from monetary care. Nevertheless, it is a fact that the day Sir William Hamilton died marked the end of Emma's prosperity. Henceforth we see the clouds menacing and ever more heavy. Her history is one to which it is unnecessary to add moral reflection. He who runs may read, and, reading, may well be dismayed. No better illustration is ever likely to be forthcoming of the evanescent nature of fortune won by means inconsistent with virtue.

The first effect of her husband's death was to deprive her of the ostensible guarantee of what the world calls respectability. To a certain extent it had been necessary and politic to accept the guarantee given by Sir William's countenance that the friendship between her and Nelson was platonic. Blenheim might imitate Windsor in refusing to receive Lady Hamilton, and Canterbury might take the cue from Blenheim, but not one of the three could prove that that which satisfied

Emma's husband was just cause for their condemnation. They had to rely for her exclusion, as they could do securely enough, on her ill-conduct prior to her marriage. But with the death of Sir William Hamilton the polite world felt itself released from the obligation of longer maintaining the fiction, and the claims of Lady Nelson to her husband's society were now again put forward. It is a misfortune that they were pressed in such a manner, and at such a time, for it seemed a concerted attack on one who, for the moment at least, was unable to defend herself. Nelson's reply was vigorous and complete. He had done with Lady Nelson for once and for ever. He would not pretend otherwise, nor 'offer her a consideration which she had ever denied to him and his friends.'

Emma was not inconsolable at the death of her husband, yet disposed to offer more than a show of resistance to Nelson's decision that as soon as her mourning would permit she should accompany him to Merton, and take up her position there definitely and for ever. Nelson neither in battle nor at any time had respect for formal convention, but was possessed of a kind of honest courage very different from bravado, which, had the woman of his choice been worthy of him, might have won for her eventually the respect he claimed. But this was not to be.

Greville did his share towards making Emma's next step inevitable. The breath was hardly out of his uncle's body before he threw off all restraint in his dealings with the widow. He had now come thoroughly to dislike her, and had no longer scruples in showing it. He gave her notice that she must at once quit the late ambassador's town house. As executor he was prepared to satisfy her claims; as purist, moralist, formalist, as Charles Greville in short, he would not countenance her staying there one hour in the enjoyment of Nelson's company. Nelson would have hurried her to Merton, but at Merton Gibilmanna was established, and she could not face the position she had herself created. Her one hope was that she might buy off the Sicilian with money. He often said he hated England and longed for his own country. The more she cared for Nelson and clung to his regard for her, the more was the scoundrel able to work upon her fears. She would not go to Merton until she had received from Greville the means to persuade him away. She removed to a small house, No. 11, Clarges Street, there to wait the proving of Sir William Hamilton's will, and the distribution of the objects of virtu he had accumulated. Nelson fumed and fretted at the delay, but she was able to soothe him.

At length everything was in order and Emma had money enough at her command to satisfy even Italian cupidity. She went back to Merton with Nelson to take up her abode there openly as his mistress. Gibilmanna was given £800 for all the letters in his possession and the relinquishment of any claim to her society. It was like Emma's imprudence that she neither checked nor counted what he restored to her. She had never known the full extent to which she had been robbed, she only knew the full extent to which she had been terrorised. She paid him all that he asked, seized the packet he gave her, and destroyed it. Now she could face Nelson and her future. And indeed for a time it seemed as if she would behave prudently. She had Nelson and her child, and Merton was an over-growing interest.

But the disregard shown to public opinion by the open way they were living together as man and wife increased the disapprobation of the Court and the Ministry, and decreased Emma's chance of obtaining pecuniary recognition of any claims she might make upon the Government. Whilst Nelson lived this did not trouble her greatly; at least we cannot lay to her charge that she was mercenary.

It is not part of our scheme to follow Nelson's rapid movements in pursuit of the French fleet, or to detail all he did prior to his culminating triumph and glorious death in the Bay of Trafalgar. During all the period covered by these high affairs he was of necessity often absent from his Emma. With a sense of discipline contrasting favourably with his sense of morality, he ever refused her reiterated, if somewhat insincere, entreaties to let her join him on his ship. How ardent his love for her was, how constantly his thoughts were with her, his frequent letters show.

'You, my own Emma, are my first and last thoughts, and to the last moment of my breath they will be occupied in leaving you independent of the world, and all I long in the world that you will be a kind and affectionate Mother to my dear daughter Horatia. But, my Emma, your Nelson is not the nearer being lost to you for taking care of you in case of events which are only known when they are to happen and to an all wise Providence. I hope for many years of comfort with you, only think of all you wish me to say, and you may be assured it exceeds if possible your wishes. May God protect you and my dear Horatia prays ever your most faithful and affectionate.'

Horatia suffering from an attack of smallpox, her father was in an agony of apprehension.

'My beloved, how I feel for your situation, and that of our dear Horatia, our dear child. Unexampled love, never, I trust will be diminished, never; no, even death with all his terrors would be jubilant compared even to the thought. Dear wife, good adorable friend, how I love you, and what I would not give to be with you at this moment, for I am for ever all yours.'

And once more:

'My own dearest beloved Emma, Your own Nelson's pride and delight. I find myself within six days of the Enemy, and I have every reason to hope that the sixth of June will immortalise your own Nelson, your fond Nelson. May God send me victory, and us a happy and speedy meeting. Adl. Cockrane is sending home a vessel this day, therefore only pray for my success, and my Laurels I shall with pleasure lay at your feet, and a sweet kiss will be an ample reward for all your faithful Nelson's hard fag, for Ever and Ever I am your faithful, ever faithful and affectionate   NELSON AND BRONTE.'

He did not live long enough to realise that his love was expended on a woman who every day, almost every hour, was proving herself unworthy of it. Emma had already begun to take spirits, her kindness to her child became intermittent, and she found occasion to quarrel with many of her friends and neighbours. In every way she was showing the effect of that loosening of moral fibre incidental to her mode of life. Unstable in her habits, given over to the pleasures of the table, her figure and complexion began to suffer; the former became gross and the latter blotchy. Her last attempt to improve the one, and correct the other, antedated Nelson's last voyage.

She went again to Southend for the sea-bathing that had so often stood her in good stead. There, by a strange coincidence, she met that very Jane Powell who had been her fellow-servant and companion at Mrs. Budd's. Jane exclaimed at her portliness, and Emma retorted with the other's wrinkles, the prominence of her bones, the thinness of her hair. Jane tells us that she found Emma in every way altered from the good-natured, good-hearted girl she had known. Jane was at the zenith of her career as a great artist, and, having no cause for jealousy, may well be accepted as a veracious chronicler.

It was whilst at Southend exchanging confidences with Jane Powell, and incidentally exhibiting herself as a changed and deteriorated character, that Emma heard Nelson had anchored at Spithead. She knew he would be displeased she had left Horatia, only recently recovered from her illness, and needing sea-bathing at least as urgently as her mother. She hurried back with all speed to Merton, in order that he should find her at her post. She greeted him with extravagant demonstration of affection. She kept herself well in hand all the time of his visit, abstaining from spirits and holding her temper in check. But perhaps the restraint she put upon herself made it easy for her, when his summons came, to urge him to obey it.

'Your country calls you, Nelson, and you must go,' she exclaimed grandiloquently.

'If there were more Emmas there would be more Nelsons,' he answered huskily. It never entered his head that already his company irked her, that she found his goodness and simplicity alike uncongenial, and the dutifulness he expected was a mere mask to her impatience of restraint. He never doubted or distrusted her. His love was as loyal as his nature, and no greater praise can be accorded it. He had been months in search of the elusive Villeneuve, incidentally enduring untold hardships of cold and sea-sickness and the always increasing maladies of a body that matched his spirit so ill. The repose at Merton with Emma seemed happiness almost too great; it was calm after storm, harbour after open sea. He was engrossed, too, with Horatia; fatherhood was extraordinarily precious to him.

But when the call came it found him ready. At half-past ten at night, after a farewell to both of them, the poignancy of which we need not chronicle, he entered his post-chaise, and started for Portsmouth on the first stage of his last journey. Here is his own record:

'Friday night at half past ten, drove from dear, dear Merton, where I left all that I hold dear in this world, to go to serve my King and country. May the great God whom I adore enable me to fulfil the expectations of my country, and if it is His good pleasure that I should return, my thanks will never cease being offered up to the throne of His Mercy. If it is His good Providence to cut short my days upon earth, I bow with the greatest submission, relying that He will protect those so dear to me that I leave behind. His will be done. Amen. Amen. Amen.'

At Trafalgar he found the foe he sought. His plans were perfected and completely prepared. In his cabin he prayed once more.

'May the great God, whom I worship, grant to my country, and for the benefit of Europe in general, a great and glorious victory; and may no misconduct in any one tarnish it, and may humanity after victory be the predominant feature in the British fleet! For myself individually I commit my life to Him who made me, and may His blessing alight on my endeavours for serving my country faithfully. To Him I resign myself and the just cause which is entrusted to me to defend. Amen. Amen. Amen.'

For a brief space he turned his attention to the worldly affairs of Emma and Horatia, *specially recommending them to the care of his country.* He deemed it unnecessary to mention his relations, for whom he had already made ample provision. He spent the last moments before going on deck to engage in battle, in writing to the love of his life.

'My dearest beloved Emma, the dear friend of my bosom, the signal has been made that the enemies' combined fleet is coming out of port. May the God of Battles crown my endeavours with success; at all events I will take care that my name shall be always most dear to you and to Horatia, both of whom I love as much as my own life; and as my last writing before the battle will be to you, so I hope to God that I shall live to finish the letter after the battle. May Heaven bless you, prays your

NELSON AND BRONTE.'

Cetera quis nescit? From the world-famous signal to the parting sigh, 'Thank God I have done my duty,' every word and incident is stored up in the treasure-chamber of England's national inheritance.

'Take care of my poor Lady Hamilton. Kiss me, Hardy.' '*Remember that I leave Lady Hamilton and my daughter to my country.*'

Emma had yet nearly ten years to live. How they were spent can be briefly chronicled. For with the end of her connection with the great gentleman who made her his wife, and the greater hero who threw the halo of his name around her tarnished reputation, her real interest ceases. And henceforward the relation of her career is one unbroken record of darkness, disaster, and downfall.

The decade beginning by Nelson's open grave on January 10th, 1806, and ending beside her own on January 15th, 1815, is seen as a period of wild extravagance and wilder dissipation, of sordid debt, ever-increasing difficulties, and disregarded appeals. Everyone, it appeared to her, was to blame for her distresses, the true cause of which was hidden from her. Canker in the bud, flaw in the flower, that was the beginning and end of the explanation. The evil, as we have seen, was anterior to her birth; it was the root itself that held a worm in it.

It would be wholly unprofitable to examine the details of Emma's life during these ten disastrous years. Those that stand out, and fitly end our chronicle, are sufficiently indicative to permit any of our readers who are curious in morbid degeneration to divine the others; all the material is at hand. *Facilis descensus Averni.* Emma was no exception to the rule. Already she had descended far on the road; now were her steps to gather impetus. There are persons who seem unable, by nature of their temper and constitution, to live within limits of propriety at any time or under any circumstance. Lady Hamilton was one of these. The death of Nelson left her with Merton unencumbered and an income that would have seemed fabulous wealth to her grandmother, Mrs. Kidd of Hawarden—a great fortune even to that father who misbegot her and suffered for his sin at Nesse. To Emma it was alike insufficient for her needs and incompatible with her claims. She mourned Nelson as one who had the right to mourn, publicly, and with the intention to draw the eyes of the world to herself and the share she had had in his greatness. One picture of her shows her hovering like an angel over his tomb. This she herself caused to be painted, and the caricaturists quickly prepared another, which is probably familiar to all our readers.

When 'Emma forlorn and weeping for Nelson' was treated as a jest she threw off her mourning garb. Now she resumed her former association with such of her neighbours and the fashionable world as maintained their friendship with her. When these proved few and fickle, she sought the society of those literary, musical, artistic, and theatrical persons whose morals were more akin to her own. Her generosity was as extreme and wanting in prudence, and even justice, as it had always been. Countless claims, never refused while she had it in her power to satisfy them, were made upon her purse by former recipients of Nelson's bounty, and by a host of needy Neapolitans who had known her in Naples and had suffered in the Revolution.

Greville used every means at his command to increase her embarrassments; delaying payments and making deductions, in a manner calculated to inflame her temper and irritate her, as it did more than once, into telling him to keep his money.

Yet might she have been only inconvenienced and not distressed, but for the return of Gibilmanna to the attack. It seemed that whilst at Merton he had found or stolen other letters, Nelson's own, and these, he told her, he was now about to publish. Nelson's name was on all tongues, and the scandal had like to be outspoken in the extreme, and many now in office would be scathed if they saw in print in what low esteem the nation's hero held them. Emma had still sufficient prudence left her to know the harm that might accrue, and still sufficient regard for one who had so truly cared for her, as to desire to shelter his memory. Gibilmanna played his game well. He quickly saw that in her at present unprotected condition she would be the prey of the first adventurer who came along. He it was who now charged himself with her affairs, and brought them from bad to worse. Extravagance followed extravagance, and when her resources failed she was for ever importuning the Government to recognise what she had done for Italy and Nelson!

The next few years show a sequence of passionate appeals to Ministers to give as a right what they might have been disposed to grant as an act of grace had her life been less flagrant. We have it on record that she made overtures to the old Duke of Queensberry, for many years her admirer, an amorist by nature and habit, and a man of large means. But age had rendered his Grace cynical, and it may well be, unequal to the gratification of appetites almost lost. Emma had beauty still, but her bulk was increasing, and she was now more than forty. He told her plainly she had outstayed her market; had nothing left worth giving. He promised, however, to remember her in his will, amiably prophesying that she would not have to wait long for her legacy. But, though he kept his word, leaving her an annuity of five hundred pounds and obligingly dying next year, Emma never received a penny of the money, for litigation over his last testament followed his demise, and before that was settled Emma's own troubles were over.

Her last comfort perished with her mother. Well, according to her lights, had that honest woman kept the promise made to her dying husband so many years before. She had never faltered in her loving watch over her erring daughter. From the time she joined her in Edgeware Row, until the day when she breathed her last, she had combined in her one person all the functions of mother, nurse, companion, housekeeper, confidante, friend—had discharged every service that woman can render to her sex. Never obtruding herself in the company of the great, she had, nevertheless, won their esteem and even their affection. The King of Naples called her an angel, the Duke of Sussex was her friend. Emma did not exaggerate when she declared that she had lost the best of mothers, and that her wounded heart, her comfort, all, was buried in her grave.

Merton had now to be given up, but could not be let, and for a long time was impossible to sell. It was only by vague assertions of the intentions of Ministers to grant her prayers that she was able to stave off the importunity of tradespeople. Gibilmanna, having sucked her dry, deserted her at the only time he might have been of use to her. For it needs a lawyer to circumvent one of his own craft, and it was lawyers now who swam like sharks in the waters of affliction to which she had been brought. The moment came when she who had been the wife of an ambassador, and the friend of a queen, was arrested for debt, and thrown into prison like any common malefactor. It was the humblest of her friends who came to her assistance. Alderman Smith of Merton it was by whose graces she was liberated from the rules of the King's Bench. He, good man, would have no reward from Emma for his generosity. He even shrank from an interview, knowing to what depths she had fallen, not wishing to look upon her in her degradation. But, when she was almost immediately re-arrested, at the instance of a coachbuilder, and he heard that there were other creditors only awaiting their opportunity, he took upon himself the task of arranging her affairs. All her possessions, including her presents from the Queen of Naples, and those from Nelson, were sold. She had the satisfaction presently, if it were a satisfaction to such as she had become, of knowing that her creditors lost nothing, although she herself had lost all.

It would have seemed that the lowest depths of her humiliation had now been reached. But there was more to come. With a depth of meanness only possible in one of foreign extraction Arnodeo Gibilmanna now proceeded to obtain from a publisher that which he had received again and again from Emma in order to avoid publicity. In the autumn of 1814 Messrs. Thomas Lovewell and Co., of Staines House, Barbican, announced 'The Letters of Lord Nelson to Lady Hamilton,' with a supplement of 'Interesting Letters by Distinguished Characters.'

Emma in her enfeebled health and broken spirit, could not face the hubbub that immediately arose. Everyone had guessed, now everyone would know, what manner of life she had lived. The fiction of Horatia's parentage, the fact of Sir William Hamilton's connivance, the story of her transference from Greville, her adventures with Captain Willett Payne, would be all disclosed. She put her hands to her ears and found them burning. She did not know what letters of hers had been destroyed, nor what would be in these two shameless volumes. There was nothing for it but flight, and upon flight she decided.

Taking boat in the Thames, the unhappy Horatia by her side, she started for Calais. She meant to lie *perdue* until the storm blew over; but she was seized with internal pains in the short voyage and arrived in a pitiable condition. Then, not because her resources were exhausted, but because she was ever unfit to manage her own affairs and was now reduced by illness, she caused herself to be carried to a poor lodging in the Rue Française, where, a prey to melancholy confirmed by ill-health, she passed six miserable months. She drank deeply, and proved herself unfit in every way for the care of a child.

Mr. Cadogan, the nephew who had taken her father's place with his uncle at Hawarden so many years ago, came to the rescue of one whom he had always been willing to acknowledge as kinswoman. But he arrived too late. The wages of sin is Death, and in the miserable lodging at Calais had they already been paid to Emma, Lady Hamilton. Dropsy intervening upon a chill, in the second week of the New Year, in the presence of Horatia and one faithful servant, she rendered up her account.

For the rest, reflections crowd upon the mind; the vanity of worldly success, the evanescence of power based on beauty, the unreliability of friendship founded on self-interest, the rarity of human gratitude. With these our self-appointed task ends, and we close the volume, trusting that its veracity will commend it to the student, and its moderation to the critic. Much has been omitted that might offend the susceptibilities of those to whom truth is less grateful than delicacy. Nothing has been added to distort the picture of one who having betrayed its hero had still the temerity to ask the favour of his country.

THE END.

Printed in Great Britain
by Amazon

32687650R00175